Poland in the Twentieth Century

POLAND

in the twentieth century

M. K. DZIEWANOWSKI

COLUMBIA UNIVERSITY PRESS
New York

Library of Congress Cataloging in Publication Data

Dziewanowski, M K
   Poland in the twentieth century.

   Bibliography: p.
   Includes index.
   1. Poland—History—20th century.   I. Title.
DK4382.D9   943.8   76-51216
ISBN 0–231–03577–2

Columbia University Press
New York   Guildford, Surrey

10 9 8 7 6 5 4 3 2

To Ada, Basia, and *Jaś*

Preface

THERE ARE FEW COUNTRIES that generate as much violent controversy and diametrically opposed passions as does Poland. For indeed, this country is, and always has been, a puzzling paradox.

Absent from the political map of Europe for over a century as a result of the vivisections performed on it at the end of the eighteenth century, Poland reappeared in 1918 like the mythical phoenix. Its resurrection belied the predictions of some of the most astute and "realistic" statesmen of the world. Many of these sophisticated minds continued to regard Poland for years as a fly-by-night phenomenon. Yet, in 1920, soon after having regained their independence, the Poles again astonished the world when they scored one of the most unexpected and decisive victories of twentieth-century history: they smashed the seemingly irresistible advance of the Red Army, which was then at the gates of Warsaw distributing bulletins about the fall of the Polish capital and the establishment of a Communist government. The victory, which a British diplomat called "the eighteenth decisive battle in world history," allowed not only Poland, but all other countries west of Soviet Russia, to survive and consolidate their independence during the following two decades. The memories of these twenty years of freedom are still with the peoples of the area. As a result of this, their more complete absorption into the Soviet imperial structure after World War II was made virtually impossible.

The interwar period in Poland was a time of important cultural achievement in fields as diverse as literature and mathematical logic. From the mathematical school of Lwów came Stanisław Ulam, a co-inventor of the hydrogen bomb. During the 1920s and early 1930s, Poland managed to play an international role quite out of proportion to its forces and resources, a role facilitated by the momentary weakness of the country's two powerful neighbors. The reckless balancing act between Nazi Germany and Communist Russia ended in catastrophe in September 1939. The Poles have been greatly admired for being the first to fight Hitler arms-in-hand, and then condemned by the very same people for refusing to submit to Soviet domination at the end of a war that had broken out allegedly in defense of Polish independence. Poland has been called both "the inspiration of the world" and "a constant source of trouble" by an American president who, in a cavalier manner, settled the nation's fate over after-dinner drinks. In 1945, at Potsdam, the country was physically moved westward, but politically it was forced into the Eastern orbit and saddled with a Communist-dominated government that had little to do with the wishes and sentiments of a great majority of the Polish people.

After having lost every fifth man, woman, and child, and more than half of their educated stratum in the holocaust of World War II, the Poles have astonished the world by their zest and vitality in reconstructing and industrializing their war-ravaged country. They shocked many people by rebuilding their historic monuments before they rebuilt their ruined homes. Their cultural creativity aroused curiosity and, not infrequently, won the admiration of many foreign observers, including many Soviet intellectuals. In a recent interview in the Paris monthly *Kultura,* the Russian dissenter Andrei Amalrik said: "a large segment of Soviet intelligentsia is keenly interested in Poland. This is true not necessarily about the opposition-minded intelligentsia. Many of them read and speak Polish, and Poland is for them a window, a small window on Europe. They believe that the Poles are much better informed, that their periodicals are on a much higher level, and more interesting, that they publish many worthwhile books, etc. Very often when I visit someone, I can see Polish books and periodicals. . . . And the Polish films! Polish movies have had considerable influence on the Russians. For instance, Wajda's 'Ashes and the Diamond,' what a magnificent film!''

Amalrik's admiration is not an isolated phenomenon. The intensity, versatility, and exuberance of Poland's cultural life, the puzzling combination of tradition and avant-garde, of pathos and irony, of sentimentality and whimsical wit, does not cease to astonish many Western intellectuals. The music of Penderecki and Lutosławski, the theater of Grotowski and Tomaszewski, the literary works of Witkiewicz, Gombrowicz, and Różewicz, Herbert and Hłasko, Miłosz and Mrożek, the films of Wajda and Polański, are now familiar items to the educated people of the world. What astonishes still more is the fact that the Germans, who for generations had denied the very existence of Polish culture, and during the last war did everything to extirpate it root and branch, are now among its greatest connoisseurs and propagators. Since the war they have translated, for instance, over a thousand Polish books into their language—more than any Western nation. The extensive use of Polish architects and art restorers to rebuild some of the destroyed German art treasures is another paradox of the two countries' postwar relations.

It is also paradoxical that the Poles have been accused by some people of congenital anti-Semitism, when Poland has in fact produced the most philo-Semitic literature in the world. Modern Polish prose (Orzeszkowa, Żeromski) and poetry (Mickiewicz, Norwid, Wierzyński) are replete with sympathetic references to Jews and their life and destiny. Which other literature can claim that its main national epic (Mickiewicz's *Master Thaddeus*) and its most important dramatic play (Wyspiański's *The Wedding*) have as their major protagonists a Jewish musician and a daughter of a Jewish innkeeper?

Poland is the only Communist country with a dynamic Roman Catholic church, a church that now has more clergy than before the war and is probably the only one in the world where religious vocations outgrow the number of places available in the seminaries and where the number of candidates for overseas missionaries is expanding. In the city of Lublin is a flourishing Catholic university, the only private academic institution between East Berlin and Vladivostok. The university functioned even at the peak of the Stalinist era.

At the time when all other satellites were licking the boots of the Tyrant, the Poles were the only ones not to erect a monument honoring him. Poland is, moreover, the only Soviet-controlled country where peasants still tend their individual plots. Although a member of

COMECON, it trades mostly with the West; although a member of the Warsaw Treaty Organization, it has the only army that has largely retained its prewar uniforms and badges.

The Poles are the only Soviet-controlled people who twice in one generation, in October 1956 and in December 1970, managed to change the ruling party and government team by means of two daring popular revolts. The upheaval of 1956, the "Polish Spring in October," represented a challenge and a clear rejection of the principle of universality of the Soviet experience. The emphasis on the "national road" to a reformed, more humanized Communism was, for years, a beacon and a stimulus to other Communist parties the world over, a call for them to reexamine the objectives and methods that had been largely shaped by Stalinism. By this means the "Polish October," next to the Yugoslav revolt of 1948, was an important turning point not only in the history of Soviet-dominated Europe, but also in the annals of the Communist movement. The present-day "Euro-Communism" cannot be fully understood without first comprehending the Yugoslav as well as the Polish revolts.

Despite all this, Poland still remains an enigma to most English-speaking people, one of those faraway countries about which they know very little. This work is an attempt to interpret to an intelligent Western reader the complexities of a country that exists in a unique aura resulting from the mixture of grim geopolitical realities and the deeply rooted, historically conditioned yearnings of its people.

Before writing this book, I visited Poland four times, in 1958, 1969, 1972 and 1973, and talked with many people. Parts of my manuscript were read and criticized by some of my friends. Among them I would like to mention, with thanks, the following: Francis Murray Forbes, Michał Gamarnikow, William Harwood, Leszek Kołakowski, Jan Nowak, Tadeusz Nowakowski, Peter Raina, and Marek Żebrowski. While I am grateful for my friends' observations and suggestions, the responsibility for the book is entirely mine.

In preparing the manuscript, I was assisted by my wife Ada, who typed an early draft and helped with the proofreading. Some of the typing was done by the staff of the Russian Research Center of Harvard University, with which I have been connected since 1949. The resources of the Center, and its stimulating seminars, where I met many of my sources of information, have been very helpful in researching and writing my monograph. My special thanks go to the editor of the book, Richard Steins.

Boston University   M. K. Dziewanowski
December 1976

Contents

Poland in the Twentieth Century

CHAPTER ONE

Roots of the Present

The history of Poland seems extravagant and full of incongruities: a huge state which for centuries stood up to the Teutons, Turkey, and Moscovy but . . . literally fell apart while its once weaker neighbors partitioned it and erased it from the map of Europe for some one hundred and twenty years; an astonishingly vital people who sink easily into moronic apathy and who show their virtues only in circumstances which would crush and destroy any other human group; a refinement of taste, which produced lyrical poetry comparable to that of Elizabethan England . . . but always threatened by drunken torpor and parochial mumblings; habits of religious and political tolerance which gave way, as a result of collective misfortunes, to wounded, morbid nationalism. This chaos of elements seemingly so disparate, yet interrelated by a logic of their own, may contain some lessons of universal portent.

Czesław Miłosz

A PERCEPTIVE BRITISH OBSERVER of contemporary Poland has remarked that whenever a Pole wants to explain some aspect of his work, or of the present situation, he starts, as a rule, by talking about Polish history. And, in many cases, this may be the proper way to begin, for Polish life is characterized by a pervasive sense of historic continuity.[1]

The early history of Poland was profoundly influenced by geopolitical circumstances: the Slavic tribes of the Oder and Vistula valleys, progenitors of the modern Poles, were isolated on a vast plain beyond the natural wall of the Carpathians, where they lived beyond the reach of the Roman legions. The Poles, therefore, never directly ex-

1

perienced the Pax Romana, or the fructifying influences of Greco-Roman culture; in the middle centuries of the first Christian millennium, when Celtic missionaries were carrying the Gospel and the surviving rudiments of Latin culture to western Europe, the Slavs of the northern plain, living in forests and marshes, clung to their original paganism.[2]

It was not until A.D. 963, one year after Otto I had proclaimed himself successor to Charlemagne and Holy Roman Emperor of the German nation, that a chronicler became aware of the Slavic peoples of the Vistula and the Oder, who, under the leadership of Duke Mieszko I (r. 922–92) of the Piast dynasty, were struggling against the Germans for control of the mouth of the latter river. Tenacious as they were, the pagan, primitive Poles were defeated by the better organized, more disciplined, and far better armed Teutons. Responding to this challenge, the politically wily Mieszko married a Czech princess in 966 and accepted Roman Christianity. The Poles thus accepted membership in the Christian community initially as a stratagem to counter the missionary as well as colonizing zeal of their Germanic neighbors.

While Poland was gradually emerging from paganism, the community of Christian nations of Europe witnessed the polarization of the two chief rivals of the Middle Ages: the papacy and the Holy Roman Empire. This growing antagonism was paralleled by the widening of the gap between Western and Eastern Christianity, between the Latin and Greek churches. Consequently, from the dawn of its existence, Poland faced the dilemma of siding with one or the other of the two opposing centers of civilization, Rome and Byzantium. By accepting Latin Christianity through dynastic connection with Bohemia, Poland chose Rome and thus allied itself with the West. Twenty-three years later, in 989, the neighboring Slavs of Kiev sided with Byzantium.

By the end of the tenth century, the eastern neighbors of the Empire—Poland, Bohemia, and Hungary—had achieved a measure of political consolidation under outstanding native rulers. In view of this development, it was impossible for the Empire to continue the expansionist policy initiated by Emperors Otto I and Otto II. Their succes-

2

sor, Otto III, had his own idea of an *Ostpolitik:* he wanted the Empire reorganized as a federation of free and equal Christian princes, to be led by both the Holy Roman emperor and the pope. This universalistic plan had its fierce opponents in Germany. According to Otto's formulation, the Polish state, which had become too strong to be subjugated (as was the case with the quarreling Elbe Slavs), might be tolerated by the Germans provided it remained politically and ecclesiastically dependent upon the Empire. Otto's grand design was rejected by his successors, who, at the beginning of the eleventh century, embarked on a policy of military expansion in the Slavic regions of Eastern Europe. Medieval Poland managed to withstand these attacks largely because of its cooperation with other equally threatened nations as well as with the papacy.

During the controversy in the eleventh century between Pope Gregory VII and the German monarch Henry VI, the Polish ruler, Bolesław II (Bolesław the Daring; r. 1058–79), consistently supported the papacy and its plans for ecclesiastical reform against the Empire. For this he was rewarded by the pope with the royal crown in 1076. From that time on, there developed in east-central Europe a pattern of international relations in which Bohemia was drawn increasingly into the orbit of Germany, while Poland, in alliance with Hungary, opposed not only the expansion but even the nominal overlordship of the Empire.

Until the middle of the twelfth century the young Polish state, in spite of occasional reversals, fared relatively well. It was true that the Poles were unable to prevent the Slavic lands between the Elbe and the Oder from being absorbed by the Germans, nor were they able to stop Bohemia from falling into the orbit of the Empire. Nevertheless, by holding firmly to their territory between the Carpathians and the Baltic, and between the valley of the upper and middle Oder and that of the Vistula, the Poles were able to absorb the rudiments of Christian culture and preserve their political independence. By the twelfth century certain basic principles of national policy had been established: first, that Poland could strive to be independent of the Empire by supporting its strongest antagonist, the papacy; and second,

3

that in order to pursue this policy successfully Poland must face Germany not singlehandedly, but as a member of a coalition of smaller nations of the region. The Empire was willing to tolerate the existence of national states like Poland, Bohemia, and Hungary, provided they remained relatively weak.

During this period, Poland became consolidated, internally unified, and gradually Christianized. Having no well-developed pagan religious heritage, the Poles soon identified themselves with the new creed without any reservation. By the thirteenth century, Poland had produced numerous missionaries and saints and was soon to become a bulwark against the Tatars and, later on, against the Turks. This was the origin of the still-popular notion of Poland's historical mission to defend Western Christian culture against the hostile forces threatening it from the East.

During the twelfth century some of the characteristics of the country's social structure began to take shape. From the pagan period the Poles had inherited a strong clan system with a tendency toward equality among its members, in some ways similar to the Scottish clans. In Poland, this clannish tradition prevented the formation of the feudal structure common to most European societies. Also from the pre-Christian past came the trend toward unanimity in decisions concerning vital issues pertaining to the community as a whole. This tendency was to degenerate in later years into the liberum veto a practice that bestowed on every member of the community the right to freely proclaim dissent from decisions of the majority and the right to enforce the rule of unanimity.

Despite the primitive tradition of equality, class differentiation began to develop. The head of the clan and his family, especially if they managed to acquire some wealth, were prone to emphasize their superior social position, thus forming a socioeconomic stratum distinct from the rest of the population. This group was soon reinforced by the deposed or ruined chieftains of the disintegrating tribes and by the more able and enterprising members of the ruler's suite. These

4

advisers and soldiers, who were often endowed by the chieftain for their services with more land, bounty, and prisoners than the rest of the retinue, formed the nucleus of the knighthood, the nobility of Poland. On the other hand, a class of slaves developed composed of prisoners of war or of debtors whose arrears had changed into a perpetual rent that became a form of serfdom. Thus, in addition to the mass of free men—either independent farmers or tenants—there developed in the twelfth century a group of knights and a relatively small stratum of serfs and slaves. Soon the knights came to be regarded as the szlachta, the men of allegedly better stock who were entitled to lead the country. Since in Poland, like Hungary, the principle of primogeniture never took root, every descendant of a nobleman was himself considered a nobleman. Consequently, in both countries the gentry became more numerous than in other European countries; by the end of the sixteenth century, the Polish gentry class formed some 10 percent of the population and was referred to as "the nation," since only they enjoyed full political rights.

Such was the slow evolution of social and political institutions east of the Oder when the Germans, in the persons of their two empire builders, Henry the Lion, duke of Saxony and Bavaria, and Albert I (Albert the Bear), margrave of Brandenburg, renewed their expansionist drive eastward against the Slavs of the Elbe and Western Pomerania. The task of creating a unified Poland was retarded not only by the bitter struggle against the Drang nach Osten, but also by the division of the country among numerous princes of the ruling Piast dynasty, the descendants of Bolesław III (Bolesław the Crooked-mouth). The plan, ingeniously devised by Bolesław to prevent fraticidal fights among his descendants, failed to serve its purpose; quite the contrary, it led to progressive atomization of the country, to the subdivision of the state into petty principalities, and, ultimately, to civil war and internal chaos. Although these disturbances never assumed the catastrophic dimensions of the strife then prevailing in the Kievan territories, they nevertheless caused Poland considerable damage. The family feuds among the princes of the Piast dynasty weakened the country's international prestige to such an extent that the Holy Roman emperors intervened in Poland's domestic affairs and seized its western territories with impunity. A more lasting subjugation of Poland was avoided only because of the Empire's struggle with the papacy and the gradual decay of the Empire itself during the thirteenth and fourteenth centuries. The Polish church survived the appanage divisions and the fratricidal feuds among the Piast princes; its unifying role was reflected in the special position of the primate of Poland, whose latter-day role as interrex (temporary head of state between royal elections) is directly related to the part the church played in this period of national disaster as the symbol and bulwark of national unity.

The quarreling Polish appanage princes, each eager to conquer the royal capital of Cracow and eventually dominate the entire country, were unable to cope with the nation's many external problems. Among other things, they were unable to subdue eastern or Gdańsk (Danzig) Pomerania or to keep in check the pagan Prussians who constantly invaded ancient duchy of Mazovia. In 1226, Duke Conrad of Mazovia, preoccupied with internal struggles and considering them more important than guarding his northern borders, summoned the semimilitary Order of the Knights of the Hospital of St. Mary of the Teutons of Jerusalem—more popularly known as the Teutonic Knights. In exchange for their assistance in subduing his unruly Baltic neighbors and converting them to Christianity, Conrad promised to grant the Knights some land, although his sovereignty over the original grants as well as future conquests was to be preserved.

Acting with supreme ruthlessness and brilliant military dispatch, the Knights soon established an autonomous state comprising the entire region between the Vistula River on the west and the Niemen River on the east. Thus, the domains of the Order became a menace to Poland and to neighboring pagan Lithuania. By merging in 1237 with the Livonian Brotherhood of the Sword, another military order that had previously conquered the provinces of Courland and Livonia, the Teutonic Knights gained control of most of the southeastern shore of the Baltic, and by the end of the thirteenth century, had effectively blocked the estuaries of the Vistula and the Niemen and barred Poland and Lithuania from their natural access to the sea. Both the Poles and the Lithuanians at first tried to resist actively, but were defeated and had to fall back on the defensive.

The establishment of the Teutonic Order on the Baltic created a severe problem for Poland, but a more devastating calamity was soon to overcome all Eastern and Central Europe: the area was overrun and ravaged in 1241 by savage warriors from central Asia, the dreaded Tatars. Challenging the invaders in the ferocious battle of Legnica (Liegnitz) in Silesia, Duke Henry II (Henry the Pious), at the head of Polish and German contingents, managed at great cost to slow the Tatar advance. A potential unifier of Poland, Henry perished in battle along with a large number of the Silesian nobility. Because of internal disputes, however, the Tatars had to withdraw, and as a result, Poland, unlike the eastern Slavs of the former Kievan federation, never fell under the Mongol yoke.

The devastation of Poland resulting from succeeding Tatar invasions further contributed to colonization of the depopulated country by German settlers. The previous century had seen a gradual influx of colonists from the overpopulated regions of western Germany into the western borderlands of Poland (especially Silesia), but after the Tatar withdrawal this trickle became a flood. The settlers brought with them a more scientific method of land cultivation and a superior legal system. In order to attract settlers from Germany, the Polish princes and landlords offered favorable conditions, including a fairly long rent-free period. A similar liberal procedure was applied to the founding of new towns, but they were customarily granted an even wider measure of self-government, and some were thus able to develop into flourishing communities. The fourteenth and fifteenth centuries were a period of considerable prosperity for Polish towns, many of which had large German populations, and, as members of the Hanseatic League, shared in the profitable Baltic and Levantine trade.

Prosperity reached its peak under Casimir III (Casimir the Great, r. 1333–70), the last Piast prince on the throne of Cracow. A brilliant administrator, he carried out currency reform, codified the law, fos-

7

tered trade, protected peasants from exploitation by the gentry, and strengthened the country's defenses by building some forty fortresses. In 1364 he founded the University of Cracow, the second such institution north of the Alps and east of the Rhine.

German colonization, as advantageous as it initially was, brought in its wake grave ethnic and political conflicts. To understand the violent character of the reaction against the growing German influence in Poland, one only has to consider the position of the country in relation to its neighbors at the beginning of the fourteenth century. To the north was the rapidly expanding monastic state of the Teutonic Order. To the southwest ruled the unsuccessful pretender to the Cracow throne, John of Luxemburg, King of Bohemia. King John was a constant menace because of his collaboration with the two Germanic outposts in Poland: the Order and the Mark of Brandenburg, the latter of which had gradually expanded its territory on the lower and the middle Oder. To the northeast were the domains of Lithuania, still pagan and equally menaced by the Order, but antagonistic toward Poland because of the clash between the southward expansion of Lithuania and the Polish eastward drive. In the southeast lay the politically enfeebled Ruthenian principalities and, beyond them, the Tatar Empire of the Golden Horde, extending from the Carpathians eastward to the Urals and the Crimea.

Driven from the lower and middle Oder, barred from access to the Baltic Sea, and deprived even of the use of the mouth of its chief river, Poland by the fourteenth century was engaged in a life-and-death struggle with the Germanic princes encircling the nation on three sides. Since Poland was much too weak to face this danger alone, the country's rulers saw clearly that the help of similarly threatened nations would be needed in order to survive. Accordingly, the policy of confederation or federation (then termed "union") was developed. The only potential ally against the Teutonic Knights was Lithuania, the possessor of a vast heterogeneous empire that had been created by the genius of brilliant leaders and rapidly extended far beyond the confines of Lithuania proper into the territories of the Dnieper valley formerly belonging to the Kievan state. The principalities of the Dnieper valley, present-day Byelorussia and the Ukraine, had their own Slavic and Byzantine civilizations which, although stagnant, were more advanced than that of their Lithuanian conquerors. Ruthenian Greek-Orthodox missionaries had made some inroads among the Lithuanian aristocracy, but until the end of the fourteenth century, most of the aristocracy, as well as the overwhelming majority of the Lithuanian people, remained pagan. Nevertheless, the Lithuanian ruling class did assimilate Ruthenian, or Byelorussian customs (as they are now called), and, to a large extent, the local Slavic language, which was at the time much more developed than the Lithuanian vernacular.

After more than a hundred years of intermittent warfare with the Order, both the Poles and Lithuanians found themselves by the late fourteenth century blocked from access to the Baltic by the militaristic monks entrenched at the estuaries of the Vistula and the Niemen. And with the growing power of the Muscovite state looming large in the east, it was obvious that Lithuania, like Poland, would have to unite its forces with those of a neighbor in order to survive. The question was which ally the boyars of Vilnius would choose. In 1384–85, intelligence was received at Cracow that a marriage was being negotiated between the Lithuanian Grand Duke Jagiełło (Yagailo) and a daughter of Dimitri Donskoi (Dimitri of the Don), the Grand Duke of Muscovy, and that the marriage was to be followed by a close alliance. This imminent danger gave rise in Poland to the daring idea of forestalling the Muscovites and achieving a confederation with Lithuania by means of the personal union of two dynasties, accompanied by the conversion of the still pagan areas of the Lithuanian empire. In 1386, Jagiełło was baptized and married to Queen Jadwiga of Poland. On behalf of Lithuania, Jagiełło (who would rule Poland as Ladislaw II) promised to embrace the Roman Catholic faith, to join all his lands with the crown of Poland, and to regain the territories lost by both states. Thus, by peaceful means and adroit diplomacy, the greatest missionary deed of the late Middle

9

Ages was achieved.[3] As a result of the union, the frontiers of Western civilization were shifted considerably to the northeast. Following the gradual conversion of Lithuania, Polish social and political institutions, and in later years the Polish language, slowly penetrated into Lithuania and its Ruthenian provinces.

The Polish-Lithuanian union considerably altered the balance of power in Central and Eastern Europe. The Hussites of Bohemia offered to cooperate with Poland; Moldavia became a Polish fief and both nations gradually became drawn into the affairs of the Black Sea region, where the rising might of the Turkish empire was already casting its shadow over Byzantium and the southern Slavs. At the same time, the union with Lithuania involved Poland, a country hitherto oriented to the west and the south, in the affairs of the Lithuanian-Ruthenian empire. The latter was gradually being drawn into conflict with the Muscovite state for the control of the Dnieper River valley (the Kievan "inheritance"). The conflict between Lithuania and Muscovy, "the gatherer of the Russian soil," was, in a sense, a struggle for leadership between two centers of the East Slavonic world.

Despite the union with Lithuania, the position of Poland at the end of the fourteenth century was still precarious. Because of the simultaneous growth of Luxemburg, and, later on, of Hapsburg power in Bohemia and Hungary, Poland still had two German frontiers: one in the north, another in the south and the west. By the beginning of the fifteenth century, therefore, the newly created Polish-Lithuanian commonwealth had to allot most of its resources to the coming struggle with the Teutonic Order, which had allied with other Germanic forces of Central and east-central Europe. Their vital interests threatened, the Poles and the Lithuanians decided to fight. In 1410, the forces of the Order were decisively crushed at the battle of Grünwald and Tannenberg by the joint armies of Poland and Lithuania, assisted by some auxiliaries from Smolensk as well as by the Czech Hussites.

The Polish-Lithuanian victory, scored over the greatest military power of the time, represented a profound shift in the balance of power in Central and Eastern Europe. The common victory put an end to the expansionist plans of the Order and the Luxemburgs; it broke the predominance of the German element in the Baltic area; and it transformed the Polish-Lithuanian confederation into a great power. The military triumphs of the confederation were paralleled by diplomatic successes. At the Council of Constance (1414–18), one of the great diplomatic conferences of the Middle Ages, the Poles were accused by the Teutonic Knights of having entered into league with pagans against Christians. The accusation was connected with the question of whether it was permissible to use force to spread Christianity among heathens and Jews. The Order was in favor of the use of force, whereas Poland's representative, Paulus Vladimiri (Pawel Włodkowic), rector of the University of Cracow, opposed this approach. He submitted to the Council his memorial, entitled *De potestatae papae et imperatoris respectu infidelium,* in which he formulated his, and his country's, thesis that Christianity should not be forced upon infidels, and that all forcible conversion was immoral. The thesis was accepted by the Council. The belief of Paulus Vladimiri that *fides ex necessitate non est debet,* i.e., that only voluntary conversion was valid, is at the origin of the principle of self-determination. His works, which revised the traditional Christian doctrine of the "just war" (*Bellum justum est justa executio*) while justifying only purely defensive wars, laid down the foundations of modern international law over two centuries before Hugo Grotius and one hundred years before Francesco De Vitoria. International mediation and arbitration and an international tribunal for the peaceful settlement of conflicts among nations were also advocated by Paulus.[4]

The new power of the Polish-Lithuanian union was reflected in the prestige of the ruling dynasty: the second representative of the Jagiello dynasty to sit on the Polish throne, Ladislaw III, was offered both the Czech and the Hungarian crowns; in 1440, he chose to rule Hungary. The Polish-Hungarian union was created to serve a double purpose: first, to drive the Turks out of Europe and to liberate besieged Constantinople; and second, to promote and consolidate the merger, agreed to at Florence in 1439, of the two branches of the Christian church. Had the new crusade succeeded, had Constantinople been freed and the Turks driven back into Asia Minor, the Union of Florence would have had a reasonable chance of succeeding. The fate of Europe and of Christendom depended on the outcome of the campaign. However, at the battle of Varna (1444), on the Black Sea, a superior Turkish force defeated the army of Ladislaw III. The young king was killed on the battlefield, and his head, preserved in honey, was sent home as a gift for the sultan. Constantinople fell to the Ottoman Turks in 1453, at which time both the Polish-Hungarian union and the merger of the branches of Christianity collapsed.

The growing prosperity of the Polish-Lithuanian state and the liberal policies of the Jagiello rulers presented a stark contrast to the oppressive rule of the Teutonic Knights in their lands. In 1454, the Prussian Estates revolted against the Order and requested to be incorporated into Poland. The ensuing thirteen-year war resulted in the decisive defeat of the Order. The treaty of Toruń (Thorn), which ended the struggle in 1466, divided the domains of the Order into several separate parts. Of these, West Prussia (Royal Prussia), comprising Pomerelia with the city of Gdańsk, and Ermeland (Warmia) with the city of Elbląg (Elbing), were directly incorporated into Poland, thus providing the long-sought access to the Baltic. The remaining territory, later called Ducal Prussia (East Prussia), was left to the reorganized Order as a fief of Poland.

The Polish monarchy had to pay a heavy price for the victory over the Teutonic Knights. To secure the military aid of the nobles, King Casimir IV had been forced in 1454 to issue at Nieszawa the statutes that were later to be acclaimed as the Magna Carta of the Polish nobility. Under their terms, the king pledged to make no new laws nor to proclaim general mobilization without consent of the gentry's representatives. The gentry were, for the first time, legally admitted to share in the framing of legislation. In the fourteenth century the nobility had been freed from any military and financial obligation to the crown, except for those voluntarily undertaken through vote of the provincial assembles or the dietines. The new laws, a distinct diminishment of royal authority, did not affect Poland immediately. The country was prosperous and self-confident, and the prevalent civic spirit prevented the nobility from overly exploiting their privileges. From a historical perspective, however, it is clear that the statutes of Nieszawa were a further important step in the process that was to eventually render the Polish monarchy impotent.

🖋 🖋

When King Casimir IV died in 1492, and Christopher Columbus was discovering America, the Jagiełło dynasty ruled over most of east-central Europe. At its greatest extent, the territory under their control extended from the gates of Moscow to the Black and the Adriatic seas. In addition to the kingdom of Poland and the grand duchy of Lithuania, they ruled in Bohemia (including Moravia, Silesia, and Lusatia), and in Hungary (which at that time embraced Slovakia, Transylvania, and Croatia), and held Prussia and Moldavia as fiefs.

Yet, the political horizon was beginning to darken. While Casimir IV was pursuing his dynastic policy in Bohemia and Hungary, Ivan III (Ivan the Great), Grand Duke of Muscovy, had consolidated his power by crushing the independent republic of Great Novgorod (1476), an ally of Poland-Lithuania. Muscovy had also successfully attacked the eastern approaches of the commonwealth, gradually eroding its position along the upper Dnieper. The Muscovite rulers claimed that Poland-Lithuania had annexed the western areas of the former Kievan state at the time of its destruction. It was the policy, therefore, of the tsars of Moscow, as the rightful heirs of Rurik, to retrieve parts of the Kievan patrimony, "the lands where the blood of Rurik once ruled." The Muscovites hoped to free their Orthodox brethren from the Latin yoke and unite with them in one state. The Poles believed, however, that the lands had been included in the Polish-Lithuanian commonwealth by means of a series of voluntary unions and incorporations. Protected against the Tatars by the Poles, organized and civilized by them, the lands had thus become an integral part of the commonwealth. "This Slavonic domestic feud," as the great Russian poet Alexander Pushkin wrote in 1830, was des-

13

tined to plague the relations of the two neighboring states up to our day.

While the eastern borderlands of the commonwealth were threatened by Muscovy, the southern approaches to Poland-Lithuania were increasingly exposed to the danger of Ottoman Turkish aggression. Despite these mounting problems, Poland had, by the sixteenth century, achieved respectable material and cultural progress. The Polish "constitution," which was in fact a conglomeration of fundamental rights, privileges, and immunities issued since the fourteenth century, guaranteed many impressive privileges to the large gentry class. Besides the fiercely contested right of limited taxation, they enjoyed freedom of speech and print, immunity from authoritarian seizure of property, and inviolability of domiciliary rights. Moreover, by the close of the sixteenth century each nobleman, rich or poor, had the undisputed right of personally voting in the election of the king. The privilege *Neminem captivabimus nisi jure victum* (none may be arrested unless sentenced by a law court), issued as early as 1433, gave to the Polish nobility what Englishmen were to receive legally only in 1685 by the Act of Habeas Corpus. The Polish constitutional system, despite its weaknesses and limitations, was by the sixteenth century in the vanguard compared with the constitutions of most other countries. Diplomatic reports of the time by foreign observers in Poland often expressed admiration for the well-balanced Polish political system, the *monarchia moderata*.

During this "Golden Age," Poland reached a high level of cultural development, stimulated in part by the new spirit of Renaissance humanism then penetrating from Italy, and by the intellectual ferment stemming from the Protestant Reformation. The royal capital of Cracow became a cultural and political center of considerable importance. Throughout the sixteenth century the University of Cracow was overflowing with students, most of whom came from poor families. The sons of the wealthy were able to travel abroad to attend the famous universities of Western Europe, especially those of Paris, Padua, and Bologna. The University of Cracow, where the great astronomer Nicholas Copernicus studied, spread its influence over the

14

whole of Central and Eastern Europe. It was in Cracow that Copernicus achieved the first insights that were to be finally embodied in his epochal *De revolutionibus orbium coelestium,* the revolutionary reconstruction of the Ptolemaic theory of the earth as the center of the universe and its replacement by the heliocentric concept. Among Copernicus's other influential works was the treatise *De Moneta,* which suggested numerous ways of improving and standardizing Polish currency. It was in Cracow, too, that Jan Długosz wrote his pioneering work in modern historiography, the twelve-volume *History of Poland.* The impact of Western culture in sixteenth-century Poland can be seen in the fact that Latin became the second tongue not only of the intellectual elite but of the entire gentry.[5]

Polish political literature during the "Golden Age" achieved a remarkable level of development, amply reflected in numerous penetrating works on political theory. The treatise *De Republica Emendanda* (On Reforming the Republic), by Andrew Frycz-Modrzewski, an enlightened political thinker, favored a progressive scheme of political, educational, and social reforms, defended the peasants against abuses, and advocated the equality of all citizens before the law. In some ways similar to Thomas More's *Utopia,* it differs from that famous work by its pervading sense of reality and seriousness of purpose. Poland's "prince of poets," Jan Kochanowski, the Polish Ronsard, united in his work both the spirits of humanism and traditional Christianity. Although he wrote mainly in Polish (a language considered at this early date to be colloquial, or a *lingua vulgaris*), Kochanowski was also one of the most distinguished Latin poets of Europe in a century claiming brilliant practitioners in the classic tongue. Writing to his friend Decius in 1523, Erasmus of Rotterdam praised Poland in these words: "I congratulate this nation which used to have a bad reputation for its barbarity and which now, in sciences, jurisprudence, morals, and religion, and in all that separates us from barbarism, is so flourishing that it can rival the first and most glorious of nations."

The mood of the ruling class during Poland's "Golden Age" was affected not only by the long series of military victories and political successes, but also by the nation's substantial material and cultural progress. In the light of these achievements one can understand the pride and, indeed, the arrogance of a Polish nobility convinced that Poland was the freest, most advanced nation of the world. Also prevalent was a suspicious attitude toward the Hapsburgs and a fear of *absolutum dominium,* similar to contemporary fears of totalitarianism. It is not surprising that an obscure Polish squire, a deputy of the Diet, could publicly defy the sternest monarch of the sixteenth century, Stefan Bátory. When the king, annoyed by the deputy's loud criticism of his parliamentary speech, shouted at him: "Tace famulus!" ("Silence, servant!"), the latter replied boldly: "Non sum famulus sed elector Regni et detrusor tyrranorum!" ("No servant am I, but a kingmaker and a deposer of tyrants!")

Political freedom was paralleled by religious and ethnic tolerance without equal in a Europe where religious nonconformists were burned at the stake. While fierce denominational disputes and bloody religious wars raged in the rest of Europe during the Reformation, Poland was a "haven for the heretics." The principle that no one could be prosecuted (let alone persecuted) for his religious belief had always been tacitly recognized in Poland and became law in 1572. Religious tolerance would not become part of French law until 1791. One of the Catholic statesmen of the time, Jan Zamoyski, the chancellor of the realm, said: "I would have half of my life if those who have abandoned the Roman Catholic Church would voluntarily return to its vale; but I would prefer giving all my life than to suffer anybody to be constrained to do it, for I would rather die than witness such an oppression." King Sigismund Augustus, addressing the Diet on the subject of religious freedom, declared bluntly: "I am not the King of your souls." "A state without stakes" was the appropriate name given to early modern Poland.

Although Poland has traditionally been a Catholic country, non-Christians, including Jews and Muslims, were permitted to settle freely in Polish territory throughout most of the nation's history; and each group was allowed to practice its customs without any hindrance on the part of the state. The great influx of Jews began in the four-

16

teenth century, when stern persecution drove thousands from Germany. They sought refuge in Poland, where King Casimir III granted them special privileges; as "Servants of the Treasury," or *servi camerae,* Jews were placed under the special protection of the crown.[6]

Was old Poland a "Jewish Paradise" (*Paradisus Judeorum*) as a sixteenth-century saying alluded? A Harvard scholar does not think so, but he writes that while

> elsewhere they were molested by city mobs and students . . . Poland was attracting [Jews] from other countries, and during the sixteenth and the first half of the following century their numbers grew rapidly—from about fifty thousand around 1500 to half a million a century and a half later. Life was simply more tolerable for Jews in Poland than elsewhere. In the first place, except for an inconsequential attempt in Lithuania, by the end of the fifteenth century there were no mass expulsions, nor any massacres. Moreover, the Jews enjoyed a much greater degree of self-government in Poland than in any other country.[7]

An American student of Polish history, Robert H. Lord of Harvard, writing soon after the end of World War I, characterized the historic importance of the Polish-Lithuanian commonwealth as a structure of peculiar civic nature:

> The old Polish State was . . . the first experiment on a large scale with a federal republic down to the appearance of the United States. In the sixteenth and seventeenth centuries this republic was the freest state in Europe, that state in which the greatest degree of constitutional, civic, and intellectual liberty prevailed. . . . Like the United States today, Poland was at that time the melting pot of Europe, the haven for the poor and the oppressed of all the neighboring countries—Germans, Jews, Greeks, Magyars, Armenians, Tartars, Russians. . . . Finally the oldest republic represented an effort to organize the vast open plain between the Baltic and the Black Seas—a region containing so many weak and underdeveloped areas and a region so much exposed to Germanic ambitions on the one side and the Turco-Tartar onslaughts on the other side—into a compact and powerful realm, which was directed indeed by the strongest and most

17

advanced voice within its borders . . . but which in its better period allowed a genuine equality to the other voices and extensive self-government of some of them.[8]

Although undoubtedly a rather sympathetic and somewhat over-idealized picture of the commonwealth, the essential features of the description are correct. Despite its shortcomings, the federation endured for over four centuries (1389–1791), longer than any other similar structure in European history with the exception of the Danish-Norwegian Union (1357–1814).[9]

But neither the growing prosperity, the spread of education, nor the boisterous self-confidence of the nobility could stave off the numerous foreign and domestic problems besetting the Polish-Lithuanian commonwealth. In the domestic sphere, the growing power of the nobility was stifling both the crown and the other social classes. In foreign affairs, the commonwealth was unable to solve the problem of the Ukraine and Dnieper Cossacks. These were a combination of free settlers in the Polish "Wild East," and of military colonists, often used by Polish kings as auxiliary military force in the wars against Muscovy and the Ottoman Empire. Mostly Ukrainian and Orthodox people, they resented the rule of Catholic Polish squires who wanted to enserf them. In 1647–48 the Cossacks allied with the Tatars and rose against the Poles.

The revolt of the Cossacks did not initially have irredentist aims. Its goal was to secure the repeal of unjust laws and the restoration of Cossack privileges. The Cossack leader, or hetman, Bohdan Khmelnitsky, was originally not opposed to rapprochement with Poland, but he was unable to reach any modus vivendi with Warsaw. Accordingly, he turned to Muscovy for support, and in 1654 the Ukraine was proclaimed a Russian protectorate.

Four years of Muscovite rule proved much sterner than that of Warsaw, and in 1658 the Cossacks realigned with the Poles. An attempt to reorganize the Ukrainian provinces as a separate "Ruthenian Duchy," equal to the Polish and Lithuanian segments of the commonwealth, failed because of Muscovite military intervention. The commonwealth, then involved in repelling a Swedish invasion and unable to undertake a two-front war, accepted a compromise. Under the terms of the treaty of Andrusov (1667), the Ukraine was divided between Poland and Muscovy.

The Cossack wars lasted for two decades and ended with Poland losing the left-bank Ukraine to Muscovy. The economic and social consequences of the Cossack and Swedish wars may be compared only with the effects of the Hundred Years War on France or the Thirty Years War on Germany. Soon after the treaty of Andrusov, the Ukraine right bank was integrated into the Muscovite state. The "Cossack liberties," in the name of which the struggle had been launched in 1648, were suppressed by the Muscovites, and by the time of Peter the Great and Catherine II, Ukrainian autonomy had been dealt its final death blow. The Cossack host was abolished and most of its members scattered throughout the vast stretches of the tsarist empire, while serfdom was extended "to that land of peasant proprietors." The inability of Warsaw to turn the dual Polish-Lithuanian state into a tripartite federation and thus satisfy the longings of its Ukranian segment was one of the contributing causes of the partitions of the eighteenth century.[10]

≋ 〆

A striking phenomenon of the seventeenth century was a deepening constitutional crisis that threatened the country with paralysis. Since the close of the fourteenth century, the Polish monarch had no power to increase the taxes of the gentry beyond an insignificant sum that decreased over the years with the devaluation of currency. Moreover, the king could not send the mobilized nobles beyond the frontiers of the state without granting them an indemnity. Because of the limited resources of the treasury, the standing army was hardly sufficient for the defense of vast, open frontiers. By a law enacted in 1454, the monarch promised not to introduce new laws or declare war without the consent of the provincial dietines, which were elected by the nobility of each province. In 1573, after electing the French prince Henry of Valois to the throne of Poland, the nobility further limited the monarch's power and reduced the role of the king to that of a mere figurehead.

The ascendancy of the gentry was paralleled by the progressive deterioration of the socioeconomic position of the peasantry. By 1466 the opening of the Vistula for Polish grain export through Gdańsk to northern Germany, the Netherlands, and England, where cereal prices were high, provided new opportunities to the landed Polish knights. Land became more valuable, and more intensive farming under the gentry's own management proved profitable. Consequently, from the sixteenth century on, the landowners, increasingly in control of the Diet and the whole machinery of the state, proceeded to pass bills upsetting the old, traditional agrarian settlement that dated back to the colonizations under German law. Village self-government was first curtailed, the role of the elder was then gradually limited, and finally, the office was abolished. The elder's lands and privileges were then taken up by the squire, who emerged as the local magistrate as well. In 1520, the Diet enacted a law requiring tenants to work on the squire's estate. At first this duty was apparently not burdensome, amounting to one day's service a week, but by 1563 the requirement had increased to three days. The expropriation of peasant land, similar to the English enclosure, continued uninterrupted, increasing the size of the rural proletariat. After depriving his villagers of self-government, the landowner had limited their freedom of movement and tied the peasantry to the land. By the seventeenth century the Polish peasant, although considerably better off than his Muscovite counterpart, was in a pitiable position.

The fall of Constantinople in 1453 closed the eastern Mediterranean to European commerce and brought about profound changes in lines of communications. With the economic center of the continent gradually shifting northward toward France, the Netherlands, England, the Baltic region, and the Scandinavian countries, the Baltic Sea became of paramount importance. By the end of the sixteenth century, the conquest of southern Livonia and the introduction of more intensive methods of cultivation in Lithuanian-Ruthenian lands had turned the commonwealth into a large exporter of agricultural products.

The enserfment of the peasantry had far-reaching consequences for the entire economy. With more and more free labor at his disposal, the squire proceeded to set up his own factories and endeavored to manufacture whatever he could for his own and his subjects' needs. By forbidding his serfs to purchase the products not manufactured on the master's estate, the landowner created a monopoly of trade. As a result, the large estates became almost self-sufficient, and the towns lost a great deal of their trade. As early as 1493 the nobility had granted itself the right to import goods for its own consumption without payment of duty. Since the omnipotent Diet regulated prices in the interests of the ruling class, the merchants tended to export their wares abroad. In order to lower prices at home, however, the nobility passed a law forbidding the export of all goods manufactured in Polish towns, while reserving for itself the profitable grain export monopoly.

With peasants becoming serfs, burghers growing impoverished and losing political influence, and the monarch being limited to the role of the crowned president of a royal republic, the gentry emerged all-powerful. Poland-Lithuania became a federation of powerful local dietines, with the national Diet in Warsaw as its supreme political organ. The commonwealth, despite its name, became a state run by the nobility for its own class interests.[11]

The corrupting effects of the overwhelming political power exercised by the gentry were not slow in appearing. The traditional rule of unanimity, which until the middle of the seventeenth century was interpreted in the sense that a minority eventually had to submit to the will of the majority, began to be applied literally: one vote of protest could stop any measure from being voted by the Diet. The liberum veto gave opportunity to vested factional or local interests—and to foreign agents as well—to paralyze the entire machinery of state. The civic and martial virtues of the fourteenth and fifteenth centuries, which had made Poland a great power and the center of attraction for

21

its smaller neighbors, were now corrupted by the lure of material gain. Besides politics, drinking, hunting, and gambling became the chief preoccupations of much of the nobility. Some magnates kept private armies numbering thousands of men and fought large-scale private wars. The vigorous discipline and the Christian asceticism of the medieval period were challenged by an Eastern-influenced ostentation and luxury that knew no bounds.[12]

The Protestant Reformation, which in other countries often spawned a period of social austerity, generally produced the opposite effect in Poland, where it had almost no theological impact, but gave impetus to centrifugal and anarchic tendencies found among the ruling class. The all-too-easy victory of the Roman Catholic church over its opponents—not unlike the facile triumph of the gentry over the other classes—also had a demoralizing effect. Deprived of any intellectual challenge, Polish Catholicism relapsed into passivity and ritualism. Religious toleration had been observed fairly scrupulously until the beginning of the seventeenth century. The situation changed, however, during the Cossack and Swedish wars. The assistance granted to the Swedish invaders by some Protestant sects caused sporadic outbursts of anti-Protestant sentiment. By the middle of the seventeenth century many Poles came to believe that there could be no true national unity without religious orthodoxy, and that members of schismatic and heretic (i.e., non-Catholic) groups were not trustworthy citizens. Incidents of discrimination against religious dissenters grew increasingly frequent, and nonconformists were more and more denied the political equality enjoyed during previous times.

≈ℜ ℜ≈

The Swedish, Cossack, and Muscovite wars of the seventeenth century had seriously undermined Poland's prosperity and stability. Yet, at the end of the century the country experienced a brief period of revival as a result of the brilliant victories of King John III (John Sobieski) over the Turks. At the beginning of the eighteenth century, Poland-Lithuania was still a great power, but its position was considerably weakened by the nation's participation in the Northern War

22

(1700–1721). During much of the war, the commonwealth was ruled by the unpopular Augustus II (r. 1697–1733), elector of Saxony. Fighting against Charles XII of Sweden, Poland allied with the Russia of Peter the Great; the outcome of the conflict proved destructive not only to the status of Poland as a great power but to its sovereignty as well. Using the treaty of alliance concluded in 1700 with Poland-Lithuania, the Russian tsar repeatedly interfered in the domestic affairs of the commonwealth, stationing Russian troops on its territory, systematically bribing deputies of the Diet, and encouraging the anarchic proclivities of the nobility. In 1717 the "golden liberties" of the gentry were reaffirmed and incorporated into the constitution of the commonwealth. But now these liberties were to be guaranteed by Russia. Like a permanently defeated nation, the commonwealth, surrounded by the three most militaristic powers of Europe, was compelled to disarm and to limit its forces to 24,000 soldiers, 18,000 of whom were to be maintained by Poland and 6,000 by Lithuania.

The Northern War brought advantages only to Russia, which acquired Livonia (for the recovery of which Augustus II had entered into the alliance with Peter), as well as Ingria and Estonia. The resulting shift in the balance of power in northeastern Europe was significant: Sweden was driven from the southern shores of the Baltic, Poland was weakened, Russia became a great European power, and Prussia made considerable progress toward becoming the second powerful German state and thus a potential rival of the Hapsburgs.[13]

After the Northern War, Peter the Great continued to interfere in Polish affairs. Successfully playing the game of divide and rule, he pitted the nation against the monarchy and used religious dissenters, especially those who were Orthodox, for his own ends. A master at the art of cajoling and coercing, he was able, when necessary, to paralyze and exploit the Diet through the intervention of bribed deputies who would act as his agents and use their veto power to serve his ends. By keeping Poland-Lithuania as a protectorate buffer state and a potential ally against both Turkey and Sweden, Peter was able to dominate and dictate its foreign policy. However, Peter did not completely press his advantage, for no attempt was made to acquire any part of the Byelorussian and Ukrainian territories on the western banks of the Dvina and the Dnieper.[14]

The first sixty-six years of the eighteenth century, the years of the rule of the Saxon electors in Poland-Lithuania, were among the most demoralizing in the country's history. During these years the commonwealth ceased to have a foreign policy of its own and had no unified internal administration. The executive power hardly existed, education was neglected, superstition and religious fanaticism were widely spread, and dissipation and drunkenness thrived:

> Under the rule of the Saxon king
> Loosen your belt, and eat and drink. . . .

ran a current saying sanctioning the early local version of *la dolce vita*.

The accession of the ambitious Frederick II (Frederick the Great) to the throne of Prussia in 1740 opened an era of armed conflict that was to shake the foundations of the old European order. Since the Peace of Westphalia (1648), Prussia had been in possession of both the middle Oder and a part of West Pomerania; by the end of the Northern War it was also in control of the mouth of the Oder. To complete the conquest of the Oder valley, Frederick had, by the middle of the eighteenth century, annexed the upper course of the river and the surrounding regions of lower and middle Silesia, with Breslau (Wrocław) as the capital city, all at the time under Austrian control. This annexation was a part of Frederick's plan to consolidate Prussia's scattered lands and to annex the Polish western provinces of Pomerania and Posnania. The Polish acquisitions were considered by Frederick to be an indispensable first step toward conquest of the provinces of Brandenburg and East Prussia. He believed, in addition, that Prussia would be able to achieve its goals only on a step-by-step basis, and was fond of quoting what King Victor Amadeus of Savoy had repeated to his son Charles Emmanuel: "My son, it is necessary to eat the Milanese like an artichoke, leaf by leaf. Sometimes a city, sometimes a district, until all is eaten."

Frederick's policy initially clashed with the Russian desire to keep

Poland weak but intact as a buffer state and a Russian dependency. Tsarina Catherine II and her foreign minister, Nikita Panin, continued to pursue the Polish policy of Peter I. In 1764, Catherine placed on the throne of Poland Stanislas August Poniatowski, a former Polish ambassador in St. Petersburg and her discarded lover. A man of brilliant mind but weak character, he was, as Stanislas II, to be the last king of Poland.

Soon after Poniatowski was placed on the throne, a revival of nationalistic feeling swept the land. The Russian and Prussian intervention during Poniatowski's election had shocked many patriotic Poles out of their habitual complacency, and had precipitated a widespread dissatisfaction and a demand for reforms. Under the leadership of the powerful Czartoryski family, the procedures of the Diet were simplified and the liberum veto was curtailed, commissions were set up to deal with financial, military, and economic reforms, and colleges and libraries were founded. Between 1761 and 1763, Stanisław Konarski, a reformer in the fields of education and parliamentary reform, published his monumental four volume work, *On Effective Conduct of Debates,* a devastating attack on the liberum veto. The study also contained a plan for constitutional improvements based mainly on the English model. The influential and widely respected Czartoryskis also devised a system of gradual, cautious reforms for the entire governmental system.[15]

Berlin and St. Petersburg, both committed to the task of keeping Poland weak and prostrate, watched these developments with suspicion. In response to the Czartoryski reforms they attempted to divide the nation by using religious issues as a driving wedge; the Poles were pressured to grant immediate equal political rights to dissenters, the Orthodox, and the Protestants (including the right to hold public office), a change that would require time and tact. The Russian and Prussian demands, coupled with threats, were regarded by most Poles as provocations and were met with great indignation. Indeed, disturbing news soon reached St. Petersburg: an anti-Russian resistance group, an armed confederation of noblemen, had been formed in 1768 in the town of Bar in Polish Ukraine, near the border of Turkey.

The purpose of the Confederation of Bar was to defend "the Holy Roman Faith," allegedly threatened by the concessions made to the dissenters, and to end Russian interference in Polish affairs. The struggle, which lasted about four years, plunged Poland into anarchy and proved greatly embarrassing to the Russians. Catherine's involvement in Poland was taken advantage of by the Turks, who declared war on Russia in 1768.

The protracted Balkan campaign, combined with growing domestic troubles and a threat of Austrian intervention, made Catherine doubt whether Russia could maintain an exclusive protectorate over Poland. The turning point came late in 1770, when Frederick II put forward a proposal to share parts of Poland's territory with Prussia and Austria. On August 5, 1772, the solemn ceremony of the partition agreement between Russia, Prussia, and Austria took place in St. Petersburg. As the soldiers of the three powers moved into Poland, the respective countries published manifestos proclaiming their firm resolve to protect the peace of Europe against the contamination of "Polish anarchy." As a result of the First Partition, Poland lost nearly one-third of its resources. Prussia obtained most of Polish Pomerania, and was thus able to bridge the gap between Brandenburg-Prussia and East Prussia. However, because of Catherine's veto, Frederick was denied the rich commercial centers of Gdańsk and Toruń. Austria appropriated the lion's share, receiving most of southern Poland with the exception of Cracow. Russia acquired Polish Livonia, the northeastern part of Byelorussia, with Polotsk, Vitebsk, and Minsk, or the area east of the Dvina and the valley of the upper Dnieper.

The shock of dismemberment stimulated a process of national regeneration throughout the commonwealth. The two decades separating the First Partition from the Second (1793) were years of remarkable progress in many areas. The state income was doubled; new industries were created and expanded; the educational system was modernized and expanded (by 1793, Poland had the only ministry of education in all of Europe); the arts revived; and the armed forces were reorganized and reequipped.

By the end of the eighteenth century, the Russo-Prussian alliance had not been renewed. Austria, drawing closer to Russia, joined in a military pact directed against the Turks. In 1787, Catherine II got involved in her second Turkish war, thereby encouraging Sweden to attack Russia. The Swedish attack, in turn, emboldened the restless Poles, who by this time had been under Russian domination for more than three generations. Since the First Partition, local patriots had been encouraged in their ambitions by the Prussians, who were hoping to obtain from Poland both Gdańsk and Toruń. With Prussian support, the Poles instituted a series of far-reaching domestic reforms and demanded the removal of Russian troops from their territory. Catherine, embroiled in two wars, had to acquiesce. At the same time, the Poles proceeded to further dismantle their obsolete government and to modernize their social structure. The result was the constitution of May 3, 1791 (the May Constitution), which considerably strengthened the commonwealth by abolishing the election of kings and converting Poland into an hereditary monarchy with a regular cabinet of ministers and ministerial responsibility. The liberum veto and the right of confederation were nullified; finances were reorganized, and the army was expanded to 100,000 men; serfdom was limited and peasants were put under protection of law and the government of the country; and townsmen were to be represented in the Diet and given the benefit of the privilege *Neminem captivabimus,* or the right not to submit to arrest without a warrant, previously enjoyed only by the nobility. The introduction of the 1791 constitution appeared at the time to be a considerable step forward in the process of Poland's regeneration; while the French Revolution was destroying monarchy, the Polish upheaval was making it stable and respectable. Edmund Burke, the conservative critic of the French Revolution, commented that "Humanity must rejoice and glory when it considers the change in Poland."

Russia tolerated the upheavals in Poland as long as the Turkish war continued. By 1792, however, Catherine had defeated both the Swedes and the Turks and was free to deal with the Poles. Even before the end of the Turkish war, Catherine had made arrangements with a small band of Polish noblemen who supported the Russian intervention and were opposed to the progressive changes brought about by the constitution of 1791. Deprived of the essence of liberum veto and their traditional privileges, or what they considered as the "golden liberties," resentful of not being able to elect their king, and fearful of losing control over the serfs, these reactionaries, who epitomized the worst vices of old Poland, met and formed a new confederation at Targowica in the Ukraine. The leaders of this group asked for Russian protection and for the restoration of the old constitution. With this semblance of legality, Catherine on May 14, 1792, ordered her army, led by Alexander Suvorov, into Poland.

In the face of Russian aggression, the Poles turned to their Prussian ally, but the Prussians refused to come to their aid. After a series of indecisive battles, Suvorov's troops reached Warsaw, which was captured and sacked. The May Constitution of 1791 was abolished and the old order, including the old type of serfdom, was reinstated.

In 1792, Prussia and Russia agreed to partition Poland for the second time. Austria, involved in fighting against revolutionary France, did not join the division. As a result of the Second Partition, Russia appropriated most of Lithuania, Byelorussia, and the Ukraine. Prussia seized Gdańsk and Toruń, and the rest of western Poland. While the First Partition had left Poland a potentially powerful state, the Second Partition dealt the decisive blow to independence, leaving a powerless rump state. In an attempt to justify their policies, St. Petersburg and Berlin stated that the partition was necessary to uproot the spreading evil of "Jacobinism" in Eastern Europe. Poland had been divided in 1772 because it was near anarchy; it was despoiled in 1793 because it was successfully reforming itself. If the projected reforms had been fully carried out, Poland would have, in all probability, preserved its sovereignty. The half-reformed Polish republic collapsed in 1793 not because of a lack of original and practical political concepts, but because of the inability to carry them out in the face of Russian and Prussian opposition.

In response to the Second Partition, a popular uprising broke out in April 1794 under the leadership of General Tadeusz Kościuszko.[16] On May 7, 1794, he declared all peasants personally free and thus able to move from their native villages. Obligatory labor was radically limited and those peasants who joined the insurrection were to be freed from all obligations to their masters. The prospect of such revolutionary changes spreading to other countries of Europe caused apprehension in Berlin and led Prussia toward direct military intervention against Poland. The crushing of the insurrection by the joint intervention of Russia and Prussia was followed by the Third Partition (1795), which erased Poland from the map of Europe and put a dramatic end to a series of progressive reforms begun in 1791. "The epidemic of Jacobinism" was to be torn out by the roots. In 1796, Russia, Prussia, and Austria made reciprocal pledges never to use the term "Kingdom of Poland" in official documents. It was to be "Finis Poloniae."

𝄞 𝄞

No other event in modern European history produced such lasting changes in the balance of power as the extinction of a country situated at the crossroad of East and West and larger than France or Germany. By the partition of Poland, the guardians of the old regime and the status quo had violated the very principle of legitimacy for which they had fought revolutionary, and were later to fight Napoleonic, France for a quarter of a century. As a result of the partitions, Russia, which had acquired the largest share, pushed its frontiers deep into east-central Europe to within two hundred miles of Berlin and Vienna.[17] The dramatic expansion and rounding out of the Prussian possessions by the incorporation of Pomerania and Posnania allowed the Hohenzollerns to significantly strengthen their position within Germany and to embark upon the course that eventually led to the foundation of the Second Reich of Bismarck.

29

Roots of the Present

But in addition to land, the partitioners had also acquired a most embarrassing internal problem, a disrupting element that was to continually upset their mutual relations as well as those with the Western powers. The "Polish question," from 1795 on, became the most delicate, persistent, and highly explosive problem of European diplomacy.

CHAPTER TWO

In Search of the
Lost Independence

If you cannot prevent your enemies from swallowing you, at least do not allow them to digest you.

Jean Jacques Rousseau's advice to the Poles

When a bullet strikes a wall, it halts and generates heat. In mechanics this process is called the transforming of mass motion into molecular, of what was outward into an inner force. Something like this happened in Poland after the cruel quelling of the insurrection [of 1863–64]. The nation as a whole woke up, ceased to fight and to conspire, and began to think and to work.

Bolesław Prus

THE THREE VIVISECTIONS of the Polish-Lithuanian commonwealth, followed by the settlement of Vienna in 1815, did not resolve the Polish question; they merely changed its character. Thenceforth the Poles became a divided and oppressed people struggling, often arms in hand, to preserve their cultural identity as well as to regain unity and political independence. This desire was demonstrated dramatically by the Polish participation in the Napoleonic wars on the French side, and by the three major uprisings of 1794, 1830–31, and 1863–64. Each uprising, as well as the so-called Spring of Nations (the revolutionary ferment of 1848–49), not only caused profound embarrassment to the partitioning powers, especially Russia, but also threatened them with serious international complications. After the third insurrection (1863–64), the Polish question was swept under the carpet for two generations by the common effort of Russia, Germany, and, to a lesser extent, Austria-Hungary. The problem of Poland, however, was resurrected by the clash of the partitioning powers in World War I.

While struggling for independence over a period of four generations, Poles took part in most international conspiracies and revolutionary movements in contemporary Europe. The Paris Commune of 1871 had well over a thousand Poles among its participants, among them two leading generals, Jarosław Dąbrowski and Walery Wróblewski; and the Socialist movement in Europe, in all its varieties, was full of Polish adherents. According to Alphonse Lamartine, then head of the French provisional government, the Poles in 1848 were "a ferment of Europe." [1]

While bitter polemics about the issue of why independence was lost were going on among politically active Poles, neither social reformers nor soldiers gave up the struggle for the national cause. Shortly after the Third Partition, Stanisław Staszyc, a leading thinker, writer, and scholar declared: "Even a great nation can fall, but only a worthless one can perish." Regaining "independence," which many understood in the context of political sovereignty, became the central preoccupation of most Polish politicians of the nineteenth century. Many problems, not only political but also social, economic, and even cultural, were approached in terms of their effect on the prospects of national liberation. Even the legitimacy of social revolution, despite frequent and vocal protestation to the contrary on the part of Polish leftist parties, was largely debated in terms of national liberation.

Meanwhile, the work of political rebirth, which had been started by the eighteenth-century reformers and culminated in the constitution of May 3, 1791, was continued during the existence of the Duchy of Warsaw (1807–15). Napoleon had established this state after his victories over Austria, Russia, and Prussia to reward the Poles for their assistance and to have his military outpost in east-central

Europe. His defeat spelled the liquidation of the duchy and its replacement by the Kingdom of Poland, a state established by the Congress of Vienna. The so-called Congress Kingdom (1815–30), a nominally autonomous state in personal union with the tsar of Russia, tried to maintain the reform traditions of the 1791 constitution. The survivors of the reform generation, statesmen like the Prince Adam Czartoryski and Stanisław Potocki, together with their spiritual heirs among the younger generation, set about using the advantages granted to citizens of the Kingdom to rebuild the fabric of their political, cultural, and business life along more modern lines.[2] The liberal constitution of the Congress Kingdom set new standards for political and civic relations in east-central Europe: equality of all citizens before the law, personal freedom of peasants, involvement of the burghers in political activity, and promotion of popular education.

Under an enlightened Tory, Prince Ksawery Drucki-Lubecki, the minister of finance, industries of the Congress Kingdom were developed, new mines and foundries were established, farming was modernized, roads were built, and the postal service was reorganized. Between 1820 and 1826 the textile factories of Łódź increased by tenfold the export of their wares to Russia. A respectable network of schools and teachers colleges was organized; in 1818 the University of Warsaw was founded, and in 1828 the Bank of Poland was established in Warsaw. The population increased rapidly and Warsaw, a city of some 60,000 around 1830, virtually doubled its number of inhabitants every twenty years. The remarkable economic progress of the Kingdom, however, did not channel the energies of a restless, romantic youth dreaming of complete independence. The July revolution in Paris and the subsequent upheaval in Belgium triggered an insurrection in Warsaw in November 1830.

The failure of the uprising of 1830–31 and the suppression of the liberal, constitutional regime of the Congress Kingdom by Tsar Nicholas I interrupted, for a generation or so, the development of Russian Poland. Social, economic, and cultural progress continued, however, in western Poland, which was then under the control of a liberal Prussia. During the 1840s and 1850s various schemes were developed which were to remedy one of the most acute weaknesses of Poland's social structure: the lack of a healthy, energetic middle class. The remedy was largely the work of a young medical doctor, Karol Marcinkowski, who organized several schools that provided vocational education for Polish youth. Marcinkowski also created an association of patriotic, concerned citizens who through scholarships helped poor boys train in arts and crafts as well as commercial and mechanical skills. At the same time, he worked hard at establishing Polish banks, stock companies, real estate firms, and cooperative associations of all kinds.

The industrial development of western Germany in the nineteenth century, especially the Rhineland, created profitable markets for Posnania's farm products and made the province "the granary of Prussia." The pioneering work of the burgher Marcinkowski was supplemented by the labors of an aristocrat, Count Edward Raczyński, a book collector and art lover as well as a successful country squire. By establishing an impressive public library and organizing a vibrant publishing company in Poznań in the 1840s, Raczyński soon made the city the most important cultural center of Poland.

Poles in exile in the early nineteenth century contributed not only Romantic poetry (Adam Mickiewicz, Juliusz Słowacki, Zygmunt Krasiński, and C. K. Norwid) and music (Frederic Chopin), but also political ideas of lasting significance. In 1832, a group of Polish émigrés, former soldiers of the uprising of 1830–31, formed a political party known as the Democratic Society. In its manifesto of 1836 the society declared that in order to regain state independence, Poland must rely not on the illusory help of any foreign power, which might be eager to use Poland as a pawn, but on its own forces and resources. Furthermore, the society maintained that to keep independence Poland must be democratic and progressive: "Europe is alive with new conceptions of the social order. It is being organized on new foundations. . . . In order to live in Europe Poland must do the same." The manifesto inspired most Polish political parties of the late nineteenth century as well as groups in the twentieth century, especially the Polish Socialist party, and the peasant, or populist movement.

⤳ ✍

The turmoil that occurred during the Spring of Nations slowed down beginnings of the social, economic, and cultural advances that were made in Posnania during the 1830s and 1840s. After the Crimean war, during the late 1850s, the center of gravity of Polish national life shifted again to the Congress Kingdom. There, the period of liberal reforms initiated by Tsar Alexander II in 1855 allowed the patriots of Russian Poland some temporary leeway. The tsar's concessions gave rise to the hope of Polish-Russian conciliation, an idea preached by Aleksander Wielopolski. In 1857 the tsarist authorities permitted Count Andrew Zamoyski, who represented another brand of enlightened Polish conservatism, to form the Agricultural Society in Warsaw. The society not only stimulated farming by fostering new methods of cultivation and by providing animals and seeds, but soon became a center of cultural and political activity. It also became something of a quasi parliament, eagerly debating such controversial and hitherto forbidden issues as the emancipation of serfs and Jews and the reestablishment of the University of Warsaw. In 1861–62, St. Petersburg allowed a far-reaching repolonization of local self-government as well as the school system of Congress Poland.

A considerable expansion of trade and industry took place in Russian Poland in the 1850s. Railroads were built, starting with a line connecting Warsaw with St. Petersburg and Vienna. The population of the textile center of Łódź doubled and the city's industrial output more than tripled in a decade. In 1859 the first textile mill to use steam power was built there, with 18,000 spindles and 100 looms. Gas lights were put on the streets, and soon other industries began to develop. Łódź became one of the most important industrial centers of the empire, a "Polish Manchester," exporting its manufactures not only to Russia but to Far Eastern markets as well. In 1869 the value of industrial production in Russian Poland amounted only to some $15,000,000, but by the end of the century it was more than ten times that amount. The number of towns in the Congress Kingdom with over 10,000 inhabitants went up from seven to thirty-six, while the total population by 1897 exceeded 10 million.

Economic expansion was temporarily interrupted by an ill-timed and badly prepared uprising in 1863–64 against tsarist rule. The young people who precipitated the insurrection were permeated with liberal and progressive ideas, and they rose to struggle for Poland's independence against a despotic and imperialist regime. The uprising had as a visionary slogan, "For your freedom and for ours," which signified that the insurrectionists intended not only to liberate the Poles from the Russian yoke, but also to help other subjugated nationalities of the tsarist empire, including the Russian people themselves. Following Mickiewicz's saying, "He who cares only about the interests of his own nation is an enemy of Liberty," the leaders of the insurrection took a keen interest in the fate of other oppressed ethnic groups. The conspiratorial national government abolished serfdom and proclaimed the renewal of the old federal ties previously uniting the Poles with the Lithuanians and Ruthenians, who "despite differences of faith and language, shall enjoy equal rights in free determination of their fate." The appeal was regarded by the Russians, irrespective of their political orientation, as a mortal threat to the unity of their empire. United behind their government, they fought fiercely to suppress the "Polish menace."

The defeat of the uprising of 1863–64 was a milestone in Polish history, the dying gasp of the old Romantic Poland. Following the suppression of the revolt, the last remnant of the autonomy that Russian Poland had enjoyed between 1832 and 1864 was abolished. The so-called committee of reconstruction set to work reshaping the administrative structure of the country, with civilian and military power united in the hands of a Russian governor general. Garrisons numbering up to 300,000 soldiers were quartered in a country of some seven million people. Russian was made the official language, and Polish law courts and schools were supplanted by the Russian system and staffed with officials from distant parts of the tsarist empire. In 1869 the University of Warsaw was closed, and in 1886 the Polish Bank

36

was made into a branch of the St. Petersburg State Bank. The very name of Poland was abolished and replaced by the new term, "Vistula Land." To promote the policy of russification, St. Petersburg intensified its effort to encourage the historic antagonism existing between ethnic Poles and the Lithuanian, Byelorussian, and Ukrainian inhabitants of the old commonwealth.

The collapse of the insurrection of 1863–64 also had profound social and economic consequences for Russian Poland. The repeated attempts to regain political independence had exhausted and financially ruined a large proportion of the gentry, the class that had formed the backbone of all three uprisings. Numerous estates were confiscated by the tsarist authorities and given to their loyal servants, while several thousand members of the gentry were deported to Siberia. Many members of that ruined and decimated class flocked in search of employment into the towns, where they swelled the ranks of the middle and lower middle classes, especially the intelligentsia.

With political oppression the energies of the people were channeled into economic activity, for which, at that time, conditions were favorable. The revolutionary authorities had promised the peasants the land on which they worked. In order to counteract that scheme of agrarian reform and to woo the rural masses, the tsarist government instituted a land settlement program in the ten Polish provinces more speedily than in other parts of the empire, and in a manner much more advantageous to the Polish peasants, who received more land than their Russian counterparts.[3] As a result, Polish villages during the first years after the uprising were fairly prosperous, and this in turn had a favorable influence on the industrial development that was rapidly progressing.

Between 1880 and 1890, significant changes took place in Russian Poland. The beneficent land settlement program increased the purchasing power of small farmers, while the growth of industry created a relative abundance of goods. The removal of the customs frontier, which had separated Congress Poland from the rest of the empire until 1851, opened the vast markets of European and Asiatic Russia. The construction of railroads connecting Poland with these markets

37

enabled the products of Polish industry to come within the reach of hitherto inaccessible consumers. In 1884 a high tariff was placed on coal, iron, and steel, which meant that all the important Polish industries were heavily protected and could expand without fear of competition. The results were striking. Although by population, Congress Poland constituted only 7.3 percent of the entire Russian empire, by 1890 its industrial output amounted to about one-quarter of the total imperial production.

Despite the oppression, intellectual changes had been evolving for several years, and these changes were increasingly evident in the mood of the educated classes. The concept of permanent insurrection, of constant, almost compulsive armed struggle for national independence, an idea imposed by the genius of the Romantic poets and a handful of politicians, was now increasingly questioned. The younger generation believed that work and the acquisition of knowledge as well as wealth, and not constant bloody sacrifice, were the virtues needed for the survival of the battered nation. This new temper, which had prevailed in western Poland more than a generation earlier, now spread to Russian Poland and captured the minds of a large segment of its intellectual elite.

The industrial and commercial expansion of Russian Poland was determined not only by favorable economic conditions of the 1870s and the 1890s, but also by the changing moral and intellectual climate that took place after 1864. The insurrection of 1863–64 had formed the peak of Polish Romantic and revolutionary activity. During the decades following the suppression of the uprising, the Poles, frustrated and disillusioned in their struggle for political freedom, began to reevaluate their political methods and psychological attitudes. The shock of this third major failure caused the politically conscious groups to embark on a deep introspective analysis of the national predicament. The advocates of a new approach rejected armed struggle and violent revolutionary changes as a means of achieving

38

independence and instead urged their countrymen to work "organically" for economic and cultural improvements, i.e., for rapid modernization of every aspect of national activity, especially the economy. Rationalization of agrarian production and the growing awareness of the role of industry were stressed by the partisans of organic work. The new approach recognized the importance of patient, orderly, everyday work aimed at improving economic well-being and the educational standards of the society. The mood of the new generation was best expressed by the writer Aleksander Świętochowski, who declared: "We wish to extend work and learning in society, to discover new resources, to utilize existing ones, and to concern ourselves with our own problems and not those of others." [4]

The intellectual framework for organic work, or "positivism," was shaped by a group of journalists and pamphleteers. The most prominent among this group was Świętochowski. He was impatient with the Romantic writers, whom he denounced as dilettantes and literary parasites, deluding their countrymen with mystical messianism ("Poland is the Christ of all nations!"), and foolishly idealizing the country's past in long, complex, and often confusing poems. In his Warsaw periodical entitled *Prawda* (Truth), Świętochowski formulated a new, realistic, positivistic, secular program based on the religion of humanity and the gospel of organic work for tangible gains. He worshiped energy, hard work, discipline, and progress, and regarded the dream of national independence as senseless and unachievable and an excuse for daydreaming and idleness. The more modest and realistic goals should be the expansion of education, the development of material resources, native trade, and industry, and the achievement of cultural autonomy within the framework of the tsarist empire.

Swiętochowski performed an important and manifold task. First, he helped to shape the minds of the intelligentsia of Russian Poland, a growing class that included not only intellectuals in the strict sense of the term, but all educated and politically conscious individuals, all "people who understood." Together with merchants, artisans, and civil servants, the new intelligentsia formed the nucleus a of a middle class that had hitherto scarcely existed. In the Russian Poland of the 1860s and 1870s the intelligentsia was largely composed of people who came from the gentry class. Deprived of their estates either by the tsarist political reprisals that followed the uprising of 1863–64, or suffering because of economic conditions, they now reinforced the ranks of the "proletarians of the brains." Świętochowski urged these people to make the best of their new status and to acquire higher education.

Second, Świętochowski's ideas were to permeate the Polish intelligentsia with the modern spirit of scientific inquiry, the desire to critically examine political as well as social phenomena and to use the knowledge acquired thereby in the service of the people. He took to task the old nobility for its falsely heroic attitude, for its eagerness to fight and die, if need be, for the fatherland. What was important, he argued, was not the readiness to die, but the ability to live for one's country and to serve its interests effectively, to the best of one's ability. Thus, as in the case of the Cracow historical school, which was concurrently analyzing the nation's past and also rejecting the Romantic notion of struggle to the bitter end, the conclusion was unmistakable: conciliation and compromise were often more useful instruments of struggle for national existence than hopeless armed conflict.

The concept of organic work made a remarkable contribution to the long overdue task of reshaping the collective psyche. Its theory and practice, however, had a negative side, part of which was the acceptance of the status quo. Such an attitude of resignation condoned neglect of political work and political opportunities and led to what became known as "triple loyalty" to the partitioning powers. Triple loyalty implied political passivity, renunciation of any significant steps to change the prevailing international framework, and a basic acceptance of the existing social and economic system. In practice, it meant not only conciliation, but even servility. As was to be expected, a sharp reaction set in among the young generation of radicals and Socialists against these attitudes, which had become especially popular among well-to-do classes.[5]

☙ ❧

While tsarist Russia ignored even the modest political aspirations of its Polish loyalists, the Germany of Bismarck waged a ruthless, relentless, and systematic struggle against anything Polish in the areas it controlled. In Austrian Galicia, on the other hand, following the Austro-Hungarian compromise of 1867, conditions were soon created which permitted local loyalists to reassert themselves and even to gain the upper hand by eliciting from Vienna a measure of provincial autonomy.

The experiment in Galician autonomy was largely made possible by the earlier work of the group of historians previously mentioned, known as the Cracow school. They prepared the minds of their countrymen for acquiescence in the policy of conciliation put forward by some conservative politicians. After the disappointments of the Crimean War and the uprising of 1863–64, the mood of realism and sober introspection had also descended on Galicia. In the newly liberalized and polonized University of Cracow, a group of historians led by Józef Szujski decided that if the discipline of history were to serve as *magistra vitae,* then a rigorous stock-taking of the nation's past and its mistakes must be undertaken. The Cracow historians swept aside the arguments of their forerunners of the Romantic period that old Poland fell as an innocent victim of the three predatory powers. In a series of well-researched and persuasive monographs, the Cracow scholars advanced the proposition that Poland itself was to blame for its downfall, that internal anarchy and social and economic underdevelopment had led to paralysis and the inability to resist foreign encroachments. Weak central power, an empty treasury, the impoverished peasants in bondage, a weakened middle class barred from participation in the government, a vestigial army good for parading but not for fighting—these were, according to the Cracow historians, the main causes of the catastrophe of Poland. The enlight-

41

ened reforms of the eighteenth century, they argued, like the constitution of May 3, 1791, came too late to save a structure eroded by generations of neglect and anarchy.

The remedy for the mistakes of the past, they maintained, would not be found in new insurrections, in new bloody sacrifices that would lead the nation to self-destruction, but in internal retrenchment and methodic, well-planned work within the existing system. The inference was that the past should be forgotten and new ways found to consolidate whatever still remained. After the Prussian defeat of Austria at Sadova in 1866 and the establishment of the Dual Monarchy in 1867, there existed in a liberalized Austria, argued the writers of the Cracow school, a favorable framework for national existence; a policy of conciliation should, therefore, replace that of insurrection.

One of the men influenced by the Cracow historians was Count Agenor Gołuchowski, a lawyer by education, a former governor general of Galicia (1850–59), briefly an Austrian minister of the interior (1859), and the virtual prime minister in 1860. Gołuchowski was convinced that the Poles of Galicia must abandon their perennial conspiratorial activities, postpone the armed struggle for independence, which he considered hopeless anyway, and undertake economic, educational, and social reforms to raise the level of wealth and culture. If Poland was ever to regain its independence, Gołuchowski argued, it could be done only in cooperation with one of the partition powers. He was convinced it would be Austria. The slogan *Polonia fara da se* he considered an absurdity. Here his conclusions coincided with those of the Cracow school, which had proclaimed: "Five centuries ago our enemy was Germany; today it is Russia, and Russia only." A logical extension of this theory was reconciliation with Vienna.

The Austro-Prussia war of 1866 opened new vistas to Gołuchowski. After Sadova many people expected a European war, because of the French intervention on behalf of Austria and Russian entry into the conflict on Prussia's side. Under these circumstances Polish loyalty would be of great importance. Utilizing his good personal relations with Emperor Francis Joseph, Gołuchowski offered to secure the loyalty of his countrymen in Galicia in exchange for a series of political and cultural concessions. To prove his influence, Gołuchowski convinced the Galician diet, even before the granting of the concessions, to vote a significant address to the throne. The message, voted on December 10, 1866, ascribed to Austria the mission of a shield of Western civilization against Russia: "For centuries," the address declared, "such a mission fell to us [the Poles]. Therefore, without fear of deserting our national ideal, believing in the mission of Austria and trusting in the durability of the changes announced by the Monarch as his firm purpose, we declare from the bottom of our heart that with Thee, Most illustrious Lord, we stand and we will stand."

The declaration of loyalty was accepted by Vienna and was soon repaid in the form of a series of decrees that established Galicia as an autonomous province within the Dual Monarchy. The administration, the law courts, and the school system were thoroughly polonized. The fact that the autonomous Galician institutions had at their disposal limited financial resources restricted the scope of their work. Nevertheless, on the whole, local self-government in Galicia worked well. It allowed for a fairly extensive participation in public affairs and served as a good school of local politics for over two generations until World War I.[6] Less satisfied were the Ukrainians, who formed a majority in the eastern, ethnically mixed segment of the province, but even they enjoyed economic and cultural benefits from the autonomous status of Galicia.

After the 1860s, Galicia was fully integrated into the political life of the Hapsburg monarchy. In the years 1867–69 the province had 63 members in the imperial parliament of 353 deputies. Following the introduction of universal suffrage in 1907, Galicia had 106 out of 516 seats in the Vienna parliament; of these, 70 were held by Poles and 27 by Ukrainians. Despite a relatively slow rate of economic growth, the expansion of the school system and the struggle against illiteracy proceeded at a faster rate in Galicia than in other non-German areas of Austria-Hungary. In the educational field a special role was played by the Society of Village Schools established in Cracow in 1891. In addition to founding elementary, secondary, and vocational schools,

43

the society published school books, and founded reading rooms and adult education programs.[7]

Thus, Galicia, with a number of cultural institutions such as the universities at Cracow and Lwów (Lviv) and Polish Academy of Arts and Sciences in Cracow, became a "Polish Piedmont," a nursery of Polish scholars and artists. For their privileged position, the Galician Poles reciprocated with political support and loyalty to the dynasty, a support that remained basically unaffected until destroyed by the trauma of World War I.[8] It would be destroyed only by the ordeals of the war, the inability of the Austrian government to foster an "Austro-Polish solution," and by the growing dependence of Vienna on Berlin, which resulted in the betrayal of Polish interests to those of Ukraine at the treaty of Brest-Litovsk in March 1918.

While the Galician Poles were embarking upon an experiment in autonomy, the Poles of the western, Prussian-controlled provinces were continuing their grim everyday struggle against germanization by means of organization, hard work, and the creation of self-help institutions. The results could be seen in many spheres of activity. In 1859 a Polish newspaper was founded in Poznań. Then a loan bank for farmers was set up, followed by an industrial bank in 1863. In 1872 the scattered cooperative societies were brought together and in 1886 they were welded into a solid Union of Cooperative Banks, which by 1910 numbered 265 members with a turnover of 208 million marks. This was paralleled by the development of a net of cooperatives known as the Farmer's Circles. In 1873 there were only a few in existence, but by 1914 they numbered nearly 300 well-organized local units, collectively purchasing the essential needs of the farmer such as seeds, fodder, and machinery, while catering also to his cultural and social needs and providing him with credit. From Posnania the movement spread to Pomerania, and finally to Silesia, where by the end of the nineteenth century a remarkable national revival was under way.[9]

The founder of the German empire, Chancellor Otto von Bismarck, regarded the Polish efforts at self-reliance and organization with suspicion and anger. The Poles were hateful to him not only as Slavs but also as ultramontane Roman Catholics. The Kulturkampf was triggered mostly by his fear of a growing "Polish menace" to the unity and cohesiveness of the newly established Reich.

Polish Catholics responded to the challenge with a redoubling of their religious and national zeal. The furious Bismarck replied to this by launching a vast colonization scheme to gain more land for the Germans. His slogan was "tear the Poles by the roots." From the Reichstag Bismarck obtained a grant of 100 million marks for the acquisition of Polish estates on which German colonists were to be settled. At the same time a series of strict and outwardly well coordinated measures were introduced to limit the teaching of Polish and to strengthen the German culture in the eastern provinces of the Reich. But all these measures came too late. By the 1880s the Poles were sufficiently developed nationally to offer stiff resistance to the colonization drive.

After having successfully withstood the Kulturkampf, the Poles were able to steadily improve their economic position. Berlin, anxious to consolidate the German element in its eastern borderlands, gave large governmental appropriations and subsidies to the German colonists there. They were encouraged to buy more land and establish new shops and factories. By that time, however, the Polish cooperative banks and Farmer's Circles were strong enough to resist most German offers with counteroffers of their own. Moreover, economics were now intertwined with patriotic considerations: for the Poles thrift, hard work, and the struggle for the land became a vital part of their struggle for ethnic survival.

Bismarck's successor continued his colonizing drive. In 1898, 1902, and 1908 new appropriations were voted totaling 375 million marks, and by 1913 some half a billion marks had been spent. The mounting demand for the land sent the prices of all real estate skyrocketing: between 1880 and 1900 they nearly trebled. This motivated many German colonists, most of whom had only been lured by the government to emigrate eastward because of the generous sub-

45

sidies, to sell their farms to the highest bidder and to move back to the more congenial parts of the empire. By 1905 the Germans were losing to the Poles some 50,000 hectares of land every year. The Prussian law of 1908, which introduced various ruthless measures, including compulsory expropriation of Polish land, was a mortal menace to the Poles. Fortunately for them the outbreak of World War I prevented a full implementation of this measure.

The flight from the East (*Ostflucht*) had far-reaching consequences on the ethnic composition of Posnania. Between 1849 and 1871 the number of Germans in Posnania increased; after 1871 they began to leave the province for the greener pastures in the western parts of the German empire. Between 1871 and 1896, on the manorial estates of Posnania, the number of Germans decreased, while the number of Poles rose considerably, from 292,000 to 334,429. In 1867, 62.5 percent of population of Posnania was Roman Catholic (mostly Poles); by 1895 it had risen to 67.1, and by 1910 to 71.3. Thus, in the battle of wits and tenacity up to World War I, the Poles got the upper hand.

This social, economic, and cultural struggle also had a political side: to send as many Polish deputies as possible both to the provincial Prussian parliament and to the imperial Reichstag. The Poles were also largely successful in achieving this goal, partly because they had found some support from the Catholic party, as well as from the German Social Democrats, who were anxious to embarrass the conservative establishment. From their parliamentary tribune in Berlin the Polish deputies, free from the censorship imposed on the Polish press, were able to denounce quite openly the inequities of the local administration and the oppressive policies of the federal government. One of the most forceful and eloquent members of the Polish circle was Wojciech Korfanty, son of a Silesian miner, a man who was destined to play a vital role in the national reawakening of his people.

There were numerous similarities between events in Posnania and Pomerania and those in Silesia, more specifically, the same patient, persistent grassroots work of a handful of resourceful, determined, dedicated people, whose labor, in due time, produced amazing results. There were, however, two essential differences which made the emancipation of Silesia immensely more difficult: first, the province had been separated from Poland as far back as 1335, and consequently had fewer direct links with the fatherland; second, during more than five centuries of foreign domination, Silesia lost practically the entire educated stratum of the people through germanization. The struggle of the Silesian people for emancipation was one of the great dramas of the late nineteenth and early twentieth centuries.[10]

Until the 1740s, Silesia was under the Hapsburgs. Annexed to Prussia by Frederick II, it was subjected for over a century and a half to a systematic denationalization. After 1871, Germany embarked on an extensive scheme of economic development of Silesian national resources (including the large deposits of coal) utilizing the money provided by French war indemnities. With practically no national consciousness and minimal economic power, the Polish rural population seemed to have little chance for ethnic survival. But again the challenge of the German Kulturkampf rekindled a dormant national awareness, stimulating a scarcely flickering spark and turning it into a blazing flame. The deeply Catholic Silesian farmers and miners, faced with Prussian governmental policies that would rob them of both their mother tongue and their religion, awoke and began to fight. The struggle was as much a class struggle as a fight for national and religious rights. Korfanty, because of his skill and persistence, managed to score numerous successes. By 1902 a Polish newspaper had been established, and Polish deputies were being elected to the Reichstag in considerable numbers. In 1907 the Polish vote, which because of German administrative manipulations and economic pressures had been very small, began to catch up with the number of German ballots.

The fight of the Posnanians against germanization and colonization, a struggle which had its repercussions in both the neighboring provinces of Pomerania and Silesia, was to the Poles a challenge of the first magnitude, a struggle for survival. According to Professor W. J. Rose, "A byproduct of all this was the development of the individual citizen and the reinforcement of the social and economic order to a degree never known heretofore in Polish lands." [11]

⤳ ⤶

By the close of the nineteenth century the workers, the peasants, and the intelligentsia had emerged as the three most active strata of Polish society. This phenomenon, in turn, led to the formation of the three main political movements of contemporary Poland: Socialist, Nationalist, and Populist. Each movement developed simultaneously in Russian Poland and in Austrian Galicia, and each eventually affected the German-controlled area of Poland.

The first to form modern political parties were the urban workers led by radical intelligentsia. The early Socialist circles on Polish soil came into being during the 1870s in Galicia. But it was in Warsaw that the first Socialist party of some consequence was founded. By the late nineteenth century Socialist theory had begun to have some acceptance, a fact that was acknowledged by a memorandum of the German chancellery on August 24, 1873: "Of all lands belonging to His Imperial Majesty the Kingdom of Poland more than any other constitutes a favorable ground for the [Socialist] International."

The rapid growth of industries in Russian Poland greatly favored enterprising capitalists, "the sober and the strong." They took very seriously the slogan *"enrichissez-vous,"* and reaped considerable profits. On the other hand, the conditions of the working class, although better than in Russia proper, were unsatisfactory. The lack of social legislation left wide scope for abuse and gave the industrialists numerous advantages. As in the rest of the empire, workers were not allowed either to form trade unions or to strike. By the end of the nineteenth century the industrial proletariat in Russian Poland already numbered about 300,000 in a population of some 9.5 million; if one includes some 140,000 craftsmen and artisans, who by then played a very important role in the economy of the country, the approximate figure is 440,000 workers. Except for a small prosperous group, most of the craftsmen and artisans should be considered as an urban proletariat; and impoverished craftsmen were often a better recruiting

48

ground for radical Socialist ideas than were industrial workers. This fact was noticed by the Russian revolutionary leader Stepnyak (Sergei Kravchinski), who visited Warsaw in 1879. Stepnyak could hardly get over the zeal and the skill of the Polish revolutionaries, many of whom were craftsmen and not industrial workers:

> When all had assembled [he wrote, describing a Socialist group] in Warsaw there were altogether some fifteen to eighteen people. It was a meeting of delegates or organizers, each of whom represented a circle of fifteen to twenty persons. Thus at that moment there must have been about 150 to 200 workmen united in one organization—a number that surprised me, indeed; for I know that all this had been done in a few months, and that eighteen months before there was not a single socialist circle among the Warsaw workmen. I remembered that when we Russian revolutionists began our propaganda in St. Petersburg in 1871, at the end of the first two years we could hardly contrive to impart to a dozen workmen the notions of socialism.[12]

The first Polish Socialist party, known as the Proletariat, was founded in Warsaw in 1882 by Ludwik Waryński, but it was soon discovered by the tsarist police. Arrests, deportations, and executions followed, and by 1886 the Proletariat had ceased to exist. The next Socialist group organized itself in exile. In 1892 a group of veterans of the former Socialist circles declared itself as the political organization of the working class of Poland, struggling, however, not only for liberation of the class from capitalist exploitation, but also to free the entire nation from its political subjugation. This newly founded Polish Socialist party, according to its program, was determined to win political power for the proletariat and to set up an independent democratic republic, possibly in a federal union of Poland, Lithuania, and the Ukraine, which would form the future democratic, and eventually Socialist, Polish republic.

But even while the Polish Socialist party was in the process of being organized, opposition to its program arose in many places. The opposition was to crystallize in 1893 and take shape in a separate political party named the Social Democratic party of the Kingdom of

49

Poland and Lithuania. The new party rejected the fusion of Socialism and patriotism and emphasized close cooperation with the Russian Socialist movement. The history of the Polish labor movement after this time was largely the story of the fight between these two rival groups and their descendants, one of which was to be the Communist party of Poland.

The Polish Socialist party was the first Marxist group that explicitly and directly connected the problem of social justice with that of national liberation, and it decided to fight with equal determination for both at the same time. This policy was, perhaps, the secret of the party's numerous successes. The fact that the Polish Socialist party proclaimed its all-Polish character, irrespective of the partisan orientations, gave it added strength, because the party soon managed to gain precious allies in similar movements in Galicia, Posnania, and Silesia.

From the very beginning many people, such as Ignacy Daszyński, the eloquent son of a Galician official, and Józef Piłsudski, an ambitious, stubborn, restless, and imaginative medical student-turned-revolutionary, were attracted to the Polish Socialist party exactly because it combined the revolution against class injustice with the struggle for national liberation.

Piłsudski's socialism was sui generis: it combined the doctrines of Marx and Engels with those of Louis Blanc and other utopian Socialists, as well as with the traditions of the emigré organization known as the Polish Democratic Society. From Marx, Piłsudski adopted the idea of the struggle against capitalism on behalf of the working class. On the other hand, he was always suspicious of the exclusively materialistic interpretation of history and of doctrinaire cosmopolitanism. Unlike many of his Socialist comrades he never rejected patriotism. Quite the contrary, he took it for granted. After having participated as one of the leaders of the revolution of 1904–5 in Russian Poland, Piłsudski began to drift away from Socialism and devote himself more and more to military pursuits. On the eve of World War I his links with Socialism were already rather tenuous, although he was reluctant to denounce them openly. This pattern was

50

not unique: it applied to many contemporary leaders of national liberation movements of Eastern Europe who tried to unite international Socialism with patriotism.[13]

The combination of Socialism and patriotism was exactly what the Social Democrats despised so much. The driving force behind the new Social Democratic party's struggle against the hated "Social Patriotism" was Rosa Luxemburg. Born of a prosperous Jewish family in central Poland in 1871, she was afflicted from childhood by a hip ailment. Because of illness her energies were channeled more toward intellectual activities. While still in a Warsaw high school she joined the revolutionary circles of the Proletariat. In 1886, to avoid imprisonment, Luxemburg escaped to Zürich, which at that time was a rallying point for Russian Socialists. She decided at the outset of her activity that the Polish Marxist movement should reject the idea of national independence. How could the proletariat of Poland, she argued, create a bourgeois national state? The rebirth of such a state would contradict both the workers' own vital economic interests and the interest of the Polish bourgeoisie, who gained so many economic advantages from the fact that the industries of the Congress Kingdom served Russian markets. On the other hand, if the Polish working class had sufficient strength to overthrow the power of the three strongest governments in Europe, then it would also have enough drive to achieve social revolution. For it was only *social* revolution that could offer the hope of better conditions for the Polish proletariat.

An all-Russian constitution, with territorial autonomy for Poland, was accepted as the minimum aim of the Social Democratic party. An independent Poland was branded a utopian objective, harmful to the workers' cause. First, argued Rosa Luxemburg, independence diverted attention to aims that had nothing to do with class struggle and proletarian internationalism; second, it spelled the loss of Russian markets, which were essential to the very existence of the Polish industry and therefore also essential to the working class. Polish Socialists in German and Austrian Poland were advised to follow the example of the Social Democratic party, and to integrate their activities

51

with their respective social-democratic movements. Soon Rosa Luxemburg was to formulate her theory of the "organic incorporation" of the Congress Kingdom of Poland into the Russian state, and to expand the economic foundations of this thesis in her doctoral dissertation, entitled *Die industrielle Entwicklung Polens* (The Industrial Development of Poland), published in Leipzig in 1898.

Thus, from the very beginning, the differences between the two parties centered on the national problem. On one side were the Social Democrats, who claimed that national cultural autonomy would sufficiently safeguard the legitimate national interests of the Polish proletariat. On the other side stood the Polish Socialist party, who would be satisfied with nothing short of full political independence and severance of all ties with the Russian empire, whatever its future political structure. For the Social Democrats, forerunners of the Communist party of Poland, the international solidarity of the proletariat was a primary and decisive factor, overruling national allegiance. Such allegiance was held to be only a remnant of the receding past, to be discarded as quickly as possible in order to reach a higher stage of social development. Social Democrats rejected the idea of an all-Polish Socialist movement, and instead advocated a separate group for each of the three sections of Poland. The activities of each group would be limited to the partition frontiers, and there would be encouragement to merge, or at least federate, with their respective Russian, Austrian, and Prussian comrades. As for the Social Democratic party of Poland and Lithuania, it declared itself for a common fight with Russian labor groups for the cause of the proletarian revolution.

The revolution of 1905, which marked the entry of the Polish working class into the political arena, demonstrated the considerable dynamic power, endurance, and remarkable spirit of self-sacrifice of the proletariat of the Congress Kingdom. The working-class movement exerted some influence on other political groups: a typical proletarian form of struggle, the strike, was soon imitated by other classes of the nation. From this point on, the working-class parties played a considerable role in political life of the country. The purely material interests of the workers were also well served by the 1905 revolution. Real wages in industry increased by about 20 percent in comparison with the period prior to 1904.[14] Another valuable gain of the revolution, which resulted in the tsar granting a constitution to his empire, was the right of free association. Finally, the revolutionary struggle created a sort of legend, a proletarian epic. The price paid for this, however, was very high: the armed struggle lasted longer than the guerrilla warfare of 1863–64, and it cost more in human lives and material destruction.

The close of the nineteenth century was also the period of the political awakening of the rural population, the birth of the peasant, or Populist movement, and of the first peasant political parties. It was no accident that this movement originated in Galicia, where the economic conditions of the peasantry were harsher than in Prussian or even Russian Poland. The liquidation of serfdom, which came during the late 1840s and early 1850s as a result of the Spring of Nations, did not immediately improve the material condition of the Galician peasants, who suffered from the fragmentation of their landholdings as well as from outmoded methods of cultivation.[15]

The beginnings of the Populist movement owed a great deal to Stanisław Stojałowski, a devoted and determined Galician parish priest. Fighting against heavy odds, which included not only reprisals by an administration tightly controlled by the conservative gentry, but also the opposition of his ecclesiastic superiors, Stojałowski founded in 1875 the first newspaper for the villagers, *Wieniec i Pszczółka* (The Garland and the Bee). The purpose of the paper was to defend the economic interests of the peasants and to achieve for them better schools and the right to participate in political life. Taking as an example the work of his countrymen in Posnania, Father Stojałowski organized a Union of Farmers' Circles in 1877. This program was modest indeed, but it was the first step toward political organization of the hitherto amorphous and lethargic peasantry. And indeed, his work shook the rural masses of Galicia out of passivity and prepared the ground for the formation of the more politically dynamic Populist movement.[16]

Stojałowski's pioneering work was extended and intensified by a married couple, Bolesław and Maria Wysłouch, both of gentry origin and both veterans of the first Socialist circles in Russian Poland, where they had found themselves as political refugees in Lwów. In April 1889 they set up a special paper for peasants, entitled *Przyjaciel ludu* (The Peasant's Friend). While Stojałowski's movement was permeated with clerical influence and was based on the papal encyclical *Rerum novarum* (1891), the Wysłouches' was an independent, secular force, an expression of the peasantry's political, social, and economic aspirations. The Wysłouches, brought up in the Populist tradition, performed an enormous educational and political task, supplementing as well as superseding the pioneering work of Stojałowski, with whom they often quarreled bitterly. In 1894 delegates of various peasant organizations inspired mostly by the Wysłouches held a congress in Lwów and prepared the ground for the formation of the first peasant political group. In July 1895 the Polish Peasant party was formed at a congress held at Rzeszów. Initially the party cooperated with the Galician Socialists led by Ignacy Daszyński, but it later took an independent course.

At the beginning of the twentieth century, the Peasant party was taken over by a group of younger men educated in the schools of Stojałowski and the Wysłouches; the most prominent among them were Jan Stapiński and Wincenty Witos. Stapiński was more of an agitator and demagogue, but Witos came to be a statesman. He was born in 1874, the son of a poor peasant from the region of Tarnów. As a boy he had pastured geese and cattle and managed to acquire a limited elementary schooling. Because of his toughness, ability, and perseverance, he rose to the top. In 1905, Witos was elected to the county council of Tarnów. In 1908 he was a deputy in the Galician provincial diet at Lwów, and by 1911 he was representing the Polish Peasant party in the Viennese parliament, where he displayed remarkable skill both as a tactician and an orator. After Polish independence, he would be prime minister three times.

Despite the emphasis on the grievances of the peasantry, especially the urgency of agrarian reform, the Peasant party leaders never rejected patrotism. From the beginning they viewed the peasantry as heir to the country's historic tradition and stressed its strivings for national independence. The rise of a particular form of national consciousness among the peasantry during the nineteenth century had profoundly affected its concept of political democracy. Thus, the Populist movement played a significant role in preparing the rural population for the eventual recovery of political sovereignty. The peasant leaders often bitterly criticized the excessive loyalist zeal of their conservative opponents who, until World War I, practically controlled the administration of Galicia, and who frequently exploited their political ascendancy to perpetuate social injustices and to foster their class interests.

✍ ✍

By the close of the nineteenth century, the organic work and positivist theories, so popular after the failure of the 1863 uprising, came under attack by supporters of neoromanticism. The neoromantic school of thought was fostered by many writers and artists, including the Cracow-born painter, Jan Matejko. Beginning in the 1860s, Matejko set out to depict the glories as well as the miseries of the old Poland in a series of large paintings, some of them of considerable artistic as well as documentary value. The impact of these canvasses on the popular imagination was considerable. Together with the historic epics of Henryk Sienkiewicz, such as the three-volume novel *Trylogia* (The Trilogy), which described in heroic terms the deeds of Polish war heroes of the seventeenth century, and Stefan Żeromski's novels about the struggle for independence during the Napoleonic period, the canvasses of Matejko helped to counteract the impact of positivism and triple loyalty on Polish minds. In 1904, Stanisław Wyspiański, poet, painter, and philosopher, launched in his play, significantly entitled *Wyzwolenie* (Liberation), with the provocative words: "A nation has no right to exist unless as a sovereign state." Such battle cries gave a powerful stimulus to the simmering patriotic movement that began to take shape in the 1880s.

Disappointed with the dogmatic and often narrow positivism and loyalism of the years immediately after 1863, a group of young men gathered in Warsaw around a publicist named Jan Popławski. In 1887 they established the weekly *Głos* (Voice). Popławski held attitudes similar to those of Aleksander Świętochowski: realism, soberness, and a dislike of the melodramatic and often hysterical recitations of empty patriotic slogans and incantations. He shared with him also his condemnation of the past national uprisings, which he felt had been badly prepared, poorly led, and above all untimely. But Popławski, who thought in essentially political terms, definitely rejected Świętochowski's attitude of political resignation and his political loyalism.

According to Popławski, organic work was good only as long as it was quietly preparing for the future reconstruction of Polish statehood. While analyzing Polish history, he concluded that the main error of the fifteenth and sixteenth centuries was the country's eastward expansion, which had involved Poland in the affairs of ethnically mixed Lithuania, dragged the Poles into a protracted struggle against Muscovy, and led to the neglect of Polish lands such as Silesia and Pomerania in the north and west.

For Popławski, the main task of Polish statesmanship and the sine qua non of national survival was the regaining of these lands, especially Gdańsk and the mouth of the Vistula. The modern, efficient, dynamic Germany of Bismarck and not the semi-Asiatic, sluggish, backward, Slavic Russia was the main enemy of Poland, according to Popławski.

The ideas of Popławski were elaborated upon by Zygmunt Balicki, author of the booklet *Egoizm narodowy* (National Egoism). In his work Balicki stated the main principles of modern Polish nationalism. His theories were based partially on Charles Darwin and Herbert Spencer, but included considerable contribution of his own ideas, derived from specifically Polish traditions and conditions. For him national egoism was secret egoism, legitimate, justified, and the only way to national survival.

Popławski's and Balicki's work was continued by Roman Dmowski, who rose to be the head of the nationalist movement of Poland. Born in 1864, Dmowski was the most bitter critic of the motives and methods of the revolution which had failed in that year.

Elaborating upon and expanding the concepts of Popławski and Balicki, Dmowski not only synthesized their ideas, but put them into practice. In 1895 he founded in Lwów a theoretical journal, *Przegląd wszechpolski* (The All-Polish Review). Its program was indicated by its title: to arouse and to consolidate public opinion of a divided country in order to prepare for its unification and liberation. By 1897 a political movement was formed around the journal under the name of the National Democratic party.[17]

The party originally considered itself as revolutionary because it rejected loyalty to the partitioning powers and aimed at the overthrow of the status quo. Nevertheless, the National Democratic leadership firmly rejected armed struggle for independence, and stressed the value of unceasing grass roots work to build up national resources in every field of activity as a preparation for independence. The anti-German stand of Popławski was reaffirmed by Dmowski, who by 1904–5 emerged as the most active and fruitful of the National Democratic leaders. While outwardly rejecting the policy of conciliation, the party, from the very beginning, favored Slavic Russia against the two Teutonic partitioning powers. Although the National Democratic party was founded in Austrian Galicia, it firmly stressed its all-Polish character. Soon the party spread to the Congress Kingdom and to Prussian Poland and became a leading political institution of the country. At the beginning of the twentieth century it was probably the strongest single political force in Poland.

The party's anti-German stand had important consequences for two groups. The National Democrats ("Endeks," as they came to be called) assumed an intransigent attitude toward the Jews and Ukrainians, the two ethnic groups they considered inherently pro-German. The Jews were considered by Dmowski as the main enemies of Polish economic emancipation because of what he regarded as their intolerably powerful position in liberal professions, the arts, trade, industry, and handicrafts, and because of their pro-German leanings. The influence of Jews in Socialist movements also made Dmowski, a fierce nationalist and traditionalist, highly suspicious of them. Dmowski was a natural scientist by education and a Darwinist by conviction, and he regarded Ukrainians as an ethnic mishmash to be either assimilated or dominated by the more advanced Poles then controlling politics in eastern Galicia.

In 1902, Dmowski published his programmatic book *Myśli nowoczesnego Polaka* (Thoughts of a Modern Pole) in which he subjected his countrymen's past mores and attitudes to bitter criticism. He accused his fellow-Poles of being effeminate and incapable of persistent effort and compared them unfavorably with Germans, whom he thought of as tough, virile people. If the Poles were to survive, he argued, they had to become strong, discard their traditional softness and passivity, and imitate their main enemies, the Germans. Poles ought to educate themselves for organized, systematic political action and raise patriotism to the rank of religion. The people of Posnania, Pomerania, and Silesia had given the example to the rest of the country how to fight stubbornly and relentlessly for their ethnic survival. The rest of Poland should imitate their example. Dmowski drew logical consequences from Balicki's book on national egoism and declared himself for integral nationalism, the absolute priority of one's national interests. The book condemned Socialism as an international movement directed by Jews and Germans and therefore a menace to Poland.

$$\approx \ll$$

Thus, by the end of the nineteenth century a new generation had matured and the policy of conciliation (*ugoda*) and of triple loyalty had begun to lose its grip on the younger Polish intelligentsia. Only in Galicia, which enjoyed an autonomous status and where Polish cultural life flourished, was the policy of conciliation preached and practiced on a large scale. Although economically far behind Prussian, and even Russian Poland, Galicia was politically as well as culturally far ahead of the other portions of the divided country. Russian Poland, surrounded by protective tariffs, had metallurgic and textile industries that drew considerable benefits from the Asian markets of the tsarist empire. Moreover, an increasing number of enterprising Poles began to occupy high managerial positions in the Russian economy. According to Sir Bernard Pares, by the beginning of the twentieth century the Poles had become "the Scots of the tsarist Empire." [18] As a result the attitude of many Poles toward Russia tended to be ambivalent. They resented the political and cultural repression but at the same time enjoyed the economic benefits derived from membership in a vast empire.

An ambivalence also existed in enlightened Russian political circles toward the Polish problem. Some Russians realized that in the long run it would be very difficult to maintain tsarist rule over this area, which was becoming both a political and strategic embarrassment. On the other hand, imperial pride and prejudice played their role, and most patriotic Russians hated to part with a conquered country that was so important economically for the entire empire.[19] As Dmowski repeatedly stressed in his works, Russian rule over Poland had two important effects on the empire. First, it created a certain community of interests with Germany and thus strengthened the already powerful German influence inside Russia; this, in turn, affected Russia's freedom of movement on the international scene every time the interests of the country clashed with those of Germany. Second, Russian rule over Poland hampered the internal evolution of the empire in a more liberal direction.

Polish participation in the political life of the tsarist empire was on a far smaller scale than that enjoyed by the Poles of Galicia; but after the revolution of 1905, Russian Poles came to play a modest role in the Duma. In the second Duma, Dmowski tried to win over the Russian Constitutional Democratic party to the idea of autonomy for the "Vistula Land." He opposed vigorously and eloquently the harsh methods used by the imperial administration in Russian Poland, but emphasized his party's loyalty to the empire, a bastion of the anti-German coalition. Dmowski was afraid that a continuation of revolutionary ferment in Poland might increase the dependence of Russia on Germany and thus loosen the Franco-Russian alliance on which he staked his hopes. The "Polish Circle" in the Duma proceeded to astonish both Russian as well as Western European public opinion by voting for the military budget, approving the drafting of recruits, and

59

making numerous declarations of support for a strong Russia that would oppose the growing Teutonic danger. Despite Dmowski's parliamentary talents, the Congress Kingdom received no autonomy.[20]

Political oppression and economic exploitation by the partitioning powers had many humiliating and debilitating facets. But, however harsh, they never completely extinguished the cultural creativity of the Polish people or their will to live in freedom. Despite numerous obstacles, intellectual activity was going on in all three partition territories. The Warsaw-educated Maria Skłodowska scored worldwide renown because of her research in physics and chemistry, especially on the radiation of uranium. This led to the discovery of two new radioactive elements, polonium (so named by her in honor of her native country) and radium. After settling in Paris she married Pierre Curie, a professor of the Sorbonne, and together they were awarded a Nobel Prize in 1903. After the death of her husband she became a professor of physics at the Sorbonne. In 1911 she won a second Nobel Prize for her research that led to obtaining pure radium, thus becoming the first woman to win the Nobel Prize in her own right.

Almost simultaneously, two professors of the University of Cracow, Zygmunt Wróblewski, a chemist, and Karol Olszewski, a physicist, discovered a way of liquefying oxygen and nitrogen. Another Pole, Ignacy Jan Paderewski, achieved world fame as a composer and pianist. While on a concert tour of the United States he befriended President Woodrow Wilson, and this friendship was to have a considerable bearing on Poland's destiny at the close of World War I. Arthur Rubinstein, who was born and educated in Poland, through his virtuosity as a pianist made Polish music, especially that of Chopin, known throughout the world. The novelist Henryk Sienkiewicz became popular not only among Poles, but also abroad, where his series of historical novels were translated into some forty languages and published in millions of copies. For his novel *Quo Vadis,* one of the best sellers of all time, Sienkiewicz received the Nobel Prize for literature in 1905.

60

Some creative Poles who were unable to find a proper outlet in their oppressed country found greener pastures in Western Europe. This was the experience of the novelist Joseph Conrad (Korzeniowski) and the poet Guillaume Apollinaire (Kostrowicki), who by their works enriched English and French literature, respectively. Another novelist, Stanisław Przybyszewski, wrote both in Polish and German, but became probably more known and appreciated in Germany than in his native land.

In the field of scholarship the Poles also scored some successes on an international scale. Professor Tadeusz Zieliński wrote first in German and only later in Polish, and became a world authority on the civilization of ancient Greece and Rome. Professors Gabrjel Narutowicz and Ignacy Mościcki achieved considerable success in the fields of engineering and chemistry, respectively, and became well-established scholars in Switzerland. Both were creative, inventive minds of high caliber, and both were destined to become presidents of the reborn Polish republic after World War I. Professor Leon Petrażycki, who first taught at the University of St. Petersburg (during the 1920s he became professor of philosophy of sociology at the Warsaw University), was a pioneer in the field of legal theory. By linking the psychological aspects of all legal problems not only to the action of law, but also to its psychological causes and inner motivation, his theory of law was soon accepted as a significant contribution to legal philosophy.[21]

Although considerable social and economic progress had been made in Poland by the early twentieth century, the lack of capital and entrepreneurial skill created widespread unemployment, especially in the Austrian and Russian provinces. The result was a large-scale migration to Western Europe (mainly Germany and France) and to the Americas (chiefly the United States, Canada, Brazil, and Argentina). There was also a considerable Polish diaspora throughout the vast tsarist empire, composed of political exiles as well as of those who went east in search of better opportunities. Although the Polish migration never assumed the dimensions of the exodus from Ireland, by the time the Polish state was reestablished, about one-fourth of the

61

world's ethnic Poles were living dispersed throughout the world. (By the beginning of the twentieth century, Chicago had the second largest Polish-speaking community in the world.)

From the early 1830s on, much of the Polish intellectual and artistic community had left the country and gone abroad. Some of the most significant work of Mickiewicz, Słowacki, Krasiński, Norwid, Chopin, Paderewski, and Maria Skłodowska Curie was done in exile.

The loss of independence in the eighteenth century had produced negative consequences, both moral and material. Captivity is a bad school, degrading and corrupting its inmates. The armed uprisings scattered throughout the nineteenth century were one proof of it. Yet, the loss of statehood did not spell the end of the Polish nation. Although, in a sense, Poland did not participate fully in the social, economic, and intellectual progress of nineteenth-century Europe, the challenge of the national catastrophe brought about a painful but on the whole fruitful process of national self-evaluation and regeneration. Many vestiges of economic and social underdevelopment, and of cultural backwardness, were still haunting the largely traditionally minded society. But despite these shortcomings the Poles entered the twentieth century better organized, tougher, and more politically mature than their lighthearted, pleasure-loving ancestors who were responsible for the ruin of the Polish-Lithuanian commonwealth.

CHAPTER THREE

The Polish Phoenix

> Poland is still living
> While we are alive.
> *Polish National Anthem*

THE WORK CONTRIBUTED BY the Polish patriots during the partitions brought about a profound transformation of the society. As a result, on the eve of World War I, the Poles, although divided territorially as well as politically, and in many respects suffering from an underdeveloped social and economic structure, were a much more mature nation than before the catastrophes of the eighteenth century.

At the beginning of World War I, Polish public opinion crystallized around two rival camps, or orientations, as they were called: one pro-Russian and another pro-Austrian. The third partitioning power, Germany, had no significant supporters except for a few isolated, mostly highly conservative individuals. The Kulturkampf and the policy of extermination of the Polish element followed by Bismarck and his successors had prevented the formation of any significant pro-German movement in Prussian Poland.

Probably the strongest single political party was the National Democrats led by Roman Dmowski, former chairman of the "Polish Circle" in the Russian Duma. Several years before the outbreak of the war, Dmowski was calling for a united front of all Poles against Germany as Poland's main enemy. As a consequence of this stand,

63

the National Democrats advocated seeking the support of the tsarist empire as the most powerful Slavic and anti-German force. They argued that Russia, allied with France and Britain, would defeat Germany and her vassal, Austria-Hungary, and would thus reunite all territories inhabited by the Poles under the scepter of the Romanovs. In his book, *Germany, Russia, and the Polish Problem* (1908),[1] Dmowski argued that the tsarist regime, under the impact of internal political forces, as well as its association with the western democracies, was bound to become more liberal and hence more tolerant. In the years immediately preceding the war, this platform, vigorously presented by Dmowski himself and by a group of his National Democratic co-workers, became increasingly popular throughout the divided country. The program stressed the priority of unification over liberation. Even in Austrian Galicia, where the Poles enjoyed a generous measure of political and cultural autonomy, the all-Polish movement gained many adherents.

Those who followed the pro-Austrian trend, on the other hand, staked their hopes on the Hapsburg monarchy as the most liberal and benevolent of the partitioning powers. According to the supporters of this orientation, a victory over Russia would result in the incorporation into Austria of Congress Poland and the extension to it of all the blessings of the liberal Austrian system. Dmowski objected to this view and pointed out the rapid loss of vitality of the Hapsburg state and its increasing dependence upon Germany. The most that could be hoped for from Austria, he asserted, was the reunion of Galicia with the Congress Kingdom. This meant, however, that Pomerania, Posnania, and Silesia—i.e., the cradle of the Polish nation—would be left to the mercies of Prussia. To this the supporters of the Austrian orientation replied that Vienna would not only grant to the Congress Kingdom the liberties enjoyed by Galicia, but would most probably transform Austria-Hungary into a trialist German, Magyar, and Slavic state. Such a solution would be generous enough to act as a magnet even on Prussian Poland and as a deterrent to further germanization: the Poles of a trialist monarchy, as co-rulers of the state, would be able to exercise a moderating influence on their German ally. The price of complete unification, on the other hand, would be extension over the whole of Poland of the reactionary Russian autocracy, only slightly mollified by the sham constitutional manifesto of October 1905. The constitution was a child of defeat, granted with utmost reluctance under duress. To Russian Poland it granted no autonomy. Would a triumphant tsardom be more benevolent toward the Poles than a humbled one?

The main opponent of the pro-Russian program was Józef Piłsudski, then still affiliated with the Polish Socialist party and supported by many left-of-center groups. While rejecting the pro-Russian views altogether, he did not subscribe to the pro-Austrian program without reservations.[2] Although he was convinced that in view of the critical international situation Vienna was bound to conciliate its Polish subjects, he did not want to commit himself completely to the pro-Austrian orientation. An unconditional commitment to a cause which, in his opinion, was both alien and ultimately doomed, he considered as dangerous. In Austria, and its ally, Germany, he saw not protectors of a future Polish state, but merely the means of struggling against Russia and bringing about its disintegration, and hence the liberation of the Congress Kingdom. His own conception of things to come was most sharply expressed in January 1914 in a lecture given at the Geographic Institute of Paris. A prominent leader of the Russian Social Revolutionary party, Victor M. Chernov, reported the gist of Piłsudski's talk. Chernov was especially struck with the conclusions which Piłsudski made at the end of his lecture:

> Piłsudski clearly prophesied an Austro-Russian war for the Balkans in the near future. He had no doubts that behind Austria will stand— and even now secretly stands—Germany. He further expressed conviction that France would not be allowed to remain a passive spectator of the conflict: the day when Germany will openly side with Austria will be the eve of the day when France, by virtue of her alliance, will intervene on the side of Russia. Finally, Great Britain, he thought, could not afford to leave France to her fate. Should the united forces of France and England be not sufficient they will, sooner or later, drag America into the war on their side. Analyzing further the military po-

tential of all these countries Piłsudski clearly stated the problem: how would the war develop, with whose victory would it end? His answer was: Russia was bound to be beaten by Austria and Germany, and they in turn would be defeated by the Anglo-French (or Anglo-American-French) coalition.[3]

The defeat of all the three empires, insisted Piłsudski, would create throughout Eastern Europe a momentarily chaotic situation that would permit reconstruction of an independent Polish state. To exploit this opportunity the Poles must have at least a nucleus of an armed force. This idea was at the root of the Polish Legion that Piłsudski created in Galicia with Austrian assistance shortly before the war.

The outbreak of World War I created for the Poles a unique situation for which their leaders had hoped for three generations. For the first time all three co-partitioning powers were fighting each other in all seriousness. One of the main theaters of the contest was to extend across Poland, and more than a million Poles were mobilized on opposite sides by the belligerent powers. The first months of the war demonstrated that Poland would play a significant role in the conflict.

On August 8, 1914, a few days after the opening of the hostilities, a spokesman of the "Polish Circle" in the Duma offered the loyal cooperation of the Poles to help the Russian war effort. On August 14, Grand Duke Nicholas Nikolayevich, commander-in-chief of the Russian armed forces, published a manifesto addressed to the Poles, promising them unification and self-government under the scepter of the Romanovs, and exhorting them to join the all-Slavic crusade against the common Teutonic enemy. The manifesto, as well as the declaration of the "Polish Circle," were considered successes of Dmowski's policy and a setback for the pro-Austrian orientation.

For a while, Vienna contemplated transformation of the Dual Monarchy into a trialist one, but such a move never materialized because of Hungarian opposition. Another indication of the success of National Democratic grass roots propaganda was the fact that the call to arms to fight Russia alongside Austria, issued by Piłsudski from Galicia, found practically no response in the Congress Kingdom. This was of crucial importance to the Polish cause. We know what a vital role was played by the East Prussian offensive of the two Russian armies. Although an operational failure, it diverted enough German troops from the western front to emasculate the von Schlieffen plan and resulted in a strategic victory for the Allies. The success of Piłsudski's appeal for an uprising in Russian Poland, at this crucial stage of the war, might have spelled early German victory in France. What would have been the outcome of the battle of the Marne had the Russians been compelled to use their soldiers to suppress a Polish uprising in Warsaw, Łódź, and Kalisz instead of throwing them into East Prussia?

After Russia's setbacks in East Prussia in 1914, and its victories in Galicia in 1914–15, came the successful German offensive under Field Marshal von Mackensen's on the Galician front; the breakthrough of the Russian front at Gorlice was followed by a German victory in central Poland, including the capture of Warsaw and Wilno by the end of the summer of 1915. The triumphant Central Powers were now masters of the lion's share of historic Poland. The preponderant role played by the German and not by the Austrian forces in the military conquests had important political consequences for the future of the Polish question.

Because of the Russian reverses of 1915, and because of Petrograd's political passivity, the Russian orientation favored by the National Democratic party and by most Poles at the outset of the conflict was pushed somewhat into the background. Nevertheless, Dmowski continued his relentless behind-the-scenes diplomatic efforts. At the end of 1915, he transferred the center of his activities from Russia to London, and eventually to Paris, and started intensive diplomatic activity on behalf of his country, placing it firmly on the side of the Western powers. He submitted, for instance, to leading Western statesmen a series of comprehensive memoranda dealing not only with Poland, but with the future of east-central Europe in general.[4] Until the upheaval in Russia, however, he found little active response among European statesmen. As long as the tsarist empire was a fighting ally, the Polish question was to be considered a purely Russian domestic issue, much too dangerous a problem to be discussed openly by any Allied diplomat in Petrograd.

While Dmowski was busy abroad, in Poland more attention was being focused on the only significant native fighting force, the Legions organized in Galicia by Piłsudski. The prominent part played by Piłsudski in Poland for over two decades, from 1914 to 1935, is directly related to his meteoric rise during World War I. In 1914, Piłsudski was merely a leftist leader identified with the Polish Socialist party. Although he had achieved some fame because of his acts of terrorism and sabotage carried out during the revolution of 1904–5, he was not a national figure. But his participation in the war at the head of the Polish Legion, followed by his resistance to the Central Powers, eventually catapulted him to the position of a personality of the first rank.

At the beginning of the war, Piłsudski's position was most precarious and fraught with pitfalls. The Austrians granted his Legion the ill-defined status of an irregular auxiliary corps with no political guarantees except for some vague confidential promises given to Piłsudski. He recklessly backed an unpopular cause which, according to his own forecast, was bound to lose eventually. He gambled with the future of his country; an uprising in Russian Poland could have tipped the delicate balance that existed in August 1914. Yet, despite all these handicaps, he managed before the end of the war to extricate himself from this embarrassing association and emerge as the popular hero of an active struggle against the moribund Central Powers.[5]

It is true that favorable circumstances often played into his hands. But it seems that Piłsudski's political skill as well as his personality and his qualities of daring, foresight, and initiative had a great deal to do with his success. The war gave him a chance to test these qualities and to weld together a heterogeneous group of supporters, linked by an abiding loyalty to their chief, into a cohesive team. His first military success, the skillful use of his small force in difficult circumstances, resulted in a spontaneous identification with him. This was

68

the beginning of the Piłsudski legend, which was to play such an important role in subsequent Polish history.

The lack of response in Poland to Piłsudski's appeals for an uprising created a sentiment of alienation and even rejection among his legionnaires. They concluded that since their sacrifices were neither shared nor appreciated by the masses, they were lonely freedom fighters, a small group of superior individuals destined to lead a passive nation. This sense of aloofness eventually degenerated into a patronizing and even domineering attitude toward the rest of society. Initially, however, it was reflected only in the Legion's songs, slogans, and poems. Later on this feeling of superiority would reappear and flourish in the form of an elitist self-awareness during Piłsudski's semidictatorial period after 1926. The roots of this frame of mind are to be found during the war, if not before, during the revolution of 1904–5.[6] It is difficult to understand the mood of Piłsudski's Legion, and then of his politics after 1926, without remembering this attitude, born during the lonely underground fight against tsarist Russia, and then fostered by World War I.

While the two main contenders for Polish leadership, Dmowski and Piłsudski, were striving to achieve their respective goals, the situation in Poland was changing very rapidly. The German chancellor, Bethmann-Hollweg, had declared in the Reichstag in April 1916 that in entering the war neither Austria-Hungary nor Germany had any intention of reopening the Polish question. The course of the war, however, was forcing forward the issue of Poland, an integral part of the planned *Mitteleuropa*. The Allied blockade and the staggering casualties of the first two years compelled Berlin and Vienna to consider the possibility of Polish independence in order to court the favor of this large reservoir of manpower in east-central Europe. The supporters of the Central Powers in Poland were pressured to open a recruiting campaign in the parts of the country occupied by German and Austrian troops. But most of the Polish leaders, including Piłsudski, refused to associate themselves with the recruitment, insisting on an explicit political quid pro quo.

Realizing that no result could be achieved without some sort of political guarantees, the Central Powers decided upon a dramatic step which was to have far-reaching consequences. On November 5, 1916, they proclaimed the formation of the so-called Kingdom of Poland under the protection of the Austrian and German emperors. This rump Poland was to consist of only a portion of its former Russian part, and during the war, was to be divided into German and Austrian occupation zones. The German governor-general of Warsaw, Count Hans von Beseler, in whose hands was concentrated all political power, proceeded, with the collaboration of the Austrian governor residing in Lublin, to implement the declaration of the two emperors.[7] Of course, Paris and London, as well as Petrograd, protested this move as a flagrant violation of international law. But the Central Powers went on with their self-imposed task of creating a semi-independent Polish state under their protection. The declaration of the two emperors—a hesitant, reluctant, and modest tactical gesture—proved to be a turning point in the story of Poland's reappearance on the map of Europe as a sovereign state.

On December 5, the two governors set up in Warsaw an advisory body, the provisional Council of State. The council consisted of 25 members, appointed by the two emperors; among them was Piłsudski, as head of the council's military commission, to administer the Polish armed forces (*Polnische Wehrmacht*) and cooperate with the troops of Central Powers. Unwittingly, the two partitioning powers were proceeding step by step toward the reconstruction of a Polish state.

The relatively small group of Poles who were collaborating with the Central Powers (the "activists") were far from enthusiastic in their commitment. The Central Powers pursued a harsh occupation policy and mercilessly exploited the manpower and the economic resources of the country. The crucial question of recruitment, however, was the main bone of contention. The Poles were obviously in no hurry to supply recruits and kept insisting on political concessions. In March 1917 the German and Austrian authorities demanded that the Council of State adopt a special form of oath for the Polish Auxiliary Corps, as the nucleus of the Polish army was now termed, binding it to intimate collaboration with the German and Austrian armies. Piłsudski and most of his soldiers refused to obey. This caused the dissolution of the Polish Auxiliary Corps and the internment of Piłsudski's soldiers.

These events in Poland almost coincided with the upheaval in Russia that swept away the tsarist regime and with the entry of the United States into the war. In Russia both of the rival revolutionary centers of power, the liberal provisional government of Prince Lvov, and the Marxist soviet of workers and soldier's deputies in Petrograd, almost at once undertook to accomplish what the fallen tsarist regime had been unable to do. On March 27, 1917, the Petrograd soviet, and two days later, the provisional government, issued significant statements regarding the future of Poland. The provisional government proclaimed:

> True to the commitments toward its Allies, true to mutual plans to fight against German Militarism, the Provisional Government views the creation of an independent Polish state incorporating all territories where the majority of population was Polish, as a hope-inspiring step toward lasting peace in future Europe. In a free military alliance with Russia, the Polish state will firmly resist the pressure of the Central Powers against Slavism.

Both statements declared the partitions of Poland as null and void and emphatically stressed the inherent right of the Polish people to a free and independent existence. While the provisional government in its short proclamation emphasized no less than four times the necessity of concluding a Russo-Polish treaty of alliance under a common Slavic banner, the statement of its rival, the soviet government, unconditionally recognized Poland's right to full independence. Immediately after the declaration of the provisional government, a special ministry called the Polish Liquidation Commission was set up, and its chairman, Aleksander Lednicki, a prominent Polish lawyer and a member of the Russian Constitutional Democratic (Cadet) party, was given a seat in the cabinet. Soon a fairly large, separate Polish armed force, composed of Russian soldiers of Polish nationality, was created and organized into three army corps. At the time of the Russian Revolution there were approximately 110 generals and admirals, 10,000 officers, and about 700,000 soldiers of Polish origin in the imperial armed forces. Some of them were incorporated into the three army corps.

Even though ethnographic Poland was entirely outside Russian control by 1917, and the disputed borderlands were also quickly slipping out of reach, the declaration of the provisional government was a significant document with far-reaching political consequences. It finally freed the Allies from the necessity of treating the Polish question as a domestic Russian issue, and turned the Polish problem into a vital international issue.

The Allied powers were now free to act on Poland's behalf. On January 8, 1918, President Woodrow Wilson proclaimed his Fourteen Points, of which the thirteenth was thus formulated:

> An independent Polish state should be erected, which would include the territories inhabited by indisputably Polish populations, which would be assured a free and secure access to the sea, and whose political and economic independence and territorial integrity should be guaranteed by international covenant.

Simultaneously, Prime Minister Lloyd George declared: "We believe that an independent Poland, comprising all those genuinely Polish elements who desire to form part of it, is an urgent necessity for the stability of Western Europe."

Thus, by the spring of 1917, because of the steps undertaken by the former partitioning powers, the Poles had a nucleus of a state administration in Warsaw and Lublin as well as the beginnings of two armed forces, one in Russia and another in Poland. To this one should add the existence of the Polish National Committee headed by Dmowski, active in the West and trying to connect Poland's national cause with that of the Allies. The committee was soon to embark on organizing a third Polish armed force, composed partly of Polish volunteers from America. The pro-Russians and the pro-Austrian orientations, although outwardly working at cross purposes, were basically complementing each other and preparing, step by step, the eventual reconstruction of an independent Polish state.[8]

While cooperating with the Central Powers Piłsudski had created an underground apparatus, the Polish Military Organization, which had spread its net far and wide. The purpose of this group was to prepare for an eventual break with Austria and Germany and to wage a struggle with them at the moment of their defeat on the western front. Piłsudski's diplomatic agents were sent to the West to keep in touch with the Allies and to inform them that his collaboration with Vienna and Berlin was purely tactical. The refusal of Piłsudski and most of his legionnaires to take an oath of allegiance to the Central Powers had resulted in the liquidation of his small force. There is no doubt that his imprisonment by the Germans in July 1917 made him an overnight national hero. But his plan of escaping to Russia in order to head a large Polish army about to form there was frustrated. During the sixteen months or so which he spent in captivity, a far-reaching change had taken place throughout Europe.

By the time Piłsudski had been released by the German revolution from the Magdeburg prison and returned to Poland, his authority was great, his legend well-established. His only possible rival, Dmowski, had been far away from the country for more than three years, working first in Petrograd and then in London and Paris. At home Dmowski's National Democratic party still had considerable influence throughout the country, and the resounding triumph of the Allies strengthened its position even more. But the army organized by Dmowski in France under the command of General Józef Haller was still far away from home, as were the most resourceful and skillful National Democratic leaders.

Piłsudski, on the other hand, was close to the main scene of action and commanded the loyalty not only of the small Polish regular military units but also of some 50,000 men of the Polish Military Organization. His seemingly fantastic predictions as to the course of the war had been proven accurate. His long imprisonment added to martial glory the aura of intransigence and even martyrdom. The National

Democratic opposition against him, as a result, was not very effective.

On November 10, 1918, Piłsudski returned from Magdeburg to Warsaw. On November 14, the German-sponsored Regency Council in Warsaw resigned. In a public pronouncement, the council transferred its powers to Piłsudski, who would become provisional chief-of-state and commander-in-chief of the armed forces until the formation of a truly national government through free, democratic elections.[9]

≫ ≪

In order to appreciate Poland's difficult position as a newly restored state, one has to bear in mind the problems it faced in 1918 and 1919. The reborn republic was a precarious creation with amorphous frontiers. It consisted of the two former governor-generalships of Warsaw and Lublin, which had formed the Austro–German-sponsored Kingdom of Poland as proclaimed in 1916, plus the former Austrian Galicia together with the small Silesian province of Teschen. In the Lublin area the Austrian forces were disarmed and the administration taken over by the Poles without resistance, but in the Warsaw region the disarming proved difficult. There the German soldiers, although badly demoralized by the revolutionary ferment, were still a formidable force, and the regular Polish detachments, even with the aid of the Polish Military Organization now emerging from the underground, were no match for them. Furthermore, all of western Poland (the provinces of Pomerania, Posnania, and Silesia) was still controlled by the Germans, who hoped to retain at least some of this territory despite the defeat on the western front. The Germans also controlled the entire southeastern Baltic shore up to the Estonian capital of Tallinn as well as vast stretches of the Ukraine and Byelorussia. Moreover, since the beginning of November, eastern Galicia and its capital city of Lwów were in the throes of a fierce civil war between the Ukrainians and the Poles. Piłsudski's native city of Wilno (Vilnius) was still in German hands. At the same time Bolshevik detachments were advancing from the east and were menacing not only Wilno and eastern Poland but also the newly born Baltic states of Lithuania, Latvia, and Estonia. On January 5, 1919, Wilno was captured by the Red Army and soon thereafter proclaimed as the Soviet Lithuanian-Byelorussian republic.

The crumbling within about a year and a half of three well-established empires, those of the Romanovs, the Hapsburgs, and the Hohenzollerns, was one of the great upheavals of modern times. As a result of these cataclysms, a power vacuum was created in east-central Europe. To the west of Poland, Germany was in the throes of a revolution and its people were seething with profound resentment. In the east, in the territories of the former tsarist empire, the civil war was about to enter a decisive phase, the outcome of which was uncertain. In the south, the peoples of the old Hapsburg monarchy were restless and eager to reassert their national identity through independent states. The power vacuum would spread farther when the German forces began their gradual retreat from the conquered eastern European territories. In their wake came the detachments of the Red Army with their revolutionary slogans.

While the victorious Allies were getting ready to fix Poland's western and southern boudaries, the most urgent tasks facing the young Polish republic seemed to be in the east, where the Bolsheviks were proclaiming international civil war. The Soviet military pressure, although at first sporadic and erratic, was accompanied by the Communist infiltration, dangerous because of the unsettled social and economic conditions throughout Eastern Europe. The Red Army units were followed by teams of Communist agitators, originally mostly natives of Poland and the non-Russian borderlands, who were eager to be planted as governments of their respective countries by the "revolutionary intervention" of their Soviet comrades. Most of these nuclei of Communist governments were given at their disposal some hastily organized armed units, for instance, the Western Rifle Division composed partly of Polish Communists, partly of Poles from Russia, but largely of Russians simply assigned to the task. Thus, the external threat was coupled with the danger of a domestic coup d'état.

The Polish Phoenix

The internal situation in Poland seemed propitious for such designs. The war had ruined Poland economically and left behind a sediment of bitterness and pent-up hatred. Many factories had been dismantled and shipped to Germany. With the cessation of hostilities more industries were suddenly closed down, throwing large numbers of unemployed workers into the streets to demonstrate their wrath. Inflation, profiteering, and black marketing were rampant. The prolonged industrial unemployment resulted in an appalling pauperization and subsequent radicalization of the working class. Moreover, a large part of the Polish labor force was still abroad, evacuated to Russia in 1915 or forcibly deported to Germany between 1916 and 1918. Some of the returning workers were not only swelling the ranks of the unemployed but were preaching the dictatorship of the proletariat. Consequently, the country was passing through a period of economic chaos and social conflict, in some ways not much less acute than that of Russia or Germany.

At first sight, the reborn Poland seemed ripe for Communist revolution and, consequently, for engulfment by Soviet Russia. This was openly advocated by both extreme Socialist groups, the Social Democratic party of Poland and Lithuania and the Polish Socialist party Left, as well as by the group of Council of Workers' Delegates sponsored by these two parties. Both groups decided to seize the opportunity and redouble their efforts. In December 1918 they merged and formed the Communist Workers' party of Poland.[10] The party immediately started to organize a net of revolutionary workers' councils, as well as detachments of "Red Guards," to grab power at the approach of the Red Army. The new party, following the views of Rosa Luxemburg, pronounced itself for immediate incorporation of Poland into the emerging Soviet Socialist Republic.[11] Similar views were advocated by the Communists of Finland and of the Baltic countries of Latvia and Estonia, where civil wars were already in full swing.

To cope with the dangerous situation, the political leadership of the Polish republic had to mobilize the available resources to satisfy the immediate needs of the people and to promote long-range democratic reforms, including the redistribution of land. The first government, headed by a Socialist, immediately decreed an eight-hour working day and enacted a generous system of social security. A Ministry of Food was set up and supplies were stored, controlled, and distributed by the state. A provisional democratic constitution was promulgated and a decree of November 29 provided that democratic elections to the Constituent Assembly should take place on January 26, 1919. Elections consolidated the young republic domestically and gave a sense of confidence to its democratically elected leaders.

Before domestic consolidation could be completed, however, the problem of national frontiers had to be faced. The western borders were determined by the Paris peace treaties in keeping with Wilson's thirteenth point, and a series of plebiscites and compromises were scheduled.

Because of the efforts of Dmowski's Polish National Committee in Paris, Poland had been recognized by all the Allies as "an allied belligerent nation" on June 3, 1918. Meanwhile the committee organized in France a Polish army of some six divisions. These events made it a foregone conclusion that Poland would be represented at the peace conference as one of the victorious Allied states. The fact that there were two rival bodies claiming to represent the Polish people—the conservative Polish National Committee and the leftist government in Warsaw—was settled by a compromise in January 1919. Piłsudski was to remain head of the Polish state and a coalition cabinet nominated by him, with the world-famous pianist Ignacy Jan Paderewski as prime minister and foreign minister, was to govern. In turn, the Polish delegation at Versailles was to be headed by Paderewski and Dmowski, with a handful of Piłsudski's representatives hastily added to represent his point of view.[12]

While there was considerable disagreement, even among Poles, as to what were "indisputable" Polish territories in the east, the situation was fairly clear in the west. The German census of 1910, based on linguistic criteria, left no doubt whatsoever that the bulk of former Prussian Poland, the duchy of Posnania, Pomerania, Upper Silesia, and Opole Silesia had preserved their ethnic Polish character despite well over a century of German rule. This was true also of the northern part of Pomerania, the strip of land which German propaganda had tendentiously labeled the Polish Corridor. The only exception to the largely Slavic character of Posnania and Pomerania was the city of Danzig (Gdańsk), at the mouth of the Vistula, and a small strip of territory around it. The commission for Polish affairs at the peace conference followed the German census of 1910 and unanimously voted to restore Danzig to Poland not for ethnic, but for historic, strategic, and economic reasons. This was the only major departure from the principle of national self-determination in the projected Polish-German frontier settlement, which, otherwise, was based on linguistic criteria. Professor Robert H. Lord of Harvard, the U.S. delegate to the commission, argued that the failure to provide Poland with possession of the mouth of the Vistula would be to favor the interests of 200,000 Germans over that of 20 million Poles and would be an equivalent of handing over the mouth of the Nile, or the Mississippi, to a foreign power. On the insistence of Lloyd George, Danzig was eventually declared a free city with some special rights reserved for Poland.

Again on the insistence of Great Britain, the conference reversed its initial decision on two other points. It concluded that in the cases of Slavic Silesia and of the southern fringes of East Prussia (the Masurian Lakes district), which were inhabited by Polish Lutherans, the question of nationality would be resolved by means of plebiscites. On paper, the decision appeared fair enough. But in practice it was executed in a way that grossly favored for generations the occupying power then in control of the disputed areas. First of all, the old, oppressive German administration was left intact; it obfuscated and even actively sabotaged the wishes of the non-German majority and did not refrain from acts of deceit and terror. Moreover, in the period before the plebiscite, the German government was allowed to bring in some 200,000 Germans, born in Silesia but no longer residing there and having no vital links with the area, to cast their vote.

In the case of East Prussia the voting took place at the worst possible moment, in July 1920, while the Red Army was approaching Warsaw and the fate of Poland was hanging in the balance. The Poles made a poor showing and the Masurian Lakes district was over-whelmingly allotted to Germany. The more nationally conscious Silesians, on the other hand, were determined to have their way. They protested against the unfair, pro-German decisions of the Allies concerning the plebiscite with three spontaneous armed insurrections and demanded immediate incorporation into Poland. The first armed protest, which arose out of a mass strike movement led by Wojciech Korfanty, took place in August 1919 and ended in failure. The second insurrection, which started on the night of August 19–20, 1920, was also put down.

As a result of the Silesian plebiscite, conducted on March 20, 1921, 479,000 votes were cast for Poland, while 706,000 votes favored Germany. The role of the 200,000 former residents of the area, imported by the German authorities to cast pro-German votes, was crucial. The publication of the results precipitated the outburst of the third mass revolt of Silesian Poles. This uprising, which lasted throughout May and June of 1921, was marked with considerable success for the insurgents. Especially memorable was the struggle for St. Ann's Mountain near Opole. The uprisings were a heroic epic which demonstrated the desire of the Silesian people to be part of a Polish state.

The insurrection exerted considerable pressure upon the Council of Ambassadors, which made public its final decision in the Polish-German border on October 20, 1921. The eastern part of Upper Silesia was given by the League of Nations to Poland, while the western, together with the region of Opole, went to Germany. The fate of the southern fringes of greater Silesia, the Teschen (Cieszyn) region, was settled by a compromise imposed upon Poland by the Allies in July 1920, during the crucial phase of the Soviet invasion. As a result of the settlement Teschen Silesia was partitioned between Poland and Czechoslovakia, the latter obtaining the larger and richer area south of the Olza River. This region contained a considerable Polish majority.

☙ The Polish Phoenix

While a large measure of consent could be reached among the Poles concerning the western boundaries, agreement was more difficult on the shape of the eastern boundaries as well as on the nature of relations with the nations of the twilight zone between ethnographic Poland and ethnographic Russia, the area where Poles were mixed with Lithuanians, Byelorussians, and Ukrainians. Dmowski and the National Democrats advocated a peaceful compromise with Russia, regardless of the nature of its regime, and a division of the disputed lands between the Poles and the Russians. Piłsudski, on the other hand, was convinced that Poland was too weak either to withstand the revolutionary pressure from the east alone or to assimilate a large number of ethnic minorities inhabiting the borderlands. At the same time, he believed that Poland could not cope with the Communist challenge by military force alone, and needed partners in the struggle. His answer to the Bolshevik menace was close cooperation among Eastern European nations bordering on Poland. Piłsudski hoped that by supporting the right of the Ukrainians and Byelorussians to national independence, the Poles would gain their confidence and good will. He even hoped to persuade them to join their destiny with that of democratic Poland in the form of a confederation or perhaps even a federation.[13]

Piłsudski's federal policy of the years 1918–22 is one of the most puzzling and least-known aspects of the period. Some of his opponents, especially the Communists, denounced him as Machiavellian, a new embodiment of the age-old Polish imperialism and a willing tool of international capitalism. On the other hand, his National Democratic critics decried him as a dangerous utopian, a cosmopolitan Socialist, plotting to undermine Poland by pitting it permanently against Russia. Whatever the merits of this criticism, one should view Piłsudski's plans in an historic perspective against the background of contemporary events. In the chaos following World War I, he saw a quick opportunity to put into practice his program for the integration of Eastern Europe. Piłsudski believed that national sentiments, by and large, prevailed over ideological allegiances, including class solidarity. He was convinced that an atomized Eastern

80

Europe would maintain independence only for a brief period and would soon fall prey to more powerful neighbors, chiefly Russia, who controlled a vast colonial empire and coveted further territory, this time in the name of a new, outwardly internationalist doctrine.[14]

Consequently, Piłsudski tried to channel the outburst of energy generated in Poland by the recovery of national independence. The achievements of the highly successful year 1919, which saw the liberation of Posnania, the signing of the Treaty of Versailles, the reconquest of Wilno as well as Lwów, and the capture of Minsk from the Soviets, all seemed to show that there might have been some ground for the success of his plans. Russia was in the throes of a paralyzing civil war. Lenin seemed to offer to Warsaw an apparently advantageous compromise that would have left most of Byelorussia to Poland. At that time the White Army of Denikin was pushing north toward Moscow, and Poland's neutrality was vital. Piłsudski hesitated enough to permit the Bolshevik victory. Had he stopped there, he might have achieved at least a part of his original plan. But in 1920, mistrusting Lenin's offer as a pure stratagem, Piłsudski threw caution to the wind and embarked upon his daring Ukrainian policy, signing a treaty of alliance with the Ukraine's Socialist leader, Semion Petlura. In return for Poland's aid in establishing a Ukrainian national state on the right bank of the Dnieper, Petlura confirmed Polish sovereignty over eastern Galicia. The climax of Piłsudski's efforts came in May of 1920 when the Polish-Ukrainian troops captured Kiev and when Warsaw seemed to be determining the fate of Eastern Europe.

Contrary to some views, the Russo-Polish war of 1920 was not a marginal event, as most historians have argued. It was not only an important closing phase of the Russian civil war, but also a vital clash of two concepts of organizing the area between Poland and Russia proper. The outcome of the war decided the fate of the region for a generation or so. Lenin's strategic goal was the splitting of Russia's western neighbors with the ax of the social revolution backed by the "revolutionary intervention" of the probing Bolshevik bayonets. A Communist upheaval would rend the neighboring bourgeois states along class lines; the Red Army would then plant its commissars in the respective East European capitals. If successful, the Bolshevik plan would have created, already by 1920, what ultimately materialized in 1944 and 1945: a belt of vassal states encompassing practically all of Central and Eastern Europe.

The Red Army was to establish in east-central Europe not only a new revolutionary social order but also a new concept of state organization and international order. When the Soviets started their counteroffensive, Stalin, then the people's commissar for nationalities, as well as head political commissar of the First Cavalry Army, was already exchanging letters with Lenin concerning the future structure of the countries to be conquered.

> For the nations which formerly belonged to old Russia, our [Soviet] type of federation may and ought to be considered as leading toward unity [wrote Stalin on June 12]. The motives are obvious: either these nations had no independent existence of their own, or they lost it a long time ago; that is why they would be willing to accept without much friction our Soviet [centralized] type of federation. The same cannot be said of nations which did not make part of the old Russia, which existed as independent states. But if such states become Soviet states, they would have to establish some sort of relations with Russia. I am speaking of a future Soviet Germany, Poland and Hungary. It is doubtful whether those people which have their own governments, their own armies, their finances, would agree, even if they became Soviet states, to establish with us a federal union of that type which links us now with the Bashkirs or the Ukrainians. . . . They would consider federation of our Soviet type as diminishing their national and state independence. . . . On the other hand, I do not doubt that for those nations a confederation would be the most acceptable form of relations with us.[15]

Lenin agreed to Stalin's formula: confederation as a transition toward federation, and federation as a transition toward final unity. But Lenin's dream was shattered by the Polish victory at Warsaw in August 1920 and by the failure of the scheme for a Communist seizure of power in Poland. The battle of Warsaw largely determined the political order in Eastern and Central Europe for almost two decades, which was just enough time to give the area a breathing spell. That is why the British ambassador in Berlin, Lord d'Abernon, did not hesitate to call it "the eighteenth decisive battle in world history."

The essence of Piłsudski's plan of 1919–20 was to stop Bolshevik expansion by splitting asunder its territorial base, the former tsarist empire, by means of a strict application of the principles of national self-determination. Thus, indirectly, Piłsudski aimed at nipping the Soviet state in the bud by dividing it along national lines. By this means, a new, more stable, and enduring balance of power would be created in the eastern part of the European continent. The scheme failed largely because Poland, although militarily victorious, was too weak politically to exploit its splendid victory. The result was the compromise treaty of Riga.

The treaty, signed on March 18, 1921, divided the disputed Ukrainian and Byelorussian lands between the two contenders, with only the western fringes going to Poland. The agreement represented the end of over six years of war in and around Polish lands. It delineated what appeared at that time as a fairly satisfactory eastern frontier of the Polish republic and thus supplemented the Versailles settlement.[16] Most Poles greeted the treaty of Riga with relief and satisfaction as a realistic compromise reflecting the balance of forces existing during the early 1920s. From the point of view of Piłsudski's great design it was not a compromise but a catastrophe.[17]

In retrospect, Piłsudski's plans for Eastern Europe appear as premature, middle-of-the-road attempts to conciliate the narrow nationalistic aspirations of the Lithuanians, Byelorussians, Ukrainians, and Poles. To a war-weary and excited generation emerging from the barbed wire trenches of World War I and from many years of national oppression, his program appeared as a utopian sacrifice of many cherished desires. As faithful sons of the nineteenth century most Poles did not see beyond the national state. The outward successes scored at the Paris peace conference elated them. They forgot that their independence was largely a result of propitious circum-

83

stance, created by the simultaneous defeat and disintegration of their former masters. The potent wine of freedom and national sovereignty went quickly to their heads, and the dizziness resulting from restored independence led to an overindulgence in domestic quarrels. The Poles forgot that unity was essential in order to survive the pressure from more powerful neighbors. They quickly forgot about their earlier federal schemes, and once again the slogan *Polonia fara da se* became a battle cry.

Although a hero because of the war of 1920, Piłsudski, unlike his rival Dmowski, was never able to create a broad, modern political movement, nor did he ever control any significant segment of the Polish press. He was a loner, surrounded by a small group of faithful and uncritical admirers. It was Dmowski who was to capture the imagination of the youth with his idea of a Greater Poland, a unified, centralized state run by Poles alone. Dmowski's thinking, rather than Piłsudski's, would dominate Polish politics during the interwar period.

The Russo-Polish war, the first Polish victory in more than two and a half centuries, along with the signing of the treaties of Versailles and Riga and the incorporation of an eastern segment of Silesia lost to Poland some 600 years before, all spelled the end of the long and laborious process of the rebuilding a Polish state after some 123 years of foreign rule. The apparent successes turned many a Polish head: too much was ascribed to the spectacular military victory over Soviet Russia and not enough to the circumstances in which it was achieved. The organic work that had made the rebirth possible was underrated, and too little attention was paid to the spadework of a handful of writers and politicians who had helped prepare the Polish triumph. The national perspective was warped and Poles were lulled into a false sense of security.[18] It was in this spirit that Poland entered the third decade of the twentieth century.

CHAPTER FOUR

Experiment in Independence

> When nations have existed for a long and glorious time, they cannot break with their past whatever they do.
>
> *François Guizot*

⚞THE ESTABLISHMENT OF an independent state after a century and a quarter of subjugation generated an outburst of enthusiasm among patriotic Poles. Sir Esmé Howard (later Lord Howard of Penrith), who came to Warsaw in February 1919 as a member of the Interallied Mission, was very much impressed with the mood of excitement and with the ardent glow of patriotic zeal radiating from many Poles during the early, difficult months of their freedom. The British diplomat remarked:

> The crowds were ragged, thin, and anaemic, with sunken . . . cheeks . . . and great hollow eyes. Nothing could have seemed more gloomy and depressing than the picture they presented. Yet the enthusiasm of a people raised unexpectedly and almost miraculously like Lazarus from the dead . . . was such that it carried me, at last, away.[1]

Patriotic excitement and feverish exaltation alone were not sufficient, however, to cope with the formidable problems facing Poland from the first day of its independence. To begin with, the geopolitical situation as shaped by the treaties of Versailles and Riga was difficult and complex. Only a narrow strip of territory connected a country of well over 20 million people with the Baltic Sea. Moreover, on 60

85

percent of its frontiers Poland was bordered by Germany and Soviet Russia, antagonistic powers opposed to the very existence of the new state. In 1922 they signed the treaty of Rapallo which was, for all practical purposes, an alliance directed largely against Poland. For Germany, Poland was the hated ''upstart of Versailles''; for Soviet Russia, it was an obstacle to Communism's westward expansion, the main barrier separating the Red Army from Germany. This double enmity produced a considerable strain on the country's resources: about one-third of the state budget was devoted to national defense, thus drastically reducing the portion of the modest national income available for construction purposes. Despite the proximity to Soviet Russia there were few economic advantages for Poland. This was a new and strange phenomenon. Before World War I, the exchange of goods and services between the Polish provinces and other areas of the tsarist empire (especially the Asian provinces), had been very active, and many Polish industrial centers, such as Łódź, had been largely dependent on vast eastern markets. During the interwar period these links dwindled to insignificant proportions. Despite Poland's repeated efforts to counteract this situation, Russia's share in Polish foreign trade during the period between 1921 and 1939 amounted, on an average, to only one percent.

The frontier with Germany was not closed and was even, on the whole, rather active. From 1920 to 1925, Germany absorbed nearly 50 percent of Poland's exports. But here also political factors intervened: trying to undermine the Polish economy, the Germans forced upon Poland a tariff war that lasted for five years. Even when normal trade relations were resumed in 1930, Germany, because of basic political hostility, could never be completely trusted even as an economic partner.

The heaviest burden which Poland had to carry after World War I was the physical rehabilitation of its ruined cities, farms, industries, and communications systems. The occupying forces had left the country in a state of devastation and impoverishment. The powerful armies of Germany, Russia, and Austria had passed over Polish soil

86

several times in advance and retreat. The occupying powers had driven off cattle, removed farm implements, and stripped factories of machinery. Half the bridges, station buildings, and railroad workshops had been destroyed. One million eight hundred thousand buildings in cities, towns, and villages were demolished by fire. The losses in livestock amounted to 2 million head of cattle, a million horses, and 1.5 million sheep and goats. Nearly 11 million acres of agricultural land were put out of use by military operations, and 6 million acres of forest were totally destroyed. That which was not destroyed by military operations was pillaged, confiscated, or ruined by enforced contributions, levies, and requisitions.

Many of the country's major economic difficulties stemmed from the fact that the three regions of Poland did not form a single economic unit, and that the partitioning powers had subordinated the interests of their annexed provinces to those of Russia, Prussia, and Austria. For over a century the Polish lands had belonged to various customs units as well as to differing money and credit systems. They had different systems of civil, commercial, and fiscal legislation. Some areas were overdeveloped and some underdeveloped. The transportation and communications systems and trading facilities were not uniform. The main railroads had been constructed by the partitioning powers and run to strategic points on the frontiers, while others ran parallel to the borders in disregard of the economic needs of the respective areas.[2]

Other difficulties were related to the ethnic composition of the state. The Polish republic, as recognized by the Council of Ambassadors in 1923, had an area of 150,200 square miles (389,000 square kilometers). Of the 27 million inhabitants (1921 census), 14.3 percent were Ukrainians, 3.9 percent Byelorussians, 7.8 percent Jews, and 3.9 percent Germans. More than 6.5 million ethnic Poles lived beyond the borders of the Polish state, and, according to the German census of 1910, more than 1.5 million of these were in Germany, chiefly in the Opole, Warmia, and Masuria regions. The ethnically mixed population reflected the fact that Poland's borders had been subjected to considerable changes in the past, and that in previous centuries the country had been a haven for Jews and other persecuted minorities.

Various ethnic groups played a crucial part in the national economy. In 1931, for example, the Jews, who by that time constituted slightly over 10 percent of the total population, made up 58.7 percent of those engaged in commerce and 21.3 percent of persons in industry. They also figured prominently in the liberal professions, with nearly half of the doctors and lawyers of Jewish extraction. This resulted in a sharp competition with the non-Jewish Polish intelligentsia and the evolving middle class. Germans also constituted a prosperous group in both agriculture and industry. The social structure of the new state was thus a source of tension throughout the years preceding World War II.

One of the main problems of the interwar period was the spread of anit-Semitism, a phenomenon rooted apparently in the economic competition between the native, non-Jewish middle class and the Jews. According to Erich Goldhagen, a Jewish-American historian, this type of anti-Semitism was of an "objective" variety: it represented mainly a manifestation of hostility "born of a genuine conflict of interests between the Jews and their host people," mainly merchants, traders, artisans, as well as professional people, involved in fierce competition with corresponding groups among the Jewish population.[3]

During the interwar period Poland had the highest percentage of Jewish population of any country in the world, and "subjective," ideological anti-Semitism was not lacking. But neither the intensity nor the scope of the Polish anti-Semitic movement ever reached the proportions of similar trends in neighboring countries, such as Romania (with its large Iron Guard Fascist party) or Hungary (with its Arrow Cross), where there were far fewer Jews. Polish Fascist groups belonged to the lunatic fringe and never amounted to much. The sporadic outbursts of anti-Semitism were repressed by the government. Until their extermination by Hitler, the Jews of Poland played a considerable role in all fields of activity. They occupied numerous high

88

positions not only in the economic, professional, and scholarly fields, but also in the state administration (including the cabinet post of minister of industry and trade, held by Henryk Floyar Reichman) and in the army, where there were a few generals. (Bernard Mond was commander of the Cracow military district, and Jakub Krzemiński held several high military and civilian posts.) Jews were prominent in the artistic and literary world (Julian Tuwim, Antoni Słonimski, Józef Wittlin, and Boleslaw Leśmian are examples), some of them enjoying high official favors, including membership in the Academy of Literature. A flourishing center of Judaic studies was located at Wilno until World War II. Highly placed representatives of world Jewish organizations often praised the liberal policies of the Polish government with regard to Jews.[4] When Hitler seized power in Germany in 1933, many Jews sought shelter in Poland. Jews continued to play influential roles in Poland until the 1930s, when the situation began to change for the worse.

The bitter turbulence of Poland's political life was another reflection of the severe tensions besetting the country. During the 1920s violent struggles for power took place between rightist and leftist factions. These parties, which by and large represented the propertied classes—the National Democrats, Christian Democrats, and other small groups often allied with well-to-do small farmers—endeavored to maintain the existing system and to adapt it still further to their own social and economic interests. The National Democrats, the foremost nationalistic party, had developed over the years increasing authoritarian leanings. The non-Communist Left (the Polish Socialist party, smaller socialist groups of the various national minorities, and the peasant group called *Wyzwolenie,* or "Liberation"), opposed attempts to preserve the status quo, endeavoring to consolidate and even expand the social gains obtained during the 1918–19 period. The parties of the Left insisted on shifting the brunt of social and economic reforms to the shoulders of the propertied classes; they demanded that a radical agrarian reform be carried out and a comprehensive social security system, initiated by the first Socialist government in 1918, be further expanded.

Experiment in Independence

Until well after the coup d'état of May 1926, the hopes of the Left were fixed on the person of Marshal Piłsudski.[5] Although he had formally left the Polish Socialist party in 1916, Piłsudski remained popular during the 1920s with many Socialists, most radical democratic groups, and the national minorities, including the Jews. Until the end of 1922, Piłsudski was head of state and the chief opponent of the National Democratic party. Piłsudski's popularity was an important political factor in the struggle. Against him and his supporters stood the Right as well as the extreme Left (composed mostly of Communists and fellow travelers), both opposed to the existing democratic form of government.

Piłsudski's coup d'état was a revolt of an ambitious leader against the ultrademocratic constitutional framework designed in 1921 by the National Democrats to keep him either out of power or to prevent him from exercising it fully should he become president of the republic. In 1922 he had refused to run for president, and soon afterwards he had resigned also as commander-in-chief and gone into a reluctant retirement. When all other attempts to change the established system and to get back into political and military life on his own terms had failed, Piłsudski decided to challenge the government by force of arms. On May 12, 1926, at the head of some military units loyal to him, he appeared in Warsaw, hoping that a military demonstration would be enough to overthrow the government. His hopes were disappointed, however, and a bloody three-day struggle ensued in the streets of the capital.

Immediately after his victory, Piłsudski advanced a nonrevolutionary program embodying three main points: first, a fight against the excesses of party politics; second, a moral cleansing of public life (*sanacja*); and third, an improvement of economic conditions. Here, Piłsudski meant primarily stabilization of the currency, a balanced budget, and reduced unemployment. His task was greatly facilitated by currency depreciation and a general strike in Great Britain, as a result of which Poland was able to corner the Scandinavian and Baltic coal markets. During the summer of 1926 unemployment declined, exports increased rapidly, the budget was balanced, and the zloty

90

stabilized. A period of considerable prosperity, which was to last about three years, enhanced the prestige of the new regime both at home and abroad. The moral cleansing of public life was a more controversial issue. Piłsudski himself was beyond reproach, a selfless and incorruptible man. But his followers, while fighting against actual or alleged abuses of the parliamentary regime, soon lapsed into practices that made them open to charges of favoritism, nepotism, and back scratching.

Although Piłsudski generally followed a moderate course, he did not, at first, completely forget his old comrades of the Left. Soon after his victory, he made a bid to win their support, but his offer was accepted by only a small number. By 1929–30 the bulk of the Left had reluctantly gone over to the opposition. As a result of Piłsudski's failure to gain support from the Left, his government, which had initially pursued a middle course, increasingly revealed rightist proclivities. It disregarded parliamentary majorities and emphasized efficiency and quasimilitary discipline. Several cabinet changes amounted to no more than shifts of influence within the same ruling clique. Agrarian reform, although not abandoned altogether, was soft-pedaled, and social policy became progressively more cautious. The regime argued that a country of limited resources could hardly afford one of the most extensive and generous systems of social security. The early federalist dreams were also abandoned as Piłsudski pursued a conservative ethnic policy.

Piłsudski, however, was reluctant to apply outright dictatorial methods. The opposition parties were allowed to function openly and voice their grievances in the press, and the old parliamentary framework was basically preserved until 1935. Nevertheless, the whole political system was manipulated to suit the purposes of a regime that refused to be called a dictatorship, preferring instead the term "directed democracy." Unable to find enough support for his system, Piłsudski set up an artificial and complex structure known as the Nonpartisan Bloc for Cooperation with the Government, which was nothing but a bizarre agglomeration of political splinter groups. Although the Polish regime was considerably more progressive than that of Admiral Horthy in Hungary, there was a certain similarity between them, inasmuch as both were authoritarian without being Fascist. Yet, while emphatically rejecting Fascism as inapplicable to Polish conditions and contrary to its libertarian traditions, the *sanacja* regime tried to strengthen executive power and establish an authoritarian government; one means was the extensive use of military men in the civil administration. This deepened the chasm still further between the regime and the bulk of the people, who were bent on democratization.

In 1930 the government underwent further militarization (the "regime of colonels"), further dividing the country between those defending democratic institutions and those opposing them. Any attempt by leftist and centrist parties to form a broad coalition to oust the *sanacja* regime from power would backfire and end with some party leaders being imprisoned at the military fortress at Brześć. Almost at the same time the country entered another period of economic depression, which in Poland was deeper and more protracted than in most European countries, largely because the regime continued to adhere for over half a decade to the principles of economic liberalism. In April 1935 a new authoritarian constitution was pomulgated, designed to reverse the trend toward democratization in social as well as political life. In May 1935, Marshal Piłsudski died, leaving his followers confused and helpless.

The ideological poverty and lack of social base of the Nonpartisan Bloc and of its successor, the Camp of National Unity, was striking—even the more impartial defenders of the regime often could not deny it. Both were essentially loose coalitions of various splinter parties and political groups willing to support the existing regime. The bewildering diversity of the Bloc and Camp memberships could be accommodated only on the amorphous concept called the "ideology of Marshal Piłsudski." This was a high-sounding but empty slogan. A static, managerial theory of government imposed from above by a self-appointed group of officers and democrats not responsible to the people was not enough for a country of some 35 million, saddled with complex ethnic as well as social and economic problems. Such a body politic could not be merely administered as an estate owned by a state-bearing, charismatic elite allegedly "responsible to God and History" for nursing a nation to political maturity.[6]

Neither the Nonpartisan Bloc nor the Camp of National Unity ever controlled any significant segment of the Polish press or public opinion. The Bloc and the Camp were largely influenced by their opponents—the National Democrats, the Peasant party, and some leftist groups, mainly Socialists of various shades. The younger generation especially was under the spell of various brands of nationalistic ideas; strictly Fascist groups had small followings, while Nazism had practically no adherents except among the German minority.

The old Marshal deplored the integral nationalism of the National Democrats. They had always opposed his version of a state patriotism acceptable to all members of the republic, including almost one-third of the population that was non-Polish. He vainly endeavored to stem the rising tide of anti-Semitism and attempted to gain the support of the national minorities for the Polish state.[7] All this was largely in vain. It was Piłsudski's old opponent, Dmowski, who managed to capture the imagination of most Poles with his dream of a unified, centralized state run by Poles alone.

Contrary to the point of view often expressed in post-World War II official Polish publications, the influence of the Communists in the period between the world wars was modest and marginal. Given the social and economic structure of the country, the Communist party of Poland (CPP) had a weak social basis of support. The industrial working class, which usually provided a base for Communist activities, was relatively small. The party, cosmopolitan in its makeup and with its largely Jewish membership, had never enjoyed wide backing among the Polish working class, which was attracted to the more patriotic and native Polish Socialist party. During the interwar years the Communist party's peak membership was 12,000, of which 59 percent were classified as intellectuals and only 10 percent as industrial workers; of the remainder, 28 percent were peasants, and 3 percent farm laborers.[8]

Besides its numerical, structural, and ideological weaknesses, the Communist movement of the 1920s and 1930s suffered from the erroneous decisions made by its leaders in 1918 and 1919. Under the influence of Rosa Luxemburg, the Communist party of Poland refused to accept Polish independence and for almost five years denied the existence of the Polish republic, urging instead its merger with the USSR. This stand prevented many radically minded, yet basically patriotic Poles, from joining the party and from regarding it as a representative of native radicalism. One of the main reasons for the rejection of Communism by the Polish masses was the emphasis on proletarian internationalism and the pro-Soviet leaning of the CPP. The party was, in fact, an isolated group, a tiny sect lost in a traditional Roman Catholic country where nationalistic feelings were strong and where the memories of Russian domination were too vivid.

From the point of view of the CPP, the second republic was merely an "ugly bastard of the Versailles Treaty," a fragment of the cordon sanitaire, "the easternmost segment of Western imperialism." The new Poland was regarded as an enemy state whose foreign as well as domestic policies were determined by France, the main instigator of foreign intervention against Soviet Russia. As a pillar of the new status quo and an ally of France, Poland was a major stumbling block between Russia and the revolutionary forces which, according to the Comintern strategists, were destined to triumph in Germany. The downfall of the "bourgeois bastard," they argued, should be accelerated by an active and conscious contribution from the working class movement. The task of the Communist party of Poland was to organize and lead the revolt. The party concluded, therefore, that the Polish republic was an ephemeral creature, bound to be torn to pieces by its internal contradictions and swept away by the mounting revolutionary wave. As a semi-feudal, semi-bourgeois state, it should be fought against and eventually destroyed. As a result of this stand the

94

Communist party was declared illegal in 1919 and had to go underground, where it remained until 1944–45.

As long as there was the possibility for revolution in the Weimar republic, Moscow regarded the Polish party as a useful tool. Despite its pro-Trotsky stand during the crucial phases of the struggle for Lenin's mantle, the party was considered a vital section of the Comintern and an essential instrument by means of which Poland was to be either neutralized or paralyzed in order to facilitate future Soviet intervention in Germany. Meanwhile, the Soviet government formed an alliance with Germany, a policy that began with the treaty of Rapallo in April 1922 and lasted until 1934, a year after Hitler's rise to power. In the eyes of the Polish government, therefore, and for the patriotic man in the street, the Communists, with their insistence on Poland joining the Soviet republic outright and their willingness to give away Poland's western provinces to Germany, were considered simply as foreign agents.

Despite the official negative stand of the party leadership toward Polish statehood, under the cosmopolitan crust of "Luxemburgism," there existed among some Communists a vague and initially rather amorphous undercurrent of patriotism. The trend was brought to the surface in 1924, the year in which a young Communist writer, Julian Brun-Bonowicz, published a series of essays entitled *Stefana Żeromskiego tragedia pomyłek* (Stefan Żeromski's Tragedy of Errors). The work analyzed one of Żeromski's novels, the hero of which brings Bolshevik ideas from the Communist Caucasus back to Poland. Brun-Bonowicz concluded that the Poles should strive for a *native* revolution similar to, but not identical with, the Communist upheaval in the USSR. Soviet-Polish relations should be based on the free cooperation of the two equal, fraternal proletarian movements.

The conflict between the cosmopolitan and the nationalistic trends in the Communist movement affected the Polish party's relationship with the Communist party of the Soviet Union (CPSU) by raising a serious issue: should the Polish comrades obediently follow Moscow's dictates in every respect, or should they act on their own and thereby adapt the Bolshevik experience to the specific, local conditions of their native country? Would, for instance, the style and methods of the Soviet party be successful if rigidly applied by the Polish Communists? Brun-Bonowicz argued that Poland should follow the Soviet experiment in essence but not in every detail, rejecting those methods that were alien to Polish mentality and tradition. By this means he implicitly rejected the universality of the Soviet experience, its automatic, unquestionable applicability to Polish conditions, and asserted that there was a peculiar native way to achieve the goals of Socialism and Communism in Poland. His reasoning implied also that not slavish subordination but cooperation would be the essence of a proper relationship between the revolutionary movements of the two countries.

The national Bolshevik concept of proletarian revolution was repeatedly condemned by Moscow and by the leftist, Luxemburg-influenced leadership of the Communist party of Poland. Nevertheless, the "nationalistic deviation" struck roots in the party's rank and file. Despite frequent denunciations and ruthless purges, the tendency was never completely eradicated; quite the contrary, it gained in popularity over the years.

The party's turbulent history culminated in one of the most dramatic events in the annuals of world Communism—the liquidation of the Communist party of Poland by Stalin. From the early 1930s on the CPP became the scene of a series of witch hunts, most of them reflecting Stalin's tactical zigzags. First, there came the purge of the Trotskyites, then the line was shifted and the party was accused of hiding "nationalistic deviationists," of being led by a bunch of "provocateurs, spies, and diversionists" allegedly planted in the CPP by Piłsudski's agents. A series of purges and splits in the party followed.

The decisive blow was struck during the great purge of 1936–38, which affected the CPP more than any other section of the Comintern. Several hundred leading Polish Communists who were in Soviet territory during that period were either physically liquidated or sent to concentration camps. Those who happened to be abroad were lured back under one pretext or another and then liquidated. Among those purged were prominent leaders such as Adolf Warski-Warszawski,

Julian Leński-Leszczyński, and Wera Kostrzewa (Maria Koszucka). Also murdered were several prominent intellectuals, including Bruno Jasieński, a writer and poet of international repute and the author of a popular French novel, *Je Brûle Paris* (I Am Burning Paris).

By the middle of 1938 the decimated CPP had ceased to exist as an organized political movement. No official announcement about the dissolution of the party was ever published. Ironically, most survivors of the purge, other than those who were either too insignificant to be killed or who served with the Stalinist apparatus, owed their salvation to the fact that they were in Polish prisons. One such survivor was Władysław Gomułka, then a second rank local Communist leader from eastern Galicia.

In Comintern calculations, the CPP had been important only as a conduit of the Soviet proletarian revolution to Germany. With Hitler's triumph, the Soviet hopes for a German upheaval had evaporated. Stalin apparently then decided to reshape his strategy completely, and as a result, there was no longer any reason for maintaining as ineffective an instrument as the CPP. Furthermore, by 1937–38, with Piłsudski's successors tightening their hold on the country, the possibility of revolution in Poland seemed more remote than ever. By 1937, following the disastrous Great Depression, a period of considerable economic progress ameliorated somewhat the smoldering social and economic situation. Consequently, Stalin must have come to the conclusion that in the event of another "revolutionary situation" arising in Poland, the Red Army would do a better job than the CPP.

Stalin knew, of course, that any deal with Hitler would provoke opposition within the ranks of the CPP. The party, with its gradually decreasing but still large Jewish membership on the one hand, and its growing undercurrent of Polish nationalism on the other, could hardly accept such an agreement without a dramatic protest. Consequently, the CPP had to be disbanded and its leaders exterminated. The Polish Communist party was one of the last major casualties of the great purge and one of the first victims of Stalin's clearing the ground for an understanding with Hitler. The slaughter of most of its leading

97

members, a traumatic experience which the survivors were never to forget, was to have a profound effect on the rebirth and reform of the Communist movement in Poland after World War II.

The story of Poland's foreign policy during the interwar period is as complex as it is dramatic. During the 1920s and early 1930s the country's security rested on the alliance with France and Romania as well as on the weakness of the Soviet Union and Germany. These two countries were allied by the 1922 Rappallo treaty, but their armed forces and economies were initially weak. During the middle and late 1930s, with German rearmament and the progress achieved by the first two five year plans, the balance of forces began to change. Although the domestic crisis was the main reason for Marshal Piłsudski's decision to assume power, foreign policy developments also played a significant role. The rapid economic recovery of Germany, the Locarno treaty of October 16, 1925, which amounted to the German refusal to accept Poland's western frontier, and the renewal of the Soviet-German Rappallo pact—all were signs of Poland's deteriorating international position, and important factors that pushed the Marshal toward his momentous decision. And indeed, throughout the nine years of his semi-dictatorial rule, from May 1926 to May 1935, Piłsudski was mainly preoccupied with foreign and military affairs. In the 1930s they were his exclusive domain.

In order to partially neutralize the Rappallo treaty and to gain time, Poland signed a nonaggression pact with the Soviet Union in 1932. Within a few months after the signing of the agreement there were numerous signs of improved relations, including ministerial visits, cordial speeches, and some cultural exchanges. *Literaturnaia gazeta* (Literary Gazette) published a special Polish issue, while a leading Warsaw literary weekly, *Wiadomości literackie* (Literary News), printed an impressive issue devoted to the USSR. Through a personal envoy Piłsudski assured Stalin that Poland would never side with Germany against the Soviet Union. For a while, the year 1932 seemed like a turning point in the relations between the two countries. But, for reasons which are beyond the scope of this study, the honeymoon did not last. Apparently the lingering memories of the events of 1920 and the differences of social and political systems were too steep to overcome.[9]

Poland's relationship with France during the interwar years was ambivalent and subject to fluctuation. One of the vital goals of Piłsudski's foreign policy was the reinforcement of the Franco-Polish alliance, the alliance which he had personally concluded in 1921. Despite his frequent gestures of defiance toward Paris, he wanted to strengthen the military ties uniting the two countries by providing the military clauses of the treaty with teeth. Paris, however, took an opposite stand and aimed at a progressive loosening of the alliance through elimination of the provision obliging both partners to come to one another's aid automatically in case of a German attack. Instead, the French wanted the military obligations to be based on a vaguely defined responsibility deriving from mutual membership in the League of Nations.[10]

Piłsudski objected to this approach and, as far as can be determined from scattered and still incomplete evidence, began to nurse a scheme often referred to as "preventive war." The issue of preventive war is still controversial. Existing evidence shows that in March 1933, a few weeks after Hitler's coming to power, Piłsudski warned the French prime minister, Edward Daladier, that German rearmament was progressing very rapidly. The Marshal proposed that immediate, direct military action be launched by France, Great Britain, and Poland to crush Hitler and prevent German rearmament. He even offered to provide the necessary pretext in form of an incident at the Polish military depot at Westerplatte, in Danzig. Daladier, after consultation with London, refused so radical a step. A month later Piłsudski again reiterated his offer, but it was again turned down by the French.

What were the chances of success and the risks involved in such a scheme? In the spring of 1933, Germany's political and military position could hardly have been worse. The Third Reich was diplomatically isolated, and Hitler's domestic position was precarious. The

✑ Experiment in Independence

German Reichswehr of some 100,000 men, deprived of tanks and military aviation, was no match for the combined forces of France, Poland, and perhaps also Great Britain. Poland alone had an army of some 300,000, and the technological differences between the Polish and German forces were not that great. It was only after the failure of his two attempts to launch a preventive war that Pilsudski decided to sign a nonaggression pact with Germany. The agreement, signed on January 26, 1934, contained explicit provisions stressing Poland's loyalty toward the existing treaties binding the country, including the French alliance of 1921.[11]

After Pilsudski's death, the idea of preventive war was taken up by the foreign minister, Joseph Beck. On March 7, 1936, during the international crisis that followed the Germany reoccupation of the Rhineland, Beck summoned the French ambassador in Warsaw, Leon Noël, and submitted to him a proposal for joint action against Germany. Beck declared to Noël that in view of the clear violation by Hitler of the treaties of Versailles and Locarno, Poland was ready to carry out its military obligations deriving from the 1921 Franco-Polish alliance. Again, after consulting the British, France refused to act. While Pilsudski's initiative is far from being adequately documented, Beck's action was confirmed in the Noël's memoirs.[12]

Thus, in March 1936 the chance of overthrowing Hitler without causing a general conflagration was probably lost altogether. Ironically, Hitler had ordered the German troops to retreat from the Rhineland in case of armed resistance by the French. But the lethargic, almost suicidal reluctance to oppose first the German rearmament and then later acts of aggression was the guiding principle of French and British policy in the 1930s. Whatever one may say about his domestic policies, Pilsudski was one of the first European statesmen who perceived the Nazi danger threatening the world. He was, moreover, the only leader who was ready to take up arms and destroy the Hitler regime before it became too strong.

From 1934 on, the main effort of the country's foreign policy was to keep a balance between Germany and the USSR. Refusing any closer cooperation with the Soviets that might result from Poland's

100

adherence to the French-sponsored system of regional mutual defense known as the Eastern Pact because of the country's position between Germany and Russia, Piłsudski and his successors put all their hopes on Poland's ability and determination to resist militarily any attempt on its independence. In view of the lingering pacifistic illusions in the west, Poland's position was far from enviable. While trying to perform a balancing act between Germany and Russia, the Polish leaders hoped that an awakening of the instinct of self-preservation in France and Great Britain would make effective military cooperation with them possible in the future. There were at least two shortcomings to the policy of equilibrium. The first was the disparity of forces between Poland and its two neighbors; the second was the willingness as well as the ability of the French and the British to intervene in a new strategic situation created by the reoccupation of the Rhineland and the building of the Siegfried Line by Hitler. In Poland's geopolitical position this policy of trying to preserve a precarious balance between two aggressive totalitarian states, without adequate assurance of effective aid from the British and French, amounted to constantly walking a tightrope.[13]

There were two possible solutions to the country's predicament: either close cooperation with other nations situated between the USSR and Germany, in order to create some sort of federation, or confederation, of smaller states, or a closer association with one of the powerful neighbors, a policy of accommodation, compromise, and even concession. Either variant of the second solution would require considerable territorial concessions, and Polish public opinion—except for the CPP—was not ready for such a move.

As far as the first solution was concerned, the prosperous, industrialized Czechoslovakia, stretching along the southern frontier of Poland, could play a vital role in a possible confederation of states threatened by the aggressive neighbors. And indeed, Warsaw made several attempts at rapprochement with Prague. There were moments in 1921, 1922, and 1925, when the Poles were willing to forgo their traditional friendship with the Hungarians, forget about the conflict over Teschen Silesia, and join the Czechs, the Romanians, and

101

the Yugoslavs within the framework of an expanded and reorganized Little Entente, which would mutually guarantee its members' sovereignty and integrity. But the mistrustful Czechs, led by Dr. Edward Beneš, rejected all Polish offers of cooperation.

In 1933, Foreign Minister Beck went so far as to offer to Prague a straightforward military alliance. But Beneš, who did not consider Czechoslovak-Polish cooperation desirable, again adopted an uncompromising attitude toward Poland. He believed that Prague should not come to the aid of a country that was, in his opinion, destined to be the first victim of German aggression. Czechoslovakia, according to Beneš, was in a much more advantageous political position in relation to both Germany and Soviet Russia than was Poland, with its unsettled frontiers. This Beneš admitted frankly in a conversation with two British statesmen held in Geneva in March 1933. As Sir John Simon reported:

> Speaking very confidentially, M. Beneš said that he feared an incident between Germany and Poland. He had had a long talk quite recently with M. Beck. He had told him that Czechoslovakia would not make an alliance with Poland against Germany, because he thought it would be very dangerous to give Germany clear cause for fearing encirclement.[14]

There is no doubt that Poland's attitude toward Czechoslovakia during the Munich crisis of 1938 was a grave mistake. Warsaw's insistence on immediate cession of the Teschen Silesia was obviously ill-timed. But Warsaw's errors cannot be put on the same level as those of London and, especially, Paris. Unlike the French, the Poles had no treaty of alliance with Prague. Warsaw's decision to claim the largely Polish province of Teschen derived from the conviction, fully corroborated by subsequent events, that the western powers would not fight in defense of Czechoslovakia and would sacrifice that country to Hitler's designs for the sake of appeasement. As Professor William Rose has pointed out in his penetrating essay, ''Poles and Czechs as Neighbors,'' both countries failed to recognize their common interests and the common dangers they were facing. The Czechs were responsible for the failure during the 1920s and early 1930s, the Poles during the Munich crisis. Each regarded the other as a hindrance to its own almost equally inflated amibitions.

🖋 🖋

The aftermath of the Munich crisis ended the period of improved relations between Poland and Germany initiated by the nonaggression pact of 1934. At the end of October 1938, Hitler summoned the Polish ambassador in Berlin, Joseph Lipski, and put forward far-reaching demands concerning Polish Pomerania and Danzig. The demands, repudiated by the Poles, were reiterated by von Ribbentrop, the German foreign minister, during his visit to Warsaw in January 1939. Hitler insisted on the return of the city of Danzig and control of a strip of land across what the Germans insisted on calling the Polish Corridor. The Poles refused both demands. The second refusal was followed by the launching of a German propaganda campaign: the German minority in Poland was to be "liberated" from Polish "oppression and persecution," just as the Sudeten Germans had been freed from the "Czech yoke." By the spring of 1939, all the tactical tricks with which the world had become familiar at the time of the Czechoslovak crisis were set into motion by Dr. Göbbels against Poland.

The German occupation of Prague on March 15, 1939, brought about a reawakening of Western public opinion and revealed the true nature of Hitler's aims. British foreign policy shifted from appeasement of Germany to active engagement in the affairs of Central and Eastern Europe. On March 31, the British government extended a far-reaching guarantee to Poland. In the words of the British prime minister, Neville Chamberlain, the British government committed itself, "in the event of any action which clearly threatened Polish independence, and which the Polish government accordingly considered it vital to resist with their national forces . . . to lend the Polish government all support in their power." The guarantee was so worded that the Poles themselves would be the judges of the right cause and the right moment for resistance. A similar guarantee was

103

given to Romania. These commitments were a momentous, historic departure for British policy, which traditionally shrank from entanglements east of the Rhine. Soon, France associated itself with the British action and began to revitalize its almost moribund treaty of alliance with Warsaw. On April 6, 1939, the British guarantee was confirmed in negotiations conducted by Foreign Minister Beck during his visit in London.

Following the Munich crisis, the Soviet Union began to view the European scene with some anxiety. In the immediate aftermath of Munich a period of improved Polish-Soviet relations ensued. On November 28, 1938, the two countries in a joint declaration reaffirmed the nonaggression pact of 1932. In case of war, the Soviet Union promised to deliver to Poland military equipment as well as medical supplies. By this means, Moscow apparently hoped to stiffen Polish resistance against Hitler's demands.

The British guarantee to Poland created a new situation not unfavorable to Soviet Russia. The French ambassador to Moscow, Robert Coulondre, wrote:

> It was enough to look at the map of Europe to see what a serious diplomatic situation it [the British guarantee] had created. Rumania and Poland practically formed a continuous front from the Baltic to the Black Sea and the Balkans, a front which separated Germany and the U.S.S.R. Germany cannot attack Russia without going through Poland and Rumania, i.e., without bringing into play the Western guarantee, and without going to war against Britain and France.[15]

Whether London and Paris could have actually restrained Hitler from attacking Poland is a controversial question. Certainly, much depended upon the attitude of Soviet Russia, which obviously held a balance of power between Germany and the Western democracies. If the Red Army had added its resources to the latter's, Hitler would assuredly have thought twice before plunging Germany into a two-front war. When the British foreign secretary, Lord Halifax, informed the Soviet ambassador in London, Ivan Maysky, about the British guarantee to Poland, the Soviet diplomat expressed his doubts whether the guarantee was firm enough to deter Hitler's aggressive drive.[16]

104

On May 10, 1939, Polish hopes for the benevolent neutrality of the USSR were further bolstered by the visit to Warsaw of Vladimir Potemkin, the Soviet deputy commissar for foreign affairs. Potemkin's talk with Foreign Minister Beck was unusually cordial and encouraging. The Soviet diplomat expressed Moscow's full understanding of Poland's difficult position and assured Beck of the USSR's interest in the continuation of good relations with Warsaw. Potemkin advised Beck that in the event of an armed attack on Poland, the Soviet Union would adopt a policy of benevolent neutrality.[17]

Until the late spring of 1939, the Soviet Union was sincerely interested in bolstering Poland's resistance to Hitler while negotiating a military alliance with France and Great Britain. The Soviet draft of a three-power pact of mutual assistance submitted to the French and the British on April 17 included a military convention and a joint guarantee to all states between the Baltic and Black seas. The guarantee involved stationing of Soviet troops in the Baltic states, Poland, and Romania. All these countries, however, were afraid that Soviet garrisons, once established on their soil, would never depart. The vice-minister of foreign affairs, Count Jan Szembek, when confronted with a renewed Western suggestion to establish Soviet military and air bases on Polish territory, bluntly replied: "That is how Poland's partitions started in the eighteenth century."

The long history of Poland's relations with Russia, as well as the brutal image of Stalin's regime, were important factors in the continuing Polish suspicion of the USSR. To the outside world, and not only to the Poles, the Soviet Union in the late 1930s presented a horrible spectacle of plotting, purges, and mass deportations. Barely a semblance of a state, it was thought to be undermined by dissent and treason, yet at the same time eager to perpetuate ambitious foreign schemes motivated both by Communist ideology and by reviving nationalistic urges. The lesson of the past was clear: the permanent stationing of Russian troops was a stepping stone to eventual subjugation.

Whether Poland should have accepted the Soviet bases and garrisons on its territory, and what consequences such acceptance would have had on the outcome of the negotiations then going on in Moscow, as well as on Poland's fate, are issues that have been debated endlessly by historians. As one author wrote:

> It may be that the Anglo-Russian talks never had any chance of success, and that the Russians were attempting, from Munich on, to reach an agreement with the Germans. What seems more likely is that the Russians were weighing up the offers of both sides for an alliance, and that a greater willingness on the part of the Poles to compromise could have led to successful negotiations which, at the cost of a diminution of Polish freedom of maneuver, might have given her more chance to resist the Germans or even have deterred Hitler from war. But until the Russian documents are made available we can only speculate.[18]

Most historians now active in Poland, as well as a few among the émigrés, argue that since cooperation with Nazi Germany was unacceptable to an overwhelming majority of Poles both on moral and political grounds, cooperation with the USSR was the only choice. Acceptance of active Soviet assistance, in the form of Soviet garrisons and airfields on Polish territory, would have been a lesser evil in comparison with what was to follow. An agreement with Moscow, even if limited to stationing of Soviet troops in strictly defined regions, would have involved a blow to the country's self-esteem and eventually result in some territorial concessions on the eastern fringes of the pre-1939 territory. The final outcome of Poland's submission to the Soviet Union would have certainly been no worse, and perhaps better, than the Nazi occupation, which threatened the very existence of Poland as a nation.

The dramatic story of the Soviet-German rapprochement in the fateful summer of 1939 is well-known and needs no retelling here. In reply to the Stalin-Hitler pact, Poland issued an order for general mobilization. But, under the concerted pressure of Great Britain and France, Warsaw halted the mobilization in order "not to provoke Hitler." The cancellation of mobilization orders played havoc with Polish planning. On September 1, 1939, without a formal declaration of war, the Nazi forces fell upon Poland.

106

The Germans threw approximately seventy-five first-rate divisions with 2,400 tanks and over 2,000 planes against Poland, quickly crushing all resistance. By September 7, the Wehrmacht had reached Warsaw, by the 15th it had occupied Lublin, and by the 17th, Brześć nad Bugiem (Brest on the Bug). Warsaw fell on September 28. The Polish army continued its fight until October 3, when the last large unit capitulated. The German conquest of Poland was a perfect demonstration of the new type of mobile warfare, the Blitzkrieg. It was a combination of military operations intertwined with multifaceted political warfare and various diversionary moves. The German minority in Poland acted as a fifth column in the rear of the Polish forces, abetting the terror and disorganization. The concept of a front lost its meaning. On September 17, while the Polish forces were still fighting a series of bloody battles, the Red Army attacked from the rear, claiming to liberate the Ukrainians and the Byelorussians of the Eastern Marshes from the Polish yoke.

The Poles, naturally enough, expected offensive air operations to begin immediately following the British and French declarations of war on Germany on September 3. On September 5, the Polish military attaché in London went to the Air Ministry with an urgent request for the Royal Air Force to launch bombing raids against Germany. All requests were in vain. The same day, a conservative member of Parliament, Leopold Amery, saw the British air minister, Kingsley Wood, and urged him to set afire the Black Forest with incendiary bombs as a reprisal for the German raids on Polish cities. "Oh, you can't do that," said Wood, "this is private property." [19]

In order to do something, however, the British Bomber Command was ordered to drop leaflets on Frankfurt, Munich, and Stuttgart, informing German citizens of the true facts about Hitler's aggression against Poland. In his parliamentary speech, Wood claimed that these "truth raids" had caused the German authorities great irritation. The fact that in those tragic September days England and France abandoned Poland to face German aggression alone could have been no surprise to Hitler. He had no fear of Poland's Western allies when he launched his attack and withdrew his troops and military equipment from Germany's western borders, leaving them almost unguarded. According to the testimony of Field Marshal Wilhelm Keitel at the Nuremberg trial as well as to evidence found in other historic documents, Germany in September 1939 had barely twenty poorly prepared combat divisions on its western frontier. All the better troops, all tanks, and practically the entire air force had been thrown against Poland. Facing these meager German forces in the west were more than ninety French divisions, about 2,500 tanks, 10,000 guns, and 3,000 French and British aircraft, which were soon joined by a dozen British divisions with several thousand tanks and guns. None of this great force was used to mount an offensive. All the allies of Poland managed to do was to send a few patrols and reconnaissance flights and drop an occasional pacifistic proclamation.[20]

The most important part of the Stalin-Hitler pact signed in Moscow on August 23 was the secret protocol dividing Poland, the Baltic states, and Romania between Germany and the USSR. The territory in Poland west of the rivers Narew, Vistula, and San, was originally to go to Germany, and Warsaw, situated on both sides of the Vistula, was to be split. The secret protocol did not specify what each conquering power would do with its sphere of infleunce. On September 28, another deal was made between Moscow and Berlin in which Hitler traded Lithuania for the east-central segment of Poland, on the right bank of the Vistula. Consequently, most of the ethnic Polish lands were eventually allotted to the Third Reich, to be subjected to genocidal experiments.

Thus, attacked from the west and the east, outflanked and outgunned, Poland went down, fighting to the last moment, while vainly invoking help from its allies. The events of September 1939 were almost the worst that could have happened. Encouraged by its apparently viable alliances with France and Britain, an overconfident Poland had plunged into a most disastrous war, only to be shamelessly and rather foolishly abandoned. The destruction of Poland was soon followed by that of all other independent states of east-central Europe.

In purely material terms, the accomplishments of the interwar period were not spectacular, although a considerable measure of material progress was achieved. This was accomplished against heavy odds, without major foreign investments, and without applying totalitarian methods that were alien to a great majority of Polish people. The war-ruined country was speedily welded together and rehabilitated, and numerous new industries were established. Within a decade the obscure fishing village of Gdynia was turned into the largest and most modern harbor on the Baltic, capable of handling some 10 million tons of goods a year. The Polish aircraft industry, which literally did not exist before World War I, grew and achieved some notable successes. On an individual level, one is amazed by the number of Poles who scored highly at various international air competitions such as the Challenge and the Gordon Bennett Competition. The Central Industrial Region, built during the late 1930s along the middle Vistula, was the foundation of a new industrial area in one of the most neglected parts of the country. In terms of long-range coordinated planning, the organization was unique in non-Communist Eastern Europe and was comparable to the American Tennessee Valley Authority. Although agrarian reform was pursued far too slowly and was by no means completed when the war broke out, some 3 million hectares of land were taken away from large landowners and divided among peasants. In the area of social welfare, a rather impressive body of legislation was put into practice.[21]

There were also some worthy cultural achievements in the years between the world wars. Illiteracy, which had plagued nearly half of the people in Russian Poland in the early 1920s, was greatly reduced by 1939. Institutions of higher learning (although mainly restricted to individuals of middle class origin) were producing educated young people of respectable caliber who compared favorably with their counterparts in the West. In the creative field, Polish intellectuals won many international prizes, including the gold medals for the pavillions at the International Exhibitions of Decorative Arts in Paris in 1924, and the World Exhibition in 1937, as well as numerous prizes for graphic arts (especially posters, a field in which the Poles seem to excel). In 1924 Władysław Reymont was awarded the Nobel Prize for his powerful novel, *Chopi (The Peasants)*. At the 1938 Olympic Games at Amsterdam the poet Kazimierz Wierzyński was granted a gold medal for his collection of poems entitled *The Olympic Laurel,* while Jan Parandowski got a third-prize bronze medal in 1936 for his book about the ancient games, *The Olympic Discus.*

The painter Tadeusz Makowski played a considerable role in forming the École de Paris and achieved a reputation as a sensitive and subtle painter of children. In the field of music, Karol Szymanowski continued the development of Polish musical composition; his opera-ballet, *Harnasie,* based on Tatra folklore, was presented on many Western stages with great success. Several authors who were to gain worldwide reputations only after World War II, among them Stanisław Ignacy Witkiewicz, Witold Gombrowicz, Bruno Schultz, and Czesław Miłosz, produced some of their plays, poems, and novels during the interwar period.[22] While Gombrowicz and Miłosz developed their talents to the full extent only after World War II, Witkiewicz, although rediscovered and made famous after the war, fully belongs to the prewar period, of which he is the strange yet brilliant star.

Witkiewicz was endowed with many talents: he was an accomplished musician, novelist and essayist, playwright, and philosopher, as well as a painter and draftsman. The most intriguing achievement of this bizarre genius was the theory and practice of "theater of pure form." His ideas were explained in three books, the most significant of which was *An Introduction to the Theory of the Pure Form in the Theater,* published in 1923. Witkiewicz believed that theater was the most impure of the arts because of its composite nature. According to him, an author, rather than seeking to imitate life or other forms of artistic expression, should manipulate the theatrical elements "to create a whole whose meaning would be defined only by its purely scenic internal construction."

Witkiewicz wrote some thirty plays in which he applied his theories; the most important of them are: *They* (1920), *The Water Hen* (1921), *The Cuttlefish* (1923), *The Madman and the Nun* (1923),

The Mother (1924), and *The Shoemakers* (1934). Widely regarded as a bold forerunner of the present-day theater of the absurd, Witkiewicz rejected "programmatic nonsense." As he declared in his *Introduction to the Theory of Pure Form . . . ,* he was simply trying "to enlarge the possibilities of composition by abandoning life-like logic in art." Consequently he tried to liberate the theater from the shackles of the traditional plot based on the local cause-and-effect mechanism. He presented instead dramatic segments connected only by ad hoc laws he himself had created. His characters transcend the conventional rules of psychology and biology, physics and ethics, operating in a fantastic, grotesque world of their own. Corpses come back to life, historic characters mingle freely with those of the present day; all of them often engage in strange violent actions, mixing freely sex and murder with passionate philosophic diatribes and elaborate political debates. The free play of arbitrary forces and utter liberty enjoyed by his characters inevitably produce an antiutopian, dehumanized world haunted by demonic beasts.

During the interwar period Witkiewicz's contemporaries looked down at his nightmarish visions as products of a morbid imagination of an alcoholic and drug addict. Only after the horrors of World War II, and with the revival of surrealistic trends in art, was his strange genius rediscovered. Since the late 1950s his works have been recognized not only as a dramatic anticipation of the Orwellian nightmare, but also as brilliantly pioneering achievements in the field of the theater of the absurd. Witkiewicz was clearly the most original Polish writer of the twentieth century.[23]

During the 1920s and 1930s the Polish schools of logic and mathematics, centered mainly at the universities of Warsaw and Lwów, achieved leading positions in their fields. At the same time, in sociology and anthropology such scholars as Florian Znaniecki and Bronisław Malinowski, active mostly abroad, became world authorities, while Professor Tadeusz Zieliński of the University of Warsaw continued his brilliant work on the civilization of classic antiquity and was awarded the Goethe medal for his writing.

Despite these achievements in various fields of creativity, there can

Experiment in Independence

be no doubt that Poland's social and economic progress in the 1920s and 1930s was too slow to provide a decent standard of living for a burgeoning population, and that, despite the continuing emigration, prewar Poland was unable to provide decent employment for a large segment of its people. The large surplus of the rural population was an especially heavy burden on the country's economy. Agrarian reform was timidly enacted and the process of industrialization too sluggish to absorb the surplus population. Moreover, the relatively slow social mobility tended to perpetuate the surviving social and economic injustices.[24]

In the field of foreign relations, the failure of earlier schemes to make Poland a center of an East European confederation, and the failure to join an enlarged Little Entente, left the country too dependent on the alliance with France, a country that had lost its self-confidence and its will to assert its influence even in the areas adjacent to its borders, let alone in Eastern Europe. The Franco-Polish alliance of 1921, salutary during the initial stages of Poland's independent existence, gradually lost its vitality and, together with the British guarantee in March of 1939, merely lulled the Poles into a false sense of security. Both these distant alliances prevented them from seeing the grim reality and adjusting to it.

To sum it up, one may say that the significance of the short spell of the independence cannot be measured either in economic terms or even in terms of success or failure of Poland's foreign policy. The meaning of the years 1918 to 1939 transcends purely material values and is essentially moral. After some five generations of subjugation, these two decades constituted an experiment in political independence and democratic form of government, whatever its imperfections. The interwar years gave the Poles a breathing spell, restored their self-confidence and recharged their national energies, which had been seriously drained after more than a hundred years of foreign oppression. Moreover, twenty years of independence allowed the Poles to educate a new generation of young people in the love of freedom. Their mettle would be tested in the trials of World War II.

CHAPTER FIVE

The Time of Trial

> Pity we should have only for Germans!
> *Dr. Hans Frank*

There is not a city in the world whose soil is as bloody as Warsaw. It seemed as if every stone on the pavement we trod, under the dirt and snow covering it, must have its stains of martyrs' blood. I understand then why Warsaw was and has been and will always be the site of revolution. Until it is burnt to ashes and destroyed . . . and its citizens not allowed to settle within a score of miles, as with old Carthage—til then Warsaw may be reduced to gloomy silence, but never subdued by despotism; and at the first call of liberty they will rise in arms to one man.

> *Sergei Mikhailovich Kravchinski (Stepnyak)—1879*

THE PERIOD FOLLOWING the German invasion was among the most trying and tragic in the millennial history of the Polish nation. Left alone to fight Nazi Germany and eventually abandoned by their allies, throughout the war the Polish people faced a seemingly hopeless situation. For almost six years they were threatened with annihilation. While the military campaign was drawing to an end, Germany and Soviet Russia redrafted their Moscow pact. On September 28, 1939, a new agreement was reached between the two powers for a repartitioning of Poland roughly along the Bug and San rivers, but leaving the whole Białystok district on the Soviet side. In terms of area, the country was divided into two almost equal parts, but with the Germans keeping the bulk of the population, approximately 22

113

million people. Early in October 1939, Hitler incorporated Polish Pomerania, Posnania, and Upper Silesia and fragments of central Poland, including the district of Łódź, into the Greater German Reich. The remaining German-occupied Poland was then organized as a Government General, with Cracow as its capital and Dr. Hans Frank as its satrap.[1]

From the beginning the Germans used every means of violence and physical extermination in order to transform Poland into a colony. "From now on," said Dr. Frank, "the political role of the Polish nation is ended. It is our aim that the very concept *Polak* be erased for centuries to come. Neither the Republic, nor any other form of Polish state will ever be reborn. Poland will be treated as a colony and Poles will become slaves in the German empire."

By means of forced mass deportation, practically everything considered as Polish was removed from the regions incorporated in the Reich. Those people who remained were forced to renounce their Polish citizenship and accept German nationality. The Poles living in the Government General were to form—as Hitler said—"a reservation, a vast Polish labor camp. Poles will never be raised to a higher level. . . ." Jews and educated Poles were to be exterminated. Soon blind, indiscriminate terror became the chief instrument of German rule in the Government General. The concentration camps of Oświęcim (Auschwitz), Treblinka, and Majdanek became centers for the murder of the Jewish population not only of Poland, but of the whole of Europe. In a few cases the Jews, driven to desperation, preferred to perish fighting than to be gassed in the ovens by their German executioners. This was the case of the Jews of the Warsaw ghetto, who, threatened by the final deportation to the extermination camps, rose up in April 1943. The uprising was crushed after forty-two days of heroic fighting.[2]

The Polish intellectual elite was treated almost as cruelly as were the Jews. The war cost the country almost half of its educated stratum. The senseless brutality of German occupation authorities in Poland could be compared only with the later horrors of Nazi rule in the Ukraine and Byelorussia, but not with the relatively milder

114

regimes imposed on the occupied Western countries. The Nazis took quite literally the words of Nietzsche: "Blood and cruelty are the foundation of all things." These were the policies of genocide. They reached their peak toward the end of the war. As a Nazi dignitary, Dr. Schoengarth, put it at a session of the executive board of the Government General on April 20, 1943: "No nation has ever experienced an oppression similar to that which is now the lot of the Polish nation." [3]

While in western and central Poland the Germans were establishing their New Order, the eastern segment of the country was suffering from Stalinist policies of "social engineering" and forcible deportations. On October 22, 1939, the Soviet commander of the occupation forces ordered elections to be held in order to select a supreme soviet and local bodies. In accordance with the customary Soviet practice, the electorate had no voice in the nomination of the candidates, who came mostly from the Soviet Union and were often complete strangers to the voters. Voting was permitted only for the one candidate whose name appeared on the ballot, and Soviet occupation troops were also given the right to vote. Deputies elected to the supreme soviet were formed into two so-called national assemblies, one named Western Ukrainian and another Western Byelorussian. Each of these bodies, by a show of hands, passed resolutions providing for the "admission" of their territories into the Soviet Union and for the confiscation of big estates and the nationalization of banks and industries. Shortly after the election, deportations started anew, affecting an even greater number of people than before.

The overall Soviet policy in eastern Poland would seem to indicate that, at this stage, Stalin had no plans for the creation of a vassal government in Poland. Instead, the Kremlin's program between September 1939 and June 1941 called for extermination of all politically conscious elements, whether Polish, Jewish, Ukrainian, or Byelorussian. In addition, the eastern Polish territory which Russia had already annexed was to be incorporated into the Soviet Union. As far as the rest of Poland was concerned, Moscow resolved to leave it to the tender mercies of Hitler. Such an attitude was, of course, bound to embitter an overwhelming majority of Poles, including many genuine Communists. Both the German policy of extermination, carried out in the Government General, and the large-scale deportations by the Soviets, as well as the disappearance of most Polish officers taken as prisoners of war in September 1939, seemed to indicate that liquidation of the politically conscious elements in Poland was a goal of both occupying powers.[4]

The endemic Polish mistrust of Russia was deepened by Soviet participation in 1939 in the destruction of the Polish state. Whatever limited popularity the Communist party of Poland had managed to acquire during the Popular Front period (1935–38) now vanished overnight. Soon after the end of hostilities many surviving Communist leaders moved from the German-occupied part of the country and settled in the Soviet-occupied areas. In order to hold together and utilize the remnants of party membership and fellow travelers, some minor Communist associations were organized at this time. A literary and political monthly, *New Horizons,* was started in Lwów in January 1941. Another group of Polish Communists, headed by Stefan Jędrychowski, was active in Wilno and in the region ceded by the USSR to Lithuania, while some Communists settled in Soviet Russia.

The rule of terror prevailing in different forms in both parts of occupied Poland was bound to produce an equally uncompromising resistance that would be drawn from a broad cross-section of the population. And indeed, already toward the end of September 1939 a clandestine resistance movement was organized by the major Polish political parties in the German-controlled part of the country. To preserve the continuity of Polish statehood, a government-in-exile was formed in France by General Władysław Sikorski, who became prime minister as well as commander-in-chief. In addition to Sikorski, a former rival of Piłsudski and a man of the democratic political center, the government consisted of representatives of the Polish Socialist party, the Peasant party, and the liberal elements of the National party, i.e., the same groups that formed the backbone of the resistance movement in Poland. The government favored the broad

116

democratic reform of future Poland. The fall of France in June 1940 was a heavy blow to the Poles, who were initially staking their hopes on the French army. But General Sikorski, overwhelmingly supported by the government and the mass of the Polish soldiers fighting at the front, refused to share in the French capitulation and transferred the center of the resistance to Great Britain.

While the Poles in exile were busy preparing for the decisive struggle alongside the Allies, as well as for reconstruction of their state along democratic lines and in confederation with Czechoslovakia, in occupied Poland the foundations of a resistance movement were being laid. By 1941, the Union of Armed Resistance emerged as the strongest of all the secret military groups. The next year, the Union was renamed *Armia Krajowa* (AK), or the Home Army. The Home Army tried, on the whole rather successfully, to unify the clandestine military forces of the various political parties into one single organization. Both the extreme rightist National Armed Forces (NSZ), and the Communist fighting squads, took exception to this action. By the winter of 1940–41, when Nazi-Soviet relations had worsened, some military preparations were made on the part of small Communist groups which were active in the territory of the Government General. There, however, Communists refrained from any guerrilla or sabotage activity until well after the outbreak of the Soviet-German war in June 1941.[5]

🖋 🖋

The German attack on the Soviet Union on June 22, 1941, caused a dramatic reversal in this attitude. The slogan of a "united Allied war effort" was accepted by Polish Communists without much hesitation. Nevertheless, it was some time before they could adapt themselves to this about-face. In many respects, the period from 1941 to 1945 marked a return to the old united front policy. There were, however, important variations now. The Comintern had suspended the class struggle; charges of imperialism, leveled against the Western powers during the previous strategic phases, were dropped. The

117

Time of Trial

Communists now shared with the Allied nations a desire to defeat the Axis, and military effectiveness in the struggle against the invaders was a paramount consideration.

In order to win over the Western powers, the Soviet Union sought a rapprochement with the Polish government in London. Hitler's attack on Russia seemed a propitious moment for such a reconcilation. In his speech of June 23, 1941 (the day after the German attack on the USSR), General Sikorski expressed the hope that German aggression on the Soviet Union would create favorable conditions for Russo-Polish reconciliation. It was with this hope that he signed in London the agreement of July 30, 1941, negotiatiated under strong British pressure. It provided for a resumption of diplomatic relations between the two governments and for the Soviet Union to renounce the territorial changes in Poland provided for under the 1939 treaty with Germany. The Soviets consented also to the formation on Soviet soil of a "Polish army under a commander appointed by the Polish government in accord with the Soviet government," to be made up of prisoners of war and deportees. The two governments mutually agreed to render each other aid and support of all kinds in the war against Germany. The Polish army in Russia was to be subordinated, in the operational sense, to the Soviet supreme command, in which the Polish army was to be represented.[6]

Thus Poland, an ally of Great Britain since August 25, 1939, became also a war partner of the USSR; after July 30, 1941, a new chapter in Soviet-Polish relations seemed to be opening. But the agreement was to be a far cry from what its Polish proponent, General Sikorski, meant it to be. From the very beginning the relations between the Polish government in London and the Kremlin were bedeviled by numerous controversial questions, including the territorial issue, as well as a host of minor issues pertaining to the organization of the Polish army in Russia and the fate of the civilian deportees there. Last but not least, there was the bitter, highly explosive question of some 15,000 Polish officers who had been captured by the Red Army in 1939. Despite the highly ambiguous and evasive attitude of the Kremlin on most scores, General Sikorski was a firm

118

believer in the necessity of forming a united front of all countries mortally threatened by Hitler's Germany. Determined to preserve Allied unity, he tried to disregard the mounting obstacles and pressed for close Polish-Soviet cooperation, while preserving his friendly ties with the Western powers, including the United States, to which he journeyed three times to enlist the support of President Roosevelt. None of his trips brought much tangible success.

Meanwhile, in December 1941, General Sikorski went to Moscow to continue working on improvement of relations with the USSR and to supervise the organization of the Polish army there. While negotiations between him and Stalin were still in progress in Moscow at the end of 1941, a conference of pro-Soviet politicians was called in Saratov on December 1, 1941. The date of the conference was by no means an accident; it was specifically chosen so as to put pressure on Sikorski and show him that in its policy toward Poland, Moscow had an alternative. The conference in Saratov eventually resulted in the formation of the nucleus of the Union of Polish Patriots. The union, a motley group of leftist politicians, was dominated by the surviving remnants of the CPP, led by Alfred Lampe and Wanda Wasilewska.

Of all the problems of the Allied wartime diplomacy, none played such a crucial role as the question of Poland: it occupied a lion's share of the first two summit conferences, at Teheran (November-December 1943) and Yalta (February 1945), and still lingered at Potsdam in July and August of 1945, after Germany's defeat. The clash between the USSR and Poland revolved basically around two issues: the Soviet territorial demands, and Stalin's insistence that the country should be ruled by a "friendly" government. Both demands were stubbornly resisted by the Polish government in London, which considered them as contrary to Poland's integrity and sovereignty. In this opposition the government was supported by the non-Communist underground movement in Poland, which defended the Riga frontier of 1921 as well as its own sovereignty rights.

Of the two issues, that of the government was more vital, but the emotionally charged territorial problem overshadowed it from the beginning. From an economic point of view, the Eastern Marshes

119

contained relatively few natural resources; they were, however, Poland's only source of oil, natural gas, and potash, and much of the nation's timber. From a strategic standpoint, the river Bug, which formed both the Curzon and Molotov-Ribbentrop lines, provided less secure a barrier than the Pripet Marshes further east; moreover, the shifting of Poland's boundary to the Bug would reduce to approximately 100 miles the distance from Warsaw to the Polish eastern frontier. Consequently, General Sikorski, supported by an overwhelming majority of his countrymen, tended to see the Soviets' territorial demands as motivated less by their own strategic needs than by a desire to deprive Poland of the essential sources of energy as well as natural defenses essential to independence.

In addition to rational arguments, one must recognize the emotional attachment of the Poles to the Eastern Marches. For nearly half a millennium they were intimately connected with Poland's history, the native land of many of its greatest sons: Chodkiewicz and Sobieski, Kościuszko and Piłsudski, Mickiewicz and Słowacki, Norwid, Sienkiewicz and Paderewski. The great Romantic bard of Poland, Mickiewicz, began his work, the national epic, *Pan Tadeusz* (Master Thaddeus), with the words, "O, Lithuania, my fatherland, thou art like health. . . ." Every Polish child, for about a hundred years, had learned these words by heart; they had become an integral part of the Polish national psyche, almost a religious incantation, a prayer.

General Sikorski's Soviet policy is still a controversial problem. He undoubtedly was sincere in his professions of friendly relations with Moscow, firmly convinced that such relations were a sine qua non of Poland's future security. Yet he was determined that his country not be turned into a Soviet vassal state. He hoped that the experience of joint battle against Germany would overcome Soviet suspicions and convince them that they had more to gain by returning most of the Polish eastern provinces, especially Lwów and the oilfields. In terms of total territory, these lands were insignificant from the Soviet point of view, but they comprised over 40 percent of

120

Poland. Speaking in February 1942 to the national council of the government-in-exile in London, General Sikorski said:

> . . . An honest understanding with the Soviets should ensure a lasting security for Poland. Otherwise—as the course of history has proved—we would be doomed to simultaneous struggles on two fronts, and the prospect would be dark indeed. This understanding will be no less beneficial to the other side. A strong Poland will be capable of withholding the everlasting German *Drang nach Osten.* It will afford our neighbor an opportunity of accomplishing great tasks and furthering the development of the enormous areas and untold wealth of the U.S.S.R. Unquestionably the possibilities of Russia in this regard are boundless. I am therefore confident that the differences that still divide us will disappear. . . .

Sikorski pointed out that the alliance between Poland and the Soviet Union should be based on "mutual good faith and mutual respect for each other's national independence and sovereignty." He concluded his speech by saying: "We trust that the Soviet peoples will not forget that in the hour of their gravest trials we stood up beside them and that they realize what significance a strong and friendly Poland confronting Germany has for them." [7]

General Sikorski, well-aware of political realities and the growing Soviet influence in the Allied councils, anticipated the necessity of making some territorial concession in the east. On the other hand, he wanted Poland to remain undiminished and well-rewarded for its wholehearted and often heroic participation in the struggle against the Axis powers, especially Germany.[8] A recent Ph.D. thesis at Harvard has demonstrated that Sikorski, from October 1939 until his death in July 1943 in Gibraltar, was in favor of the Oder-Neisse boundary. The thesis also proves that he argued for such a solution within the framework of an overall reorientation of Poland's international posture based on a reconciliation with the Soviet Union. The reconciliation was to include a compromise settlement of the Polish-Soviet boundary dispute as well as a federation with Czechoslovakia. The

121

thesis, moreover, shows that General Sikorski did not conceive of territorial gains in the north and west primarily as compensation for possible losses in the east, but rather as justified in their own right by Poland's economic and strategic needs and by the needs of the proposed Central European Federation. Such a solution would be a prerequisite for the creation of a new balance of power in east-central Europe.

This policy found little understanding in Moscow. Stalin obviously had his own plans for Poland. Embarrassed to refer to the boundary established by the Stalin-Hitler pact, Soviet diplomacy constantly spoke about return to the Curzon line of 1919. The Poles could not accept this point of view because they stood to lose some 46 percent of their prewar territory to Hitler's former ally. Consequently, they fought against this concept tooth and nail. The problem of the frontier became intertwined with the issue of Poland's sovereignty and independence from the Soviet Union.[9]

The Western powers, bent on appeasing their mighty Eastern ally, promptly capitulated to the Soviet demands on the territorial issue, and were merely looking for a suitable formula to make it palatable to the Poles. The question of how to revise the Riga frontier in favor of the USSR, despite Polish protests, and how to compensate the Poles for their losses, became one of the most crucial issues of the three major interallied wartime conferences at Teheran, Yalta, and Potsdam.[10]

The Polish government in London, in its controversy with the Kremlin, counted on the support of Great Britain and the United States—in both cases in vain. While trying to preserve the appearance of mediating between the Poles and the Russians, the Western powers would occasionally warn their Polish allies about the changing facts of political life and the determination of London and Washington to preserve Allied unity. In February 1942 the then-acting foreign minister of the Polish government-in-exile, Edward Raczyński, went to Washington in the hope of enlisting American support against Soviet claims on prewar Polish territory. On February 24, when Raczyński visited Assistant Secretary of State Adolph

Berle, the latter outlined the American position on this question. As Raczyński put it in his diary:

> Berle most unexpectedly expressed the prophetic view that Russia would emerge from this war as one of the Powers and added that he thought that the granting of special demands of so great a power would probably be inevitable. He also added that it was difficult to conceive that unlimited sovereignty of smaller states, in the prewar sense of the word, could stand in the way of the natural and inevitable political and economic expansion of a great Power. [11]

At the same time, in the name of "postponing the decisions concerning territorial issues," the Western powers gave the Poles evasive answers concerning compensations on Poland's western borders. Meanwhile, the British government was negotiating an Anglo-Soviet treaty of alliance. The Poles, sensing the danger involved in the British making concessions at Poland's expense, tried to extract from the Foreign Office a pledge that the treaty would not constitute "an infringement of the spirit if not the letter of the Anglo-Polish Agreement of August 25, 1939," and would not "affect vital Polish interests." [12]

Although the British government renewed its previous assurances that it would "not propose to conclude any agreement affecting or compromising the territorial status of the Polish Republic," the London Poles remained suspicious.

🖋 🖋

While the Soviet government in Russia was nursing the survivors of the old Communist party of Poland, in the German-occupied zone preparations were being made for the rebirth of the old CPP in a form more suitable to the new situation. In January 1942, the Polish Workers' party (*Polska Partia Robotnicza*), or PPR, was created from among the survivors of the Communist movement, reinforced by a handful of new adherents. The moment chosen for this rebirth of a regular Communist party in Poland coincided with the Red Army's initial recovery from the series of defeats during the first months of

123

the Nazi-Soviet invasion. The first of the PPR's proclamations was issued in January 1942; an announcement of its central committee stated:

> The PPR is no section of the Communist International or any other international organization. Nevertheless, the PPR bases itself on the Marxist-Leninist doctrine which teaches that national liberation is possible only when it is timed with social liberation.[13]

The reason for omitting the adjective "Communist" was quite understandable: Russia's two-year occupation of eastern Poland and the reports on the Soviet regime from hundreds of thousands of deportees and prisoners had made Communism less popular than ever. Consequently, the Polish Communists preferred to act under the rather neutral name of Polish Workers' party. This was also the reason why the new party deliberately avoided Marxist phraseology and tended to blur its class character by a use of radical democratic slogans combined with such broad terms as "national front" and "national unity." The party's proclamations deplored the alleged passivity of those forces that owed allegiance to the Polish government in London, and made consistent efforts to persuade the Poles that the PPR was the main center of anti-German resistance.

During the first phase of the PPR's activity, until the end of 1942, there was little conspicuous praise of the Soviet Union and its leaders. However, the importance of developing "Polish-Soviet brotherhood" was often stressed; practically no PPR article or proclamation failed to emphasize the urgent necessity of waging unrelenting warfare against Germany and of helping the Soviet Union in its life-and-death struggle. The main accent in the program of the Polish Workers' party was on friendship with the Soviet Union, not as the fatherland of the world proletariat, but as the big Slav brother, the liberator and protector of small nations struggling against the German yoke.

As for the territorial controversy, the PPR willingly acquiesced to the loss of prewar Poland's eastern provinces and advocated instead the reconquest of the former Polish lands east of the Oder River, as

124

well as of East Prussia. Initially the PPR focussed its attention on Warsaw and its working-class population and gradually extended its party organization to the provinces. Thus, simultaneously two instruments of Soviet policy for Poland were being formed: the Union of Polish Patriots in Russia, and the Polish Workers' party in Poland. The Workers' party established its own armed detachments, the People's Guard, which confined its operations to the solidly Polish area west of the Bug River and the Ribbentrop-Molotov line. Only infrequently did it dare to cross into territory east of this point, which was regarded as already belonging to the Soviet Union; the Soviet partisans, on the other hand, were active throughout Poland.

A major turning point in Polish-Soviet relations took place after the battle of Stalingrad in the spring of 1943. While the relations between Moscow and the Polish government in London were going from bad to worse, on April 12 the Germans announced the discovery of graves of the missing Polish officers in the Katyń Forest, near Smoleńsk. German propaganda immediately accused the Russians of having been responsible for the massacre. The Polish government in London, which for nearly two years had bombarded Moscow with queries, all in vain, replied to this by asking for an investigation by the International Red Cross. At the same time the Polish government denied to the Germans the right to draw arguments in their own defense from the crime which they ascribed to others. As the Polish communiqué put it: "The profoundly hypocritical indignation of the German propaganda will not succeed in concealing from the world the many and continuously repeated crimes committed [by the Germans] on the Polish people." The communiqué ended with the words: "The Polish government denies the right to exploit all the crimes committed against the Polish citizens for political maneuvers by whomsoever is guilty of these crimes." Despite these qualifications, Moscow used the Polish application to the International Red Cross to look into the Katyń affair as a pretext for breaking of diplomatic relations with the government in London.[14]

For a considerable period of time the Polish government in London was leaning over backwards to avoid an irreparable breach with the

Kremlin. Moscow, however, was adamant and determined to pursue its own policy in Poland. The breaking of diplomatic relations between the Polish government in London and the Kremlin created a most difficult situation for the Polish underground movement. The Poles made a great effort to smooth out the relations with its powerful eastern neighbor by means of military cooperation on the spot. When the first Soviet detachments crossed the old Riga treaty frontier between Poland and the USSR, on January 4, 1944, the Polish government made a new proposal for the restoration of diplomatic relations with the Russians. Moreover, the Home Army was instructed by London to take an active part in the fight against retreating German troops, to destroy communications, and to seize strategic points. Local Polish commanders were to establish contact with Soviet commanders and place themselves under Soviet orders, stating that they were doing so on instructions from the Polish government; a similar message was issued to its civil servants operating in Poland. And, indeed, numerous units of the Home Army fought behind German lines and achieved notable success in helping the Red Army to capture Wilno, Lublin, Lwów, and a score of other small localities. But once their role as the scouts of the Red Army's advance was over, detachments of the Home Army were surrounded by the Russians, disarmed, and the officers arrested along with some of their men. Those not arrested were usually forcibly enrolled into the Polish army formed in Russia under Soviet sponsorship.

This pattern was invariable throughout Polish territory. Naturally enough, in many instances this procedure aroused opposition. Soldiers who had struggled for five or even six years against the Germans refused to be disarmed by the "allies of our allies." This spontaneous resistance was to be used later by Soviet prosecutors as a major argument during the trial of sixteen Polish underground leaders in Moscow, in June 1945; it was also to be used in numerous political trials held in Poland during the postwar years.

As Soviet forces approached what Moscow regarded as "indisputable" Polish territory, a new administration for Poland was being prepared. In March 1944 a delegation from the newly created, Com-

126

munist-sponsored National Council of Poland went to Russia, where Stalin received them in Moscow on May 22. He approved and even encouraged the policy of wooing other parties left of center. Once more the council appealed to its countrymen to intensify their resistance to the Germans and to help the Red Army. It called on the Polish forces that had been formed in Russia since October 1942 to fight shoulder-to-shoulder with their Soviet comrades.

On June 23, 1944, another step toward the assumption of political power in Poland was initiated. On that day the Union of Polish Patriots formally repudiated the Polish government in London, stating that "the Union of Polish Patriots recognizes the National Council of Poland as the representative of the nation." The council based its claim to legitimate authority on the existence of a net of local national councils, nurtured during the German occupation and now supposedly represented by the National Council of Poland.

On July 20, 1944, Bolesław Bierut, the chairman of the National Council of Poland and an old Communist stalwart, left Warsaw and with the aid of the Red Army was transported to Lublin, which had just been occupied by Soviet forces. In a similar way, the major part of the Polish Workers' party's central committee was secretly moved from the German to the Russian side of the front in order to meet the Red Army as it advanced toward the Vistula. On July 21, 1944, members of the party, together with those leaders of the Union of Polish Patriots who arrived in the wake of the Red Army (among them Wanda Wasilewska, Edward Osóbka-Morawski, Jakób Berman, and Stanisław Radkiewicz), established in Lublin the Polish Committee of National Liberation, which has come to be called the Lublin Committee. Osóbka-Morawski, a left Socialist, assumed the chairmanship of the committee, while Wasilewska and Andrzej Witos (nephew of the great peasant leader) became vice-chairman.

Seven of the fifteen members of the Lublin Committee were avowed Communists, while others were members of various leftist groups dependent upon Communist favor. The committee was to act as a "provisional executive authority to lead the nation's struggle for liberation, to secure its independence and the reestablishment of the

127

Polish state." It declared itself to be the sole Polish representative entitled to lead and coordinate all activities directed toward Poland's liberation; it also assumed supreme authority over the Union of Polish Patriots, as well as the contingent of the Polish army formed in the USSR. These troops, eventually amounting to some six divisions altogether, were about to take part in the battles of Dęblin and Puławy on the Vistula, shoulder-to-shoulder with the Soviet Forces marching toward Warsaw.[15]

The Committee of National Liberation issued its manifesto on July 22, 1944. The manifesto was a sketchily outlined program containing outwardly democratic reforms as well as an appeal to the Polish nation to rise against the Germans, to submit to the committee's power as "the sole legal source of authority in Poland," and to collaborate closely with the Red Army as it liberated the country. The committee promised "broad agrarian reforms" without compensation to former owners but failed to mention any nationalization of key industries, commerce, or banking. Private initiative was, on the contrary, to be encouraged. The manifesto stated that Poland's eastern frontiers "should be settled by mutual agreement" with its neighbors—the Ukraine, Byelorussia, and Lithuania. As for the western boundaries, the committee reemphasized that it stood firmly for the return to Poland of East Prussia, of the "ancient Polish territory of Pomerania and Silesia," as well as for "a broad access to the sea, and for Polish boundary marks on the Oder." The declaration reassured the people that the "broad principles" of the democratic constitution of 1921 were still valid. The manifesto stressed, however, that "enemies of democracy cannot be allowed to enjoy democratic freedoms." The words "Socialism" and "Communism" were not mentioned in the pronouncement.

On July 26, 1944, the Lublin Committee signed an agreement with the Soviet government which defined the relationship between the commander-in-chief of the Soviet armies and the new skeleton administration organized by the committee. The agreement left wide power in Soviet hands as long as Polish territories remained zones of military operations, and full cooperation was pledged between the

128

new regime and Russian authorities. The recently established administration was, on the one hand, based on the network of local national councils which had allegedly formed spontaneously within Poland's resistance elements; on the other hand, the new government initially shaped its administration on traditional prewar patterns but tended to put its own trusted men in key positions.

Thus, taking advantage of the military successes of the Red Army and enjoying the full diplomatic support of the Kremlin, the Communists of Poland were preparing, step by step, a complete takeover of political power throughout the country. The non-Communist underground movement, on the other hand, was at a disadvantage. It relied on a distant Polish government in London, which itself was rent by internal controversies and inadequately supported by allies anxious not to endanger the Grand Alliance.

Another crucial turning point in the struggle between the non-Communist forces supporting the Polish government in London and the pro-Soviet elements backing the Committee of National Liberation took place in August and September 1944. At the moment of publication of the July manifesto, the pro-Communist forces in Poland were still small in numbers and weak. The uprising which broke out in Warsaw on August 1 and lasted for sixty-three days was to alter this balance considerably. It is, therefore, necessary to discuss the uprising in some detail because of the effects its outcome has had on Poland even up to the present time.[16]

First of all, one should stress that, from the outset of the Russo-German war, both Soviet and PPR propaganda endeavored to incite the Poles into a military uprising. There was hardly a Communist newspaper, pamphlet, or periodical that did not contain some exhortation of this sort. These efforts grew to great intensity during and after the battle of Stalingrad; the appeals did not cease when Red troops started driving Hitler's troops beyond the frontiers of the USSR. The manifesto of July 22 also included an exhortation to intensify the armed struggle. The leaders of the Polish resistance move-

129

ment, on the other hand, advocated caution. They wanted not only to save the Home Army for the moment of the German withdrawal from Poland, to mop up the remnants of the German forces; they wished also to display the strength of the underground movement as representing the main trend of the country's public opinion. Hence the leaders of the Home Army rejected Communist appeals and opposed the idea of a premature revolt for both military and political reasons. Their goal was to preserve the vital energy of Poland for the decisive moment when it could be used to the utmost advantage. A carefully calculated plan to this effect, called "Tempest," had been prepared by the Home Army as early as 1943. The plan provided for an increase in sabotage and diversionary activity and for a series of insurrections timed to assist Soviet troops as the front moved westward. The scheme was put into operation from the moment Soviet troops entered Poland's prewar territory in January 1944.

Originally, according to General Bór-Komorowski, commander of the Home Army, the "Tempest" operation was designed to avoid fighting in major towns in order to spare the defenseless population and safeguard historical buildings. With this object in mind, the Home Army did not, at first, plan any action inside Warsaw; Home Army units from Warsaw were to be concentrated outside the city where they could attack the rear guard of German forces withdrawing from the capital. However, in mid-July, the Home Army command decided upon a modification of its plan with regard to Warsaw, and prepared to capture the capital just before the Russians entered. Such a step would demonstrate beyond any doubt the strength of the Polish resistance movement faithful to the government in London, and the will of the Polish people to remain independent.

As the front approached Warsaw, the command of the Home Army grew increasingly confident that the time was at hand for the "Tempest" plan to be put into operation. At the end of July 1944 the Red Army's offensive advanced rapidly and appeared irresistible. The Germans were showing signs of exhaustion and demoralization as their disordered retreat continued. To the leaders of the Home Army it seemed that the Wehrmacht would be unable to offer resistance

130

along the Vistula line. On July 28, 1944, an official communique from Moscow announced that Marshal Konstantine Rokossovsky's troops were advancing on Warsaw from the south and east on a front nearly fifty miles wide, and were at points within forty miles of the capital. The following day, July 29, Stanisław Mikołajczyk, prime minister of the Polish government in London, flew to Moscow to see Stalin in order to attempt a restoration of Polish-Soviet relations. On the same day the Soviet radio announced: "In Central Poland, Marshal Rokossovsky's tanks, motorized infantry, and Cossack cavalry, powerfully supported by the Red Air Force, pressed on towards Warsaw. . . ."

On July 30, the Home Army's monitoring service picked up a call from Moscow, addressed in Polish to the people of Warsaw and worded in a very explicit and emphatic way. This broadcast had first been transmitted on July 29 and was later repeated by the wireless station of the Union of Polish Patriots: "Poles! The time of liberation is at hand! Poles to arms! . . . Every Polish homestead must become a stronghold in the struggle against the invader. . . . There is not a moment to lose." The appeal apparently indicated that the Soviet command was about to launch an assault on Warsaw. As a result the leaders of the Home Army judged the situation ripe for the uprising to begin.

Inasmuch as a big Soviet attack toward Warsaw was expected at any moment by the leaders of the Home Army, the Polish government in London gave the commander discretionary powers to fix the precise moment for the beginning of the uprising. On August 1, 1944, the insurrection was ordered by General Bór-Komorowski. From that day on, Soviet broadcasts changed suddenly. For several days no mention of the struggle was made; instead, the Polish radio station operating on Soviet territory resumed its attacks on non-Communist political groups. In Warsaw, on the other hand, some of the Communists and their sympathizers behaved differently. They had been left without precise instructions from their leaders, who had hastily departed from the capital ten days previously and gone eastward to issue their July manifesto. On the fourth day of the fighting, the PPR posted a declaration calling on all its members to join in the struggle and to accept tactical orders from Home Army sector commanders; a few hundred Communists responded to the call. At the time the Home Army numbered some 46,000 men.

Meanwhile, Soviet-controlled broadcasts continued to be silent on the subject of the uprising. Moreover, the Soviet troops who, according to Moscow's own communiqué, had been about to capture Poland's capital, definitely halted their advance at the same time a parallel offensive on the Balkan sector of the front was stepped up. General Bór-Komorowski addressed numerous dispatches to Marshal Rokossovsky, asking for help and coordination of military operations. All were ignored.

On August 13, 1944, Moscow broke its two weeks' silence. While acknowledging the uprising, the official Soviet press agency, Tass, accused the Polish leaders of having failed to coordinate their move with the Soviet high command. Despite this the leadership of the uprising continued their efforts to establish contact with the Red Army, urging its command to send help in any form possible.

On September 13 the insurgents finally managed to establish liaison with the Polish divisions of General Zygmunt Berling, which then formed a segment of Marshal Rokossovsky's advancing front on the eastern bank of the Vistula. In reply to an appeal for help, Berling dispatched an infantry battalion across the river. But the lonely Polish unit was not sufficiently supported and had to be withdrawn. On September 14, when it had become obvious that Warsaw must surrender any day for lack of food and ammunition, a new, dramatic Soviet appeal to continue fighting and a promise of help was broadcast by the Lublin radio station. Moreover, during the latter half of September, some belated but scanty supplies of arms and food were dropped on Warsaw by Soviet planes. (Stalin had vetoed the idea of other Allied planes using the Soviet bases at Poltava in the Ukraine to help the Warsaw insurgents.)

On October 3, 1944, the exhausted remnants of the insurgents capitulated after sixty-three days of fighting. Hitler's revenge continued, however. Even though the German army was badly in need of soldiers for the eastern front, a considerable force was assigned on Hitler's personal orders to dynamite whatever monuments of culture were still left standing in Warsaw; this included the Royal Castle, a symbol of Polish sovereignty.

Stalin's attitude toward the uprising was also clear. For six weeks, the Soviet army was ordered to stand on the eastern bank of the Vistula, while the uprising provided them with a convenient bridge-head and a diversion on the river's western bank. Yet, the Russians cynically refused to use this chance and stood by while the Poles were slaughtered.

When, soon after the end of the war, General Eisenhower made a short visit to Poland, Arthur Bliss-Lane, the United States ambassador in Warsaw who accompanied him on his sightseeing tour, noted in his memoirs:

> I showed General Eisenhower through an arch which was still standing, a magnificent view of the Vistula River below and Praga beyond, with the dome of the Russian Orthodox Church glittering in the sunlight. I explained to him that during the insurrection of 1944 this part of town had been initially held by the Polish Home Army, which was daily expecting the Soviets to join forces with them from the other side. Emphasizing that he was speaking purely as a soldier, the general observed, "What a perfect bridgehead!" [17]

The reasons for the Polish Home Army leaders ordering the insurrection were numerous and complex; some of them were bluntly explained by the man mainly responsible for the decision, General Bór-Komorowski, in his book *The Secret Army:*

> Inaction on the part of the Home Army at the moment of the Soviet entry is likely to mean general passivity on the home front. The initiative for fighting the Germans is liable then to be taken by the PPR and a considerable fraction of the less-informed citizens might join them. In that case the country is liable to move in the direction of collaboration with the Soviets and no one will be able to stop it. Also, in that case the Soviet army would not be received by the Home Army, loyal to the government and the commander in chief, but by their own adherents—with open arms. . . . Finally, the participation of the

133

Home Army in the battle for Warsaw would definitely silence the lies of Soviet propaganda about the passivity of our country and our sympathies towards the Germans, and the liberation of the capital by our own soldiers should testify with unquestionable strength to the nation's will to safeguard the sovereignty of the Polish state! [18]

The failure of the uprising in Warsaw had disastrous results for the country: the struggle cost Poland about 200,000 victims from among the most patriotic, politically active element, and destroyed not only some 70 percent of the city but also the brain center of the most widespread and determined of Europe's resistance movements. As a result of this, the hitherto weak pro-Communist forces were given a chance to reassert themselves and fill the vaccuum. This fact was underscored by a Communist member of the new Polish government, who in 1946 said to a prominent American visitor in Warsaw:

Had General Bór-Komorowski and his underground army succeeded in liberating Warsaw, they would have been the heroes of Poland and would have formed the nucleus of the government within Poland. It would have been most difficult under such circumstances for the Soviet government to maintain in power the Lublin Committee of National Liberation. [19]

The Soviet stand during the Warsaw struggle was motivated largely by political and not military considerations. It was, simply, an effort to destroy the most active elements among the non-Communist resistance. As a consequence of the uprising the prestige and influence of the Polish government in London were undermined and new vistas were opened to the Lublin Committee. Thus, the catastrophe of the London camp considerably facilitated the subsequent Communist assumption of power. George F. Kennan has described Stalin's behavior at the gates of Warsaw as "the most arrogant and unmistakable demonstration of the Soviet determination to control Eastern Europe in the postwar period." [20]

The tragedy of the Warsaw uprising has been, from the very beginning, a subject of bitter controversy, with Communist historians taking a radically different stand than those representing a non-

Communist point of view. Only recently a work on the subject, written by one of the Home Army participants now living in exile in London, took a middle position. The author, while reemphasizing the heroism of the insurgents, also stressed that the insurrection was undertaken on the basis of false political as well as military premises. Hitherto, this approach has been the essence of Communist historiography. For the first time a Western-oriented Polish historian has revised the standard treatment of his colleagues and said bluntly:

> Irrespectively of Stalin's attitude toward the Warsaw insurrection . . . the tragedy of the capital was largely caused by political and military indolence and groundless optimism of the leadership of the London camp. . . . The fact that until the moment of the outbreak [of the uprising] an understanding with the Kremlin had not been achieved, despite strong pressure of Churchill, this condemned the insurrection to catastrophe. . . . Agreement with Russia, even on very difficult and unsatisfactory conditions for Poland, was, after the battles of Stalingrad and Kursk and the Teheran conference, the only solution of a most complex situation. Only by this means one could spare Poland excessive losses and so diminish the consequences of the march of the Red Army through Polish territory.[21]

With the wisdom of hindsight one may argue that the attitude of the government in London toward Soviet Russia reflected a lack of a proper perception of the realities of the international situation. From a historic perspective it seems to be beyond doubt that the London government, as a whole, failed to realize that its cause had been doomed the moment Soviet Russia entered the war on the side of the Allies. Yet both Sikorski and Mikołajczyk were not entirely unaware of these realities and were desperately groping for an acceptable compromise. On the other hand, one has to realize that both suffered from grave limitations. It is true that they did harbor some illusions about the good faith and determination of their Western allies to act on Poland's behalf, even to the extent of risking a worsening of relations with the USSR. But these illusions had to be viewed in a larger

135

context. The idea that Poland—which was the first to fight Hitler, which had produced the largest and most formidable resistance movement in Europe, the country which was making heavy sacrifices in the Allied cause on all fronts of the struggle, and which had never produced a Quisling—that this country should be compelled to make one-sided, unprecedented concessions to a betrayed accomplice of Hitler, appeared at that time to the Polish leaders to be dishonorable and unacceptable.

The pressure of Polish public opinion on Sikorski and Mikołajczyk was also a factor to be reckoned with. For an average Pole it was not an easy matter to reconcile himself to the loss of the Eastern Marshes, or the historic Lithuanian, Byelorussian, and Ukrainian lands. Even the prospect of gaining the much richer Oder-Neisse lands could hardly compensate for the loss of the Marshes. One should also remember that a large part of the Polish armed forces in the west was composed of the deportees from the Eastern Marshes to the USSR. The emotional attachment of most Poles to these lands was such that their abandonment by a bona fide Polish statesman would have been an act of political suicide. The signing of the treaty of July 30, 1941, for example, had resulted in serious ferment in the Polish forces, conspiracies among officers, and the danger of an attempt on Sikorski's life.

Accusations that the Poles were too stubborn and intransigent, and that they never even attempted a compromise solution, do not tally with the existing evidence. As has been already mentioned, General Sikorski made a serious attempt at reaching a compromise agreement with Moscow, an agreement that would have both preserved a minimum of Polish interests in the east and saved the face of the Polish government in London. The same was true of General Sikorski's successor as prime minister, Stanisław Mikołajczyk. In May and June of 1944, Mikołajczyk undertook a series of secret talks with Victor Lebediev, the Soviet ambassador in London. The main purpose of these discussions was to assure the Russians of military cooperation on the part of the Home Army, and as a reward, to wrest for Poland, if possible, better terms than those agreed upon by the Big Three at the

Teheran Conference. The negotiations were initially conducted in a friendly way and seemed to augur well. Lebediev made the Polish representative, Professor Stanisław Grabski, then chairman of the Polish National Council and one of the leaders of the National party, understand that the Union of Polish Patriots was expendable. He assured Grabski that Moscow would not interfere in Poland's domestic affairs, and while welcoming a reconstruction of the Polish government in London, Stalin would like to avoid any appearance of an external pressure that would offend Polish sensibilities. Although the Soviet diplomat insisted on territorial concessions ("the Soviet Union needs not only people, she needs land," as he put it), he seemed to understand Mikołajczyk's and Grabski's point of view that Poland should not emerge from the war either smaller or weaker than prior to September 1, 1939.

This not entirely unsympathetic attitude underwent a dramatic change during the meeting that took place between Lebediev and Mikołajczyk on June 23, 1944, after the latter's return from Washington. During that meeting the Soviet diplomat put forward in rude form an ultimatum that amounted to an unconditional surrender to all Soviet demands: immediate cession of nearly half of Poland's prewar territory, the reshaping of the Polish government in London in accordance with Moscow's wishes, as well as the withdrawal and condemnation of General Sikorski's request that the Katyń massacre be investigated by the International Red Cross. During the previous conversations both Mikołajczyk and Grabski had hinted that the Polish side would be willing not to press its charges in the matter and keep the tragic affair under wraps for the sake of better relations, but they could not possibly go so far as to disavow the late General Sikorski and expose themselves to humiliation and ridicule.[22] Thus the negotiations were broken off and never resumed. Since the Soviet archives are closed, one may only wonder whether the mission of Lebediev was merely a tactical trick or whether it represented a serious attempt to reach a genuine compromise with the non-Communist forces of Poland.

Meanwhile, Mikołajczyk had made his visit to Washington and

137

there pleaded with President Roosevelt to intercede in Moscow on Poland's behalf and persuade Stalin to moderate his territorial demands. What Mikołajczyk hoped to obtain was the city of Lwów and the oil fields of Drohobycz, the only source of this precious raw material in prewar Poland. It is questionable whether the Russians would have treated the Polish government in London better had it avoided seeking the mediation of the United States and relied only on Stalin's mercy. This interpretation, of course, cannot be entirely excluded, but it is purely speculative.

Most Western historians argue that the Polish illusions concerning the West played a negative role in Soviet-Polish relations, and they are certainly correct. Nevertheless, they are unable to demonstrate that anything short of an abject surrender to the Soviet demands would have saved the London government, and the cause it represented, from defeat. Stalin certainly wished for cooperation from the Poles, but only a handful of them, mostly those trained in the school of Communist discipline, could accept his terms, which amounted to complete domination.

While dust was settling on the battered ruins of Warsaw, Mikołajczyk, one of the few non-Communists in London basically willing to accept the Soviets' terms, again went to Moscow (October 1944) to see Stalin. This time the Soviet dictator attempted to represent the problem of Poland as purely an internal quarrel between rival Polish factions, and shifted the burden of negotiations to members of the Polish Committee of National Liberation who, in turn, repeated word for word the Soviet demands. Upon Mikołajczyk's return to London, his colleagues rejected his suggestion that already accomplished facts be accepted, namely Russia's annexation of Poland's eastern provinces, a general westward shifting of Poland's boundaries, and the sharing of governmental administration with the Communists. Mikołajczyk resigned as prime minister of the government-in-exile at the end of November 1944. Soon he, and a group of his followers, accepted the inevitable and returned to Poland to seek accommodation with the new masters.

Meanwhile, Stalin stressed again his determination to make the

Lublin Committee the nucleus of Poland's future government. And indeed, on December 31, 1944, anticipating the capture of Warsaw by Soviet troops, the Lublin Committee declared itself to be the provisional government of Poland. The government was composed of eight PPR leaders, three Socialists, three Peasant party members, and three politicians of the Democratic party. Only five members of the old Committee of National Liberation entered the new provisional government. On January 5, 1945, Moscow extended prompt recognition to the new Polish administration.

Less than two weeks later, on January 17, Warsaw was captured by Soviet forces supported by units of the Polish army formed in Russia. The daring decision of the provisional government to retain Warsaw, then a heap of snow-covered ruins, as the capital of the country was of considerable psychological importance: it gave a badly needed moral boost to an otherwise unpopular regime. The provisional government stubbornly clung to this traditional seat of power. Fighting against heavy odds, it soon launched a campaign to reconstruct the devastated city and rehabilitate the war-ravaged country in general.

The establishment of the provisional government was soon followed by the formalization of political ties between Moscow and Warsaw. On April 22, 1945, the two countries signed a treaty of friendship, mutual assistance, and postwar cooperation, in essence a military and political alliance.[23]

The Yalta Conference was convened on February 4, 1945, in the former summer palace of the tsars in the Crimea. Here the leaders of the anti-German coalition, acting without Poland's participation, reached an agreement in principle regarding Poland's future. While the government-in-exile was completely disregarded, the Communist-dominated provisional government was to be "reorganized on a broader democratic basis" so as to include a more representative group from Poland itself and from among Poles abroad. It was to be recognized as the de facto government of Poland and was to be

139

elected on the basis of "universal suffrage and secret ballot." In these elections all "democratic and anti-Nazi parties" were to participate freely.

The Yalta Conference proved to be a great success for Moscow because it confirmed the provisional government's sovereignty and consequently strengthened both its internal and external position. The allegations often heard to the effect that it was at Yalta that Poland and Eastern Europe were "sold down the river" are not entirely correct. The Yalta Conference merely ratified those secret decisions taken earlier as a result of the Western powers perception of the outcome of the war, and their marginal interest in the affairs of "those far away countries about which we know nothing," as Neville Chamberlain said at the time of Munich. The West had essentially conceded Eastern Europe, and Poland in particular, to the Soviet sphere of influence already at the Teheran Conference in 1943 and at the Moscow Conference of Churchill and Stalin in October of 1944—both long before the meeting at Yalta.[24]

The vague terms in which the Yalta agreement was couched were bound to spell trouble. Nowhere was it specified what criteria would be used for determining which leaders and parties were "democratic" and "anti-Nazi" and which were not. The Western leaders, on the one hand, interpreted the word "democratic" in the broader sense to mean all those parties not explicitly allied with, or sympathetic to, Nazism or Fascism. The Soviets, on the other hand, were given wide latitude for excluding as "Fascist" those forces they considered to be essentially hostile to the policy of cooperation with the Soviet Union. Another bone of contention was the matter of the inclusion of the London Poles in the government, which was in no way resolved in the final communiqué—unless, of course, one considers the extremely vague and meaningless clause calling for the inclusion of "Poles living abroad" as a solution.

It is not surprising, therefore, that the first clash between the Soviet government and the Western powers was over this very issue. In accordance with their reading of the Yalta agreements, the Americans and the British expected that a completely new government would be erected in Warsaw, with the existing pro-Soviet regime serving merely in an interim capacity; the Soviets, however, interpreted the agreements to imply a retention of the already established regime, with only a few new personalities to be added.

These two conflicting interpretations could not coexist for long. And indeed, the ink was hardly dry on the Yalta communiqué when the first conflict arose over the differing definitions of democratic and anti-Nazi. The Russians insisted upon their right to veto politicians recommended for inclusion in the new provisional government whom they considered objectionable. This immediately touched off an acrimonious exchange between Churchill and Roosevelt on the one hand, and Stalin on the other, the former demanding the right to dispatch observers for the purpose of supervising the Warsaw government's implementation of the agreements. Stalin replied that this was unacceptable, since such a dispatch of observers would be regarded by the Poles as "an affront to their national dignity." [25] These diplomatic skirmishes concerning the nature and the composition of the Polish government, as well as the problem of the free elections, greatly contributed to the spread of the mounting of international tension and eventually led to the phenomenon known as the cold war.

The situation of the pro-Soviet government in Poland was at first far more tenuous than Stalin had expected. Yet he was anything but anxious to advertise this fact to the world. In an attempt to break the back of this growing anti-Communist resistance, and at the very same time that the dispute over the representation of the London Poles in the new government was still brewing, the Soviets decided on a move which, from the point of view of the Western leaders, could only cast their motives and intentions in the darkest possible light. On March 27, 1945, sixteen key figures of the Polish underground movement were invited by the Soviet high command to participate in friendly talks aimed at devising measures to prevent conflicts between their own forces and the Soviet Army. The next day they disappeared. In May, the Soviet government announced that they were being held on charges of sabotaging Soviet military operations. [26] The imprisonment of the sixteen leaders eliminated the most promising non-Communist

141

leaders from the political scene during the crucial period of negotiations on the creation of a government of national unity.

At the same time the trial of the sixteen resistance leaders was being held in Moscow (June 18–21, 1945), a conference was held in the Soviet capital presided over by Molotov and by the U.S. and British ambassadors to the Soviet Union. Representatives of the Lublin Committee, and a few other political figures selected at random, were brought from Poland. This gathering was joined by Mikołajczyk in his capacity as leader of the Peasant party, who arrived from London with two former members of his cabinet. As a result of this conference a new provisional government of national unity was established on June 28, 1945.

The government was nominally a coalition of five parties: the Polish Workers' party, the Polish Socialist party, the Peasant party, the Democratic party, and the Labor party. Of the twenty-one government posts, seven were given to Peasant party members. Mikołajczyk himself held two posts: deputy prime minister and minister of agriculture; one of his followers, Władysław Kiernik, was given the ministry of public administration, from which, however, control of the police was withdrawn in favor of an experienced NKVD-trained man, Stanisław Radkiewicz. Sixteen posts were given to representatives of the old provisional government, while only five ministries were relinquished to Poles living abroad. In accordance with Soviet wishes, the government thus formed was promptly recognized by Great Britain and the United States on July 6, 1945.

When the Big Three met at Potsdam in July 1945, the results of this conference, at least in regard to the Polish question, were largely a foregone conclusion. At stake was merely the scope of the compensations to be granted to the Poles in the west.

≈ ≈

Nations, like individuals, can best be understood in times of crisis, for it is then that they show their true mettle. The disasters that befell Poland during World War II have few parallels in modern history. The cost of the war was staggering. For nearly six years the country

142

was ravaged and devastated, the population decimated, and the Polish nation threatened with total obliteration. Each day of the German occupation cost the country an average of nearly 3,000 dead. Besides enormous material losses, more than 6 million Polish citizens, half of them of Jewish extraction, perished during the German invasion and occupation. Of these, 5.3 million died as a result of various forms of terror and 600,000 through direct hostilities. For every 1,000 citizens of prewar Poland, 220 perished during the period from September 1, 1939 to May 8, 1945; in Yugoslavia the figures were 108 per 1,000 and in the USSR 40 per 1,000.[27] This systematic genocide was stopped only as the result of the military destruction of Nazi Germany.

While resisting the invaders at home with grim determination, the Poles continued to fight abroad on the land, on the seas, and in the air on many fronts of the global contest. In the Battle of Britain, two Polish fighter squadrons played a crucial role, shooting down more than their share of German planes. While the British pilots downed three German planes for every pilot lost, the Polish airmen had a ratio of nine German aircraft to one Polish pilot. Of the 154 Polish pilots who took part in the Battle of Britain, 30 were killed. One of the Polish squadrons, bearing the number 303, was the top scoring squadron of the Royal Air Force, with 126 German planes to its credit. The small but intrepid Polish navy earned, per capita, more British and other Allied awards than any other Western navy. During the Allied invasion of Europe in 1944, two Polish army corps were fighting in the west, scoring impressive victories at Falaise and Monte Casino. The Polish army founded in Russia also gave a good account of itself and eventually participated actively in the capture of Berlin. At the end of the war the Polish government in London alone had at its command some 200,000 men. If one adds to this the nearly equally numerous Polish forces coming from the USSR and the Polish underground movement of some 300,000 people, the Polish component of the Allied forces ranks in fourth place, behind the USSR, the United States, and Great Britain, but well ahead of France and other Allied nations with far greater resources.

Time of Trial

One of the most important contributions the Poles made to the Allies' victory over the Axis powers, especially Germany, was in the field of intelligence. After the fall of France at the end of June 1940, the Poles who had not been evacuated to Great Britain immediately organized an intelligence net, known as F2. The net, led by a young officer in the reserve, Leon Sliwiński, rendered invaluable services not only to the French, but to the Allied cause as a whole. Here one should mention also the supplying by the Polish underground movement of the original plans for the German V-rockets, as well as their captured parts. But by far the most significant Polish contribution in the field of intelligence was the reconstruction of the German coding device called "Enigma." This was done before the war by three Polish mathematicians: Marian Rejewski, Jerzy Różycki, and Henryk Żygalski. By July 1939 the French and the British were presented by Warsaw with one duplicate of this coding device with detailed instructions how to operate it. During the war the same team of engineers built many copies of "Enigma" for the Western Allies. The breaking of the German code allowed the Allies to get a fairly accurate running account of Hitler's conduct of the war. Such vital facts as, for instance, the direction of Rommel's attack at El-Alamein, Kesselring's instructions during the Sicilian landing, and Hitler's orders to von Kluge for the Avranche counterattack that was supposed to drive the Allies into the sea, were known in advance to the Allied command, thanks to their mastery of the "Enigma" secrets.[28]

Despite these numerous noteworthy contributions, despite the terrible sacrifices and unparalleled losses, the end of the war brought about an outcome which was rather different from that which most Polish people had expected and fought for. Nevertheless, their exhaustion and disappointments notwithstanding, they set out for the second time in a half century to rebuild their lives and their war-ravaged country, but this time within new frontiers and under a new regime.

144

CHAPTER SIX

Polish People's Republic 1945–1956 [1]

What we have to deal with here is a communist society, not as it has developed on its own foundation but, on the contrary, as it emerges from capitalist society; which is thus in every respect, economically, morally and intellectually still stamped with the birth marks of the old society from whose womb it emerges.

Karl Marx

THE POLAND that emerged from the war was a different country from the pre-1939 state. In accordance with the decisions of the Big Three taken during the Teheran, Yalta, and Potsdam conferences, Poland had been physically transplanted westward. The Eastern Marshes, including the towns of Wilno and Lwów, were lost to the USSR, but Poland gained the former German territories of Silesia, Pomerania, and the southwestern segment of East Prussia. [2]

As a result, Poland acquired important German industrial areas, all in exchange for the poor agricultural land lost to the USSR. Moreover, the allotment to Poland of East Prussia and the regions east of the Oder-Neisse rivers, especially the area between Gdańsk (Danzig) and Szczecin (the former Stettin), made the country less landlocked and more maritime. The western territories were more generously endowed with natural resources and industries than the old regions of prewar Poland. In the agricultural field, the acquisition of the Oder-

145

a. Poland after World War I   b. Poland after World War II

Neisse lands provided the Poles with the opportunity to shift the population and thus to create a prosperous class of small farmers similar to that which had existed in the western provinces of Posnania and Pomerania. With the acquisition of a new and expanded industrial capacity along with added agricultural lands, Poland was given the opportunity to absorb the surplus rural population, estimated as high as 8 million, which had so burdened the country's economic progress in the years before the war. Thus, despite the wartime devastations, Poland emerged with an improved base of natural resources, a better balance between agriculture and industry, and a healthier agrarian structure.

The transfer of territory was also accompanied by large-scale population shifts. In addition to the movement of some 3 million Poles from the Eastern Marshes to the newly acquired western lands, between 1946 and 1949 about 2.5 million Germans, Ukrainians, Russians, and Byelorussians left Poland. The total population of Poland fell from 34,849,000 in 1939 to 25,505,000 in 1951, while the ethnic-religious composition by the latter date was more than 98 percent Polish and about 94 percent Catholic. As a result of the wartime as well as postwar changes, Poland became ethnically and religiously homogeneous as never before in its history.

While analyzing the post-World War II period, one must bear in mind that Poland suffered more severely from the war than any other Allied country. Apart from the destruction of life, the country's material losses per capita were higher than those of any other country occupied by Germany; altogether 38 percent of the old country's wealth had been destroyed. A similar, if not worse, situation existed in the former German lands east of the Oder-Neisse. The great majority of people in these territories had either fled or been transferred to Germany. It was estimated that over 90 percent of the area's livestock, 60 percent of its industrial capacity, and 45 percent of its urban dwellings had been destroyed. The territories, therefore, had to be resettled before being rebuilt.[3]

The main aims of the party were negative: to abolish the privileges formerly enjoyed by the upper classes and to establish the rule of the

147

proletariat and of its ally, the poor peasantry. This part of the program took the form of undermining the former class structure based on the ownership of the means of production. The second stage involved the planned transformation of the economic structure by industrialization and eventual collectivization of agriculture. Some political consequences of the war were advantageous to the Communists and favored their program. The traditional social structure of the country was shattered; many non-Communist political leaders had either been killed or had fled the country, the old intelligentsia was decimated, and the prestige of the London government was weakened as a result of the disastrous Warsaw uprising. The acquisition of the Oder-Neisse lands, largely deserted, opened a vast prospect for patronage. And indeed, the new rulers of the country took advantage of the western territories to consolidate their power by distributing land, jobs, and other favors to their followers. One of the early acts of the new regime was the establishment of a separate ministry of regained territories, with the party's secretary-general, Wladyslaw Gomułka, at its head. The new lands now became a special domain of the PPR, a state within the state and an experimental ground for ''socialist construction'' and for the first agrarian ''producers' cooperatives.'' Integration and resettlement of these newly acquired territories became one of the most successful battle cries of the regime.

Despite these apparent advantages, the Polish Workers' party faced perhaps a more difficult task in establishing itself in power during 1944 and 1945 than did other Communist parties in east-central Europe. Of all the areas of the world, Poland was among those least prepared to embark upon a Communist experiment: it was overwhelmingly Roman Catholic, essentially agrarian, and had a relatively small working class. In addition, there was the historic anti-Russian sentiment, which had been greatly enhanced by the brutal Soviet actions in eastern Poland and which contributed vigorously to the general unpopularity of the Communists after the war. The collectivist doctrine of Communism was incompatible with the essentially individualistic, traditional mentality of the Polish people. Stalin himself as much as admitted this in a conversation with Mikołajczyk on

October 18, 1944. Asked whether he envisioned a Communist future for Poland after the war, he declared emphatically:

> No, absolutely not. Communism does not fit the Poles. They are too individualistic, too nationalistic. Poland's future economy should be based on private enterprise. Poland will be a capitalistic state.[4]

Moreover, out of the ordeal of the war, the Polish nation, although bled white, emerged more integrated than ever, both socially and politically. Class distinctions were largely obliterated and party differences blurred, thus blunting the slogan of class struggle. Religious sentiments were both broadened and deepened, and this tended also to increase resistance to the new and unpopular regime.

The extent of the hostility encountered by the new regime at every step may be gathered from the reminiscences of Bolesław Drobner, a leftist Socialist. Referring to his experience in the summer of 1944, he wrote:

> I found myself before the Polish teachers of Przemyśl. Their eyes burned with hate for us. We answered, "You can hate us. . . ." In August 1944, I found myself before the doctors of Lublin where we faced the same scene as at Przemyśl. Again we answered: "You can hate us. . . ."[5]

In view of this widespread hostility, combined with the initially small following of the Polish Workers' party (numbering in 1945 from 20,000 to 30,000 members), it was vital for the regime to rely on all sorts of allies, including fellow travelers and opportunists. The Germans had smashed the structure of the prewar Polish state; they had been especially ruthless with the educated classes, who, next to the Jews, were the main target of Frank's extermination policy. Consequently, lack of trained personnel was a major difficulty confronting the new administration. There were very few native-educated Communists, and some of those available were ill-equipped to assume high public office or skilled jobs in the administration. Therefore, in the initial stages of organization, positions were filled at

149

random by people who often lacked the full confidence of the authorities, but who were nonetheless deemed indispensable for the task. The new government had little choice in the matter, nor did the remnants of the prewar intellectual group who now served the regime. Each needed the other in order to survive. The half-starved urban population necessarily depended on those who controlled the distribution of the country's meager resources.

> Food, not money [noted an American observer] was the basis of life in Poland. Six free dining rooms for upper civil servants were the cornerstones of the state. . . . The wages and salaries paid in paper zlotys counted for little. Permits to eat three times a day in some dining rooms were more valuable than any amount of printed cash.[6]

Yet, material comforts were not the only means of attracting adherents. The people had just emerged from the nearest thing to hell and were grateful to all those who had prevented the catastrophe from being completed. The vivid memory of the ghastly Nazi atrocities automatically gave any anti-German regime a degree of popularity, even with people who did not approve of its tenets. There was also a widespread desire to play an active role in open political life, after five years of clandestine activity fraught with deadly perils. The patriotic slogans, widely used by the Communists, played a significant part in attracting people to the task of reconstruction and rehabilitation. But the integration of the newly acquired western territories was a powerful magnet attracting many non-Communists to the new regime.

In the absorption and consolidation of power the Polish Workers' party was helped by left-Socialist and peasant politicians, among whom were Józef Cyrankiewicz and Kazimierz Rusinek, two Socialist leaders of some prewar standing who had been imprisoned in German concentration camps.[7] Both men gave support to the previously rejected idea of the "united front," i.e., collaboration with the Communists. At first, the bulk of the old Polish Socialist party protested these tactics. Gradually, however, seeing no chance of rebuilding their old movement, many honest Socialists joined the new party despite the policy of collaboration.

Similar tactics were applied to the peasant movement. As far back as 1943 the Communists had set up a bogus Peasant party. With the return of Mikołajczyk to Poland, however, many lesser leaders of the peasant movement gradually rallied around him.[8] The overwhelming support given to Mikołajczyk by most non-Communist forces in Poland was a challenge to the Workers' party's claim of representing the broad cross-section of the Polish people. Although stressing Poland's ties with the West, Mikołajczyk emphasized that he intended to establish a government "friendly to the Soviet Union" and to have a firm Soviet-Polish alliance. He hoped thereby to convince Moscow that it would be better in the long run to have as an ally a more stable and broadly based government than one led by the Communists, who had narrow support and were thus constantly compelled to depend on Soviet bayonets.

While the Communists clearly lacked mass support in Poland in 1945, there was one man whose popularity in the country was indisputable. Did Stalin, an astute politician, realize this? At that time several courses of action were open to him: Poland could be communized or it could become a country allied to the Soviet Union, like Finland, but not completely subservient to the powerful neighbor. These ends could be accomplished either through the intermediary of the Workers' party or through non-Communist politicians like Mikołajczyk. Stalin's attitude was reflected in a conversation in 1944 with Dr. Oskar Lange, a Polish-American professor of left-wing leanings. The Soviet leader declared that "although some people considered Mikołajczyk a *kulak*, he [Stalin] considered Mikołajczyk a democrat," although "he could not say the same about all the Polish socialists in his cabinet. . . ."[9]

We obviously have no way of knowing exactly what considerations ultimately influenced Stalin's decision in 1945–46. We do know, however, that once the decision was taken, every effort was made to integrate Mikołajczyk and his Polish Peasant party into the govern-

151

ment and to domesticate him to the extent of making him a docile instrument of Moscow's policy in Poland, perhaps with the end in mind of grooming him for eventual control of the government. It seemed far more desirable from the standpoint of the Soviet leadership to have in Poland a non-Communist government sharing power with, but not dominated by, the Communists. Through this formula it was hoped that the government could attain broad popular support. Such a regime would have, of course, to join with the USSR in a mutual defense pact. This Mikołajczyk was willing to do, but he was unwilling to become a simple stooge of Moscow.

In the course of the summer of 1945, however, Mikolajczyk concluded that collaboration with the Communist elements in the Peasant party was impossible, and that he would have to withdraw and form a new party. Backed by the rank and file of the old party, Mikolajczyk, on September 22, 1945, established the new Polish Peasant party. With the tremendous popularity he enjoyed throughout the country, plus his rather exaggerated reliance on British and American support, Milołajczyk was convinced that he could afford to take this line of action. He obviously forgot that for the Soviet Union, tight control over Poland was a matter of vital strategic interest. For the Western powers, on the other hand, with their own mounting domestic problems and concerns in trouble spots like Greece, Turkey, and Palestine, Poland was a distant and annoying country about which they preferred not to bother.

In November 1945, on the eve of the first Polish Workers' party congress, Edward Ochab defined the three-fold task facing the party. First, it had to "crush the reaction," which in practice meant liquidation of the remnants of the anti-Communist resistance. Second, it had to "tighten the alliance with the peasants" while "protecting the unity of the working class," which amounted to extending Communist control over the entire working class movement while creating its own peasant party. Third, it had "to have a political platform that does not terrify the peasants." This meant that the slogan of collectivization had to be soft-pedaled to neutralize temporarily the peasant opposition. In order to control the working-class movement, the

Communists had to absorb the Polish Socialist party, which still controlled by far the largest segment of the urban proletariat and which dominated the trade unions and consumers' cooperatives. But, first of all, the Communists had to prevent Mikołajczyk from becoming the center of an opposition movement. And they had to bar any rapprochement between his new party and the PPS, which would have been dangerous for the new regime.

The test of Mikołajczyk's attitude came in the elections of 1945. The former U.S. secretary of state, James F. Byrnes, recalled in his book, *Speaking Frankly,* that during the Yalta Conference President Roosevelt had said to Stalin, "I want the elections in Poland to be beyond question, like Caesar's wife. I did not know Caesar's wife, but she was believed to have been pure." To this Stalin replied: "I was told so about Caesar's wife, but in fact she had certain sins." [10]

Whatever the sins Caesar's wife, it is perfectly clear that the elections held on January 17, 18, and 19, 1947, were anything but pure. Prior to the balloting the Communists had endeavored to get Mikołajczyk and his party to join the government-sponsored Democratic Bloc, a group composed of four parties, of which only one had any degree of real independence. It goes without saying that the Workers' party and its satellite, the new Polish Socialist party, would get the lion's share of the representation. Once having obtained an absolute majority (and how could it fail if there was no organized opposition?), the PPR would apportion the seats in the parliament on the basis of previously agreed-upon percentages. Mikołajczyk rejected the idea, and as a result, the election campaign was fierce and bloody, conducted more like a civil war.

The voting was preceded by mass arrests and raids on Mikołajczyk's headquarters throughout the country, and by the passage of a new election law that effectively disenfranchised at least a million people. In addition, the candidates of the Polish Peasant party were stricken from the ballot in ten out of fifty-two election districts in which resided approximately one-fourth of the nation's population. These measures and a host of other tricks already in effect were designed to cripple the opposition as much as possible. The elections

153

were held and, predictably enough, the Democratic Bloc received 80.1 percent of the vote compared to a mere 10.3 percent for Mikołajczyk's party.

Mikołajczyk immediately protested the outcome of the elections; the United States and British governments followed suit, declaring that they could not consider that the provisions of the Yalta and Potsdam agreements had been fulfilled. All this was to no avail. In October of 1947, fearful of rumors that a price had been placed on his head, Mikołajczyk fled to the West with the aid of the U.S. ambassador in Warsaw.

Thus, Mikołajczyk's mission was a fiasco. He had left London with the idea of participating in shaping a new reality in Poland in cooperation with the Soviet Union, but he was unable to execute his plan. He was carried away by the spontaneous, elemental current of anti-Communist public opinion and was deluded by hopes of Western support. He also failed to understand that, despite the icy winds of the cold war, the United States and Great Britain were much more interested in salvaging whatever they could of their wartime relationship with the USSR and were determined to adhere to the old line as charted at Teheran, Yalta, and Potsdam. A judicious British observer of the Polish scene remarked that Mikołajczyk was attempting an impossible task by challenging the Communists. It was a trial of strength that could not have been won. Had he triumphed in the elections, the Soviet forces would almost certainly have overrun the country, and Poland would have lost whatever meager autonomy it still retained.[11]

Like Edward Beneš and Jan Masaryk, Mikołajczyk harbored the illusion that the countries of east-central Europe could be a kind of bridge between the Soviet Union and the West; for Moscow, however, they were not bridges, but bridgeheads.

With the consolidation of political power the new regime proceeded to carry out a broad restructuring of the Polish economy, starting with land reform. To set the reform in perspective, one has to bear in mind that Poland before the World War II was a predominantly rural society. Agriculture was the most important branch of the national economy, contributing 45 percent of the net material product in 1937. In 1939 about 55 percent of those employed worked in agriculture, mostly on small farms; the urban population in 1931 amounted to only 27.4 percent of the total.

The objective of prewar reforms, voted by the Polish parliament in 1920 and 1925, had been to create "a healthy peasant class" of well-to-do farmers owning medium-size tracts of from twenty-five to fifty acres. The Communists regarded this as a reactionary attempt to strengthen the "kulak" strata in the villages.

Radical land reform without compensation to former owners, yet based on private ownership of land, was an essential item in the platforms of both the Union of Polish Patriots and the Polish Workers' party. Both groups bitterly criticized the prewar government's sluggish and conservative land reforms, which had included provisions for compensation. Although both the government-in-exile in London and the non-Communist underground resistance parties had criticized the slow tempo of reform and the high percentage of land which farmers had been permitted to retain, and while both had urged a wider and more even system of distribution, they still insisted on compensation to former owners.

The principle of a radical and broad land reform was proclaimed in the manifesto of July 22, 1944, and was implemented immediately. On September 6, 1944, the Lublin Committee issued a law expropriating all landed property exceeding 250 acres, if more than half the acreage was arable. Even before publication of the law, in fact as soon as a given region was occupied by the Red Army, teams were sent by the new regime into the villages. These messengers encouraged the peasants to seize and distribute large-size estates among themselves. Since the land was divided into very small parcels, this phase of distribution was largely an absurdity and merely a stepping stone toward a more far-reaching objective: collectivization.

Land reform turned out to be a mixed blessing. On one hand, the prewar agricultural structure of Poland was replaced by a new one which in some ways was similar to the old. Both before and after the war some 60 percent of Polish farms were smaller than twelve and one-half acres. On the other hand, the liquidation of prewar bank debts and mortgages, an increase in the amount of usable land per capita of the agricultural population, and the electrification of the countryside were all undoubtedly beneficial for the rural population. In addition, the first phase of a "cultural revolution," initiated by the new regime soon after land reform, also helped the rural areas by decreasing illiteracy and spreading technical skills throughout the countryside. Although the reforms failed to fulfill many peasant hopes, they satisfied the immediate needs of the party. The distribution of land appeased some basic peasant aspirations and thereby neutralized the countryside during a crucial period in the struggle for power.

The first months of the new regime saw a rapid process of reconstruction coupled with a hasty confiscation by the state of all large and medium-size industries, banking, and foreign trade. Foreign commerce was, from the beginning, a state monopoly, although until mid-1947 considerable latitude was given to domestic trade. All banks, with two exceptions, were taken over by the state.

Generally speaking, there was less opposition in Poland to the nationalization of industry and banking than in other country of east-central Europe. Even before the war a considerable number of the country's large industries and most of the banks were either state-owned or dependent on, if not owned by, foreign capital. As far back as 1943, all political parties (except for some of the most extreme conservative groups) had agreed that key branches of the national economy should be directed by the state. In 1937 just over 40 percent of the capital of joint stock companies was in foreign ownership. The state also played an important economic role: it had a monopoly in the production of alcohol, tobacco, and armaments, and owned the railroads and airlines, as well as nearly half of all bank and other credit institutions. Moreover, the state had a large financial stake in the chemical industry and in coal, iron, and steel production. It has been estimated that by 1932–33, state enterprises accounted for

156

nearly 17 percent of the general turnover of industry and commerce.[12]

As a consequence of the nationalization law of January 3, 1946, all industrial establishments "capable of employing more than fifty workers per shift" were confiscated. Article Three of the law stipulated that a decree of the council of ministers would be sufficient to nationalize any category of enterprise not specifically exempted. This soon became an instrument for the confiscation of all sorts of industrial organizations employing more than fifty workers per shift, as well as smaller concerns spared by the limited scope of the legislation. The principle of compensation was written into the law. But, with the exception of some foreign-owned enterprises, the owners of which enjoyed the protection of diplomatic intervention by powerful embassies, no compensation was actually paid. The law was promulgated simultaneously with another, "encouraging private initiative."

The nationalization law was the single most important step legalizing the dictatorship of the Communist-controlled state in economic matters. The old assurances concerning private initiative, and a balance between the state sector on the one hand and private and cooperative sectors on the other, now became irrelevant considering the dynamics of nationalization. More than 70 percent of the workers employed in industry and crafts and more than 80 perent in industry proper now worked for the state. By the end of 1946, the production of the "Socialist sector" of industry, that is, state and cooperative industries, was 91.2 percent of the total industrial output, while that of the private sector was 8.8 percent; in 1948, this ratio amounted to 94 percent and 6 percent, respectively.[13]

Thus by 1946, even before the Three-Year Plan of Reconstruction was launched, the "commanding heights" of Poland's economy were safely in the hands of the new regime. The period of the Three-Year Plan (1947–49) saw a great increase in industrialization and a marked rise in the standard of living as compared with that of the immediate postwar period. The ravages of war were to a large extent healed, and the new western territories were successfully resettled with 6 million

Poles, some of whom were refugees from the lost eastern provinces and others from the overpopulated areas of central and southern Poland.

The increasing emphasis on industrial rather than agricultural production is illustrated by the following figures. Although somewhat distorted because of the fact that prewar Poland was not territorially identical with the post-1945 country, they nonetheless throw some light on Poland's economic progress within the new boundaries. Considering combined output in industry and agriculture to equal 100, the production volume of industry's share in 1937 was 45.5, while agriculture's was 54.5. By 1948 the corresponding figures were 64 for industry and 36 for agriculture. The growing industrialization was indicated not only by a rapid expansion in overall industrial output, but also by a swift increase in the production of capital goods as opposed to consumer items. In 1937, 47 percent of the total industrial output represented capital goods and 53 percent consumer goods; in 1948 the production of capital goods rose to 54 percent and that of consumer goods dropped to 46 percent.

The most striking example of the industrialization of the late 1940s was the construction of the Lenin steel works and the town of Nowa Huta, near Cracow. The decision to build a large industrial complex near the country's most historic and conservative city reflected not only the regime's investment policy, with its emphasis on heavy industry, but also its political goals. Writing of the underlying motives that influenced the placement of the town of Nowa Huta, a Polish author stressed that it was intended

> . . . to create a large new and strong socialist urban working class society, which would in time influence the development of the social structure and social relations in an old and extraordinarily staid population such as existed in Cracow.[14]

Rapid industrialization caused a marked increase in the number of wage earners. In 1938 there were 2.73 million people employed outside agriculture; by 1948 that figure reached the 3.5 million mark. Wage earners formed 8 percent of the population in 1938; in 1948

158

they totaled 14.6 percent. This development, stressed Hilary Minc, ''brings an absolute and relative growth of the proletariat and strengthens the position of the working class—the leading and most progressive part of the nation.'' The social basis of the party was thus potentially strengthened in turn. The process of industrialization led to the advancement of many former workers to executive and technical positions. Moreover, it created a new, mainly peasant-recruited, working class. The class has retained, at least into the first generation, some essential features of the old peasantry, and its predominantly rural background has given rise to numerous problems, mainly those of labor discipline.

On the whole, the economic recovery of Poland during the period 1945 to 1949 proceeded at a satisfactory pace, and by the end of 1949 total industrial production substantially exceeded that of prewar Poland. The great majority of Polish people, although ideologically alien to the new regime, supported its efforts at rehabilitating the country.

⫷ ⫸

The first phase in the Communist assumption of power in Poland ended with the elections of 1947. In its attempts to consolidate power, the Workers' party had combined methods of friendly persuasion with nationalistic propaganda, Communist ideological slogans, and outright terror. Political power by the end of 1947 was firmly in the hands of the PPR, while the property-owning class and its last liberal spokesmen had been eliminated as political and economic factors of decisive importance. The country's economy was now composed of three unevenly balanced sectors: private, cooperative, and socialist. In this respect there is a certain similarity between the years 1945–47 and the period of the New Economic Policy in Russia (1921–28). These years were marked by a transformation that had certain genuinely radical democratic and socialist features, such as agrarian reform and the nationalization of large industries. The reforms, generally speaking, found a broad measured of popular support. The loss of the eastern provinces, especially the cities of Wilno

159

and Lwów, was deplored, it is true, and the subservience of the regime to Moscow was denounced and often ridiculed, but the slogan of "economic reconstruction," and establishment of Poland on the Oder-Neisse rivers, as well as on the Baltic Sea, were accepted by most Poles with a considerable amount of favor.

During this period certain gestures of appeasement were made by the government, both for the benefit of the outside world and for the overwhelming majority of non-Communist citizens. The Catholic church, for example, was interfered with less than in other people's democracies. During the first postwar years Bolesław Bierut would take part in the Corpus Christi processions, thus maintaining a tradition followed by former Polish heads of state. Peasants were repeatedly reassured that they would be allowed to continue private ownership of their land. Their role as providers of food and as the largest segment of the population was stressed. Petty tradesmen and small craftsmen were told to continue their occupations and were left relatively undisturbed. During the immediate postwar period, a certain latitude was allowed to non-Communist political and religious forces, provided they did not openly challenge the new order, "the leading role" of the Workers' party, or the fundamental principle of Polish-Soviet friendship. The degree of freedom, although insignificant in comparison with that prevailing in most Western countries and, indeed, in prewar Poland, was not negligible when compared with the Soviet Union, or even other people's democracies. "The Polish way to Socialism," a line stressed in some of Gomułka's pronouncements, was still tolerated by the ruling party, which initially favored his "mild revolution." In 1947, there still existed in Poland freedom of worship, freedom of movement and of choosing one's work, freedom to listen to the radio, even to foreign broadcasts, and freedom of *private* criticism. During the years 1945–47, Poland, according to Communist theoreticians, although now no longer part of the capitalist world, was not yet fully a Socialist state but merely a hybrid people's democracy.

Following the elections of 1947 the regime began to tighten its grip on the country. The size of the security police forces was greatly increased and by April 1947 numbered some 230,000. Censorship was tightened and political controls made more rigid. On May Day of 1947, Gomułka issued a call for the amalgamation of the two working class parties.

The methods and tactical maneuvers through which the Polish Workers' party managed to absorb its Socialist rival are outside the scope of this book. One has to stress, however, that although Gomułka advocated the merger of the two parties, on the whole he took a rather moderate attitude toward the Socialists. As a Polish patriot he sympathized with the patriotic and democratic traditions of the movement to which he had belonged before joining the Communist party. He had no objection to the existence of different parties within the "democratic" framework, provided that they did not challenge the Communist supremacy. As a Marxist, however, he argued that political parties must represent genuine class interests. Since there was only one working class in Poland, it must be represented by a single working-class party.

After a bitter struggle against the old guard of the Socialist movement, who were fiercely opposed to the absorption and sentimentally attached to the glorious traditions of their party, the merger was consummated at the "Unification Congress," in December 1948. The fusion more than doubled the membership of the ruling party, now renamed the Polish United Workers' party (PUWP). The absorption of the Socialists provided the Communists with many urgently needed administrative and executive talents. Membership in the Worker's party had numbered 210,000 in 1945. By 1950, however, the new PUWP had a membership of 1.24 million (or some 5 percent of the total population). The merger represented an amalgamation of various elements, among which genuinely patriotic non-Communist Poles were quite numerous. The new party assumed control of the country and proceeded to establish what, for all practical purposes, amounted to a one-party dictatorship. In the top leadership of the new party the Communists had complete dominance: eight of eleven

161

members of the new politburo were Communists and only three Socialists.

Soon after the absorption of the Socialists, the Communist-sponsored Peasant party absorbed the remnants of the Polish Peasant party, which had been increasingly infiltrated by pro-Communist elements after the flight of Mikołajczyk. Thus was created the United Peasant party, which was to serve as a conduit from the Communists to the peasant masses. Its ideological platform was made to correspond with that of the PUWP, including the recognition of the dominant role of the working class and its party. Another political group, the Democratic party, was tolerated as a means of transmitting the directives of the PUWP to the vestigial classes of craftsmen, petty shopkeepers, and members of liberal professions.

Gomułka, who in his capacity as secretary-general had initiated the unification of the two parties, did not participate in the consummation. His dismissal from his post came in September of 1948, a few months before the formal merger. Since he was a crucial figure of the postwar period and ruled Poland for fourteen years, a few words about him would be in order.

The son of a worker, Gomułka was born in 1905 in the oil-bearing district of eastern Galicia. Originally a member of the Polish Socialist party, he played only a minor role in the work of the old CPP prior to World War II. Whether he had ever undergone any training in Moscow is still open to question. After the Nazi-Soviet partition of Poland in September 1939, Gomułka and a group of his friends remained in German-occupied territory and appealed for Comintern support in organizing a Communist resistance movement. The appeal went unheeded, but the Nazi attack on the Soviet Union in June 1941 spurred the Communist groups in Poland to reorganize (1942) as the Polish Workers' party. Gomułka's election as secretary-general by the central committee in November 1943 evidently took place, because of ruptured communications, without Moscow's knowledge or consent.[15]

Gomułka proved to be a courageous underground leader, but his Communist orthodoxy was not always of the type expected by Stalin.

162

To remedy the extremely weak domestic position of the Polish Communists, Gomułka considered it essential to broaden their rather narrow political base. Consequently, in 1943 he made an attempt to reach an understanding with the Polish Socialist party and other non-Communist groups, and even established confidential contacts with the Polish government-in-exile in London. This conciliatory line was supported by friends, among whom were Marian Spychalski, Władysław Bieńkowski, Władysław Kowalski, Zenon Kliszko, and Ignacy Loga-Sowiński—all Communists with no significant Moscow background. They maintained that the political isolation of the PPR necessitated a compromise, and that the party must reject its Luxemburgist heritage on the national issue and take a stand placing greater stress on patriotism and on a specific "Polish way of building Socialism." Gomułka's group firmly believed in close collaboration with the powerful eastern neighbor, but they were not inclined to slavishly follow its dictates in all domestic matters.

On this basic issue of tactical alliance with the non-Communist forces and the attitude toward the USSR, Gomułka and his native supporters were opposed by the Moscow-trained group led by Bolesław Bierut, Hilary Minc, Jakób Berman, and Roman Zambrowski. The tougher line of the "Muscovites" demanded that the party, relying upon Soviet support, go it alone and shun any compromise with the bourgeois groups. The consolidation of political power revived the old question of the bolshevization of the Polish movement. Now the issues so hotly debated during the interwar period—the question of whether the Soviet methods of collectivization and industrialization should be transplanted to Poland, or whether the Stalinist style of party work should be introduced without any deviation—flared up again. In their private conversations the "natives" boasted of their deeper domestic roots or contacts with the masses, and often ridiculed the slavish obedience of their rivals toward the Soviet authorities while, secretly perhaps, envying the "Muscovites" better contacts with "the Center." While many "Muscovites" were of Jewish extraction, most "natives" were ethnic Poles.

On the whole, Gomułka and his followers argued for a "mild revo-

163

lution," with no forcible collectivization and as little terror as possible; the new regime in Poland must be basically Communist, they maintained, but it need not necessarily be a carbon copy of the Soviet model. Bierut and his supporters, on the other hand, insisted on orthodox Bolshevik methods and policies. The "Muscovites" accused the "natives" of being hypocritical "radishes," that is, red outside but white inside, whereas they themselves were true "beetroots" or "tomatoes"—red all the way through.

After the establishment of the Communist-dominated provisional government, the two rival groups continued their competition for control of the party and state political apparatus. Gomułka remained in his commanding position as party's secretary-general, concurrently becoming vice-premier and minister of recovered territories; Spychalski became vice-minister of defense in charge of army political education; Kowalski headed the Communist youth movement; and Bieńkowski directed the party cultural and educational program.

From the beginning the "natives" tried to soften the harsh effects of the Soviet military occupation, restrict looting and other excesses of the Red Army, and attempted to proceed cautiously with collectivization and repression of the opposition. This emphasis upon a specifically Polish way to Socialism did not mean that Gomułka and his followers were not loyal Communists fully dedicated to establishing the rule of the party. While their policies in the early years gave an impression of relative moderation, they were both uncompromising and unscrupulous when it came to crushing those who stood in the way of full Communist political mastery.

Indeed, while the nationalistic coloration of Gomułka's policies stemmed in part from sincere ideological convictions, it was also influenced, in part, by strategic considerations of facilitating the Communist seizure of power. Nor was the concept of a Polish road to Socialism outwardly opposed, at the initial stages, by the Moscow leaders. They apparently calculated that toleration of nationalistic slogans was one means of weakening the Polish popular opposition to Communism during the crucial takeover period. The ideal of building Socialism by a maximum of domestic effort using methods in accordance with native tradition that was more congenial to the Polish people had a considerable appeal to the rank-and-file of the Polish Workers' party, then rapidly expanding its thin cadres.

The full meaning of events in Poland in 1948 and 1949 can only be properly assessed against the background of international developments: the proclamation of the Truman Doctrine; the rejection by Moscow, and subsequently by Poland and Czechoslovakia, of aid through the Marshall Plan; and the Yugoslav defection. Because of the intensification of the cold war, Stalin appears to have decided, in 1947, to tighten and coordinate the activities of the Communist parties of the Soviet bloc nations in order to ensure ideological solidarity. In September 1947 a conference was called by Moscow in Polish Silesia and chaired by Gomułka in his capacity as the party boss of the host country. The gathering, which was attended by representatives of the Communist parties of the Soviet Union, six Eastern European states, and France and Italy, resulted in the establishment of the Communist Information Bureau (Cominform).

This institution, reminiscent of the old Comintern, must have caused some apprehension in Gomułka's mind. At the conference, on various occasions, Gomułka could not avoid expressing to his Polish colleagues some misgivings concerning Moscow's intention to enforce more strictly its control over other Communist parties. He believed that the renewed stress on dependence on Moscow could only harm the working-class movement, which he had tried to represent as an expression of native radicalism. He indirectly pointed also to the role which "the question of the western territories" could play in the future of Poland's relations with the Soviet Union. In spite of its innocuous context, his statement implied an inherent mistrust of Moscow and a suspicion of its possible intentions toward its Polish ally. Gomułka was obviously preoccupied with Poland's long-range national interests and the ever-present threat of a possible Soviet-German deal at Poland's expense.

All the time the winds of the cold war were becoming more and more icy. The Communist coup d'état in Prague in February 1948 resulted in the establishment of a Communist dictatorship in Czecho-

165

slovakia; the following month Great Britain, France, and the Benelux countries signed the Brussels treaty establishing closer ties. Soon afterwards, international tension reached its peak with the imposition of the Soviet blockade on Berlin and the surfacing of the long-smoldering Yugoslav-Soviet conflict. Stalin apparently had no doubts about his ascendancy over Yugoslavia, and Tito's defiance came as a severe shock. His morbid suspicions once aroused, he was determined to take no chances in other parts of his empire with leaders of similar temperament and tendencies.

The move to a period of tighter Soviet control in Eastern Europe was accelerated: between February and December of 1948 the Socialist parties of Romania, Hungary, Czechoslovakia, and Poland were absorbed into the Communist parties. In January 1949, as a Moscow replay to the Marshall Plan, these five countries and the Soviet Union set up the Council for Mutual Economic Assistance (CMEA or Comecon). The following April, the North Atlantic Treaty was signed, providing the foundation for NATO. During 1949–51 the scope of the Soviet control of Eastern Europe was revealed by the treason trials and purges of a number of leading Communists, including Laszlo Rajk in Hungary, Traicho Kostov in Bulgaria, and Rudolf Slansky in Czechoslovakia.

On June 3, 1948, only three weeks before the Soviet-Yugoslav dispute reached its climax with the Cominform denunciation of Tito, Gomułka assailed the "Luxemburgist nihilism" of the old Communist party of Poland at a plenary session of his party's central committee. He expressly eulogized the old Polish Socialist party for its stand on the issue of national independence, and declared: "Both for the PPS and for the PWP the independence of Poland is a supreme consideration, to which all others are subordinated." Gomułka never put it in so many words, but he could have said exactly what the Yugoslav comrades had stated so bluntly in their reply to the Soviet accusations of nationalism: "No matter how much each of us loves the land of socialism, the U.S.S.R., he can in no case, love his own country less. . . ." [16]

166

Following the open break with Tito, the "Muscovite" wing of the party leadership, at a central committee meeting from August 31 to September 3, 1948, took Gomułka to task for his statement at the June conference. Now his past attempts to compromise with other parties and his emphasis on a Polish way to Socialism were scornfully denounced as a symptom of nationalism. He was accused of favoring a conciliatory attitude toward Tito, while taking a defiant stand vis-à-vis the Soviet Union and trying to negotiate with Moscow on a level of equality. He was further charged with slowing down the tempo of collectivization and with following the Yugoslav example and prematurely dismissing some unspecified Soviet experts.

Instead of meekly admitting his guilt, Gomułka defended himself courageously and even tried to counterattack. His "errors" in the realm of ideology had, after all, been shared to some extent by practically all his colleagues in the Polish party leadership, as well as by most of the party leaders in the other people's democracies. All this was in vain: his condemnation had obviously been decided elsewhere beforehand, and the central committee was merely acting out a carefully contrived morality play, staged for the benefit of all Communist parties of Eastern Europe. After a prolonged and bitter debate, the politburo found Gomułka guilty of "nationalist deviation" and suspended him from his post as secretary-general. His place was taken by Bolesław Bierut.

The essential facts were quite simple. Gomułka's concept of a Polish path to Socialism, which Moscow had tolerated for tactical reasons during the takeover period, had now become dangerous in view of the Yugoslav revolt and the danger of its spreading throughout the Soviet bloc. Stalin undoubtedly felt that under favorable circumstances Gomułka could prove to be another Tito. This, Stalin calculated, would be a far greater disaster for the bloc than Tito's defection because of the strategic position Poland occupied with respect to Germany.

Under increasingly mounting pressure, Gomułka had to capitulate, and in 1949 he confessed his cardinal sins in these revealing words:

167

> The core of my rightist, nationalist complex must have been my attitude to the Soviet Union—to the CPSU (a). . . . . My attitude should be reduced not so much to . . . the relationship between the CPSU (b) and the Polish Workers' Party as to the relationship between Poland and the USSR as states. . . . . It never entered my head that Poland could progress along the way to socialism without being supported by the Soviet Union, but . . . it was difficult for me to shift my attitude as regards the Soviet Union to the ideological party plans.[17]

Between September 1948 and December 1949 three sweeping purges were carried out in the United Polish Workers' party to eliminate those who shared or sympathized with Gomułka's deviationist views. The purges affected practically one-fourth of the party membership, their scope and intensity clearly reflecting Moscow's conviction that nationalism represented a potentially powerful and dangerous force in the Polish Communist establishment. On August 2, 1951, Gomułka was arrested and spent the next three years under house detention near Warsaw.

Now the subordination of Poland to the Soviet Union seemed to be complete. The peasant movement was emasculated, the Socialist rivals either neutralized or absorbed, and the nationalist deviationists removed from the PUWP. The bulk of the party and government leadership was securely in the hands of those who had spent long years of their lives in the USSR and whose personal dedication to Stalin was unquestionable.

On several occasions the Soviet leaders, including Stalin himself, sought to ascertain from the new bosses of the PUWP when Gomułka would be brought to trial, presumably to be liquidated in the manner of Laszlo Rajk and others. The standard answer of Gomułka's comrades was that preparatory investigations were not yet completed. This was only part of the truth. In reality the investigators had failed utterly to break Gomułka and make him admit any guilt. Moreover, he had threatened, if placed on trial, to bare some wartime party secrets.

The Soviet control over Poland was perhaps most dramatically symbolized by the installation of Soviet Marshal Konstantin Rokossovsky as minister of national defense and commander-in-chief of the Polish armed forces. His influence and prestige were emphasized when he was made one of the deputy premiers in 1952. Under Rokossovsky, the Polish forces were reorganized along the Soviet pattern, with greater attention being paid to political education, and the oath of allegiance being altered to enable Polish soldiers to swear loyalty to the Soviet Union as well as to their own country. Most key commands and staff appointments were entrusted to Soviet officers. Thus, a country whose future in 1945 had appeared to many outside observers to be an open question, had been transformed in only five or six years into one of Russia's most subservient allies.

🖋 🖋

Meanwhile, the outbreak of the Korean conflict (1950) further escalated international tensions and thus intensified the cold war. This, again, had profound repercussions throughout Eastern Europe. While tightening political control and ruthlessly eradicating all sorts of deviations, real and imaginary, the Polish party redoubled its efforts at industrialization. The drive was aimed not so much at improving the people's standard of living as enhancing the military potential of the Stalinist empire, allegedly threatened by the imperialists led by the United States. The new spirit was reflected in the Six-Year Plan, which was to cover the years 1950–56 and continue the task of reconstruction and rehabilitation begun under the Three-Year Plan. The original Six-Year Plan provided for an average yearly increase in the nation's output from 11 to 12 percent, and an annual growth in industrial production of about 20 percent. These objectives confronted the party with an almost superhuman task. In attempting to complete "the second revolution," it had to ruthlessly mobilize every ounce of the country's energy and tighten the already stringent controls to which the nation had been subjected ever since 1948.

In the summer of 1950, after the outbreak of the Korean War, the already ambitious original targets of the plan were markedly increased, apparently under Soviet pressure. The final plan, adopted at the fifth plenum of the party's central committee (July 1950), con-

169

tained substantially higher objectives to be attained by the end of 1955: 4.6 million tons of steel, 100 million tons of coal, and 19.3 million kilowatt-hours of electric power. These revisions followed a prolonged visit to Moscow by Hilary Minc, the plan's chief architect and Poland's economic boss. He was instructed to expand heavy industry and was promised more aid from the USSR. An intricate commercial agreement, to last eight years, was signed at that time. After his return, he urged Polish economists and engineers to apply "bold, Bolshevik methods of planning and production," or *"shtur-movshchina."* Stakhanovite principles of "socialist competition of labor" were forcibly introduced: fulfillment of the higher industrial objectives became the main preoccupation of the party.

Soon after the enactment of the Six-Year Plan, private enterprise and handicrafts became the primary targets of the new policy, which aimed at the total nationalization of the economy. Collectivization of peasant plots was initially not part of Communist policy in the immediate post-revolutionary era, and any intention of this sort had been repeatedly denied. Until the middle of 1948 rumors of impending collectivization were branded as malicious, reactionary gossip, or at least an "oversimplification of the tempo of historical process." This changed rapidly after the removal of Gomułka. After 1949 a vigorous collectivization drive was unleashed. Now, unwilling peasants were driven into collective farms euphemistically called producers' cooperatives. In 1949 only 243 collective farms had been formed, but by 1956 there were already 10,600 throughout the country. Even so, at the height of collectivization only 8.6 percent of the total cultivated area was part of the "Socialist sector." [18]

While expanding the Six-Year Plan, the party attempted to create an almost mystical atmosphere, emulating to some extent that which prevailed in the Soviet Union during the first two five-year plans. Popular enthusiasm for the plan was largely dampened by suspicion that the Soviet Union probably benefited as much from Poland's progress as did Poland itself. The Soviet economic exploitation of the country, camouflaged by the slogan of "fraternal aid," was a factor which even the skillful party propagandists were at a loss to explain

170

away to the lower echelons of the movement. Under an imposed agreement of August 1945, Poland was required to deliver to the Soviet Union in 1946, at a "special price" of $1.25 a ton, 8 million tons of coal. Thirteen million tons were to be delivered annually during the years 1947–51, and 12 million tons per annum thereafter. At the same time, Denmark and Sweden were offering $12 for a ton of coal. In 1947, the amount to be delivered annually was halved to 6.5 million tons. But apart from this so-called reparation coal, the Soviet Union in 1948 paid, on an average, $14 a ton for Polish coal, whereas the market price in Western Europe was $18 to $19. In 1946, as well, Polish sugar was being sought by the Soviet Union for less than half the price Poland was then paying to import sugar from Czechoslovakia.[19]

At the same time, there were attempts to launch a cultural revolution in Poland. Socialist realism was imposed on Polish artists and writers as the only acceptable form of expression. Relations with the Roman Catholic church worsened considerably. In addition to promoting a proregime lay Catholic organization called Pax, under the leadership of Bolesław Piasecki, a former head of the Fascist Falanga movement, the government resorted to the closing of charitable organizations and religious-oriented periodicals. When these measures did not produce the expected results, arrests of clergymen and of laymen close to the hierarchy became a daily feature of the last days of Stalinism. The drive survived Stalin's demise and culminated in the arrest in September 1953 of Stefan Cardinal Wyszyński, the primate of Poland. At the beginning of 1954, nine bishops and several hundred priests were held in prison.

The last three years of Stalinism saw the shaping of what Milovan Djilas termed a "new class." With the numerical expansion and bureaucratization of the party came the abuses stemming from the wielding of total power and all its privileges. The ideological fervor of 1944–47 faded away in the face of the comforts and even luxury enjoyed by the omnipotent bureaucracy. This new class became progressively isolated from the rest of the nation by a wall of special institutions, exclusive shops with "yellow curtains," luxurious summer

171

resorts, special medical care, and numerous other perquisites. The fact that the members of the establishment often brazenly displayed their privileges amidst general pauperization, and enjoyed hitherto undreamed of pleasures, alienated the party still further from the rest of the nation.

When characterizing the peak of Stalinism in Poland, one should not forget, however, that the period from 1949 to 1954 cannot be even roughly compared with the Great Purge of 1936–38 in Russia, where millions perished in prisons and concentration camps. But even though only a few thousand died in the terror in Poland, it was a bitter blow to the nation, especially after the terrible losses of the German occupation. The supreme irony is that those who perished were, as a rule, from among the best elements of the nation, principally the former members of the underground resistance.

The increasing terror and unpopular politics created an atmosphere of acute tension, alienation, and hopelessness. The tension between the rulers and the ruled was reflected in a popular joke, widely circulating at that time among people in the street: "Question: 'What is now the best way of committing suicide?' Answer: 'It is very simple. Just jump into the gap separating the nation from the Party.' "

It was in the midst of this mounting tension that on March 5, 1953, Stalin's death was announced in Moscow.

CHAPTER SEVEN

The "Polish October" and the Era of Gomułka: 1956–1970 [1]

> We are developing Socialism in our country in somewhat different forms. In the present period under the specific conditions which exist in our country . . . we are attempting to apply the best forms of work in the realization of Socialism. We do not do this in order to prove that our road is better than that taken by the Soviet Union, that we are inventing something new, but because this is forced on us by our daily life.
>
> *Reply of the Yugoslav Communist party*
> *made in 1948 to the Soviet accusation*
> *of following a partly independent tactical line*

THE LAST THREE OR FOUR YEARS of Stalin's rule were the most dreary and depressing period of Poland's post-World War II history. Most of the country's investments had been pumped into heavy industry, while consumer goods, housing, and community services were grossly neglected. The collectivization drive resulted in curtailment of food supplies. Literature and arts were muzzled, emasculated, and subjected to party supervision. Until 1948 a certain latitude had been left to writers, intellectuals, and scholars, provided they did not openly attack the Soviet Union and the basic tenets of the Communist doctrine; now active participation in the process of building Socialism was insisted upon, and Socialist realism was imposed on

173

the arts. Sycophantic glorification and abject imitation of everything Soviet became the shortest and surest way to success. Polish books and periodicals written in the so-called numb language, the Orwellian double-speak, became unreadable, while scholarship degenerated into quoting Lenin and Stalin, preferably the latter. From 1945 on the party had been the driving force that ruthlessly imparted direction and purpose to the revolution. Under Soviet supervision the PUWP enjoyed a near monopoly of power: political control, ownership of the means of production, and all but exclusive control of communications and education. But in the process of imposing these changes, the party itself had undergone a deep transformation. After a decade or so of rule, the Communist regime in Poland, like any living political system, began to succumb to the overwhelming pressures of immediate reality and began gradually to adapt itself to local ways and sentiments. From a small group of less than 20,000 in 1944–45, it became a mass party numbering over a million people at the end of 1948. In its evolution into a mass organization the party had absorbed numerous opportunistic elements having little to do with Communism, while the merger with the Polish Socialist party introduced into the PUWP a large number of patriotic individuals who decided to accept the inevitable, but who nonetheless did not alter their previous beliefs. While the swelling rank-and-file tried to preserve their ties with the people, frequently sharing their complaints and even anti-Soviet sentiments, the leadership stuck to its rigid, dogmatic line of policy and to its tyrannical methods. This created a great deal of tension within the party, a tension that could not be suppressed for long.

The death of "Number One" in March 1953 was bound to affect the whole Soviet empire, but the consequences of his demise were not felt at once. For a year or so everything appeared unchanged. The climax of the struggle with the church, the arrest of Cardinal Wyszyński, came in September 1953, six months after Stalin's death. Nevertheless, a variety of phenomena both inside Poland and in the Soviet Union was already gradually eroding the unbearable Stalinist system.

The progress of the "thaw" in Poland can only be properly understood if viewed against the background of a series of developments. Immediately after Stalin's death the new Soviet leadership declared that the Soviet Union would in the future be governed in accordance with the principle of collective leadership. Later in the same year, Lavrentii Beria, who a few months before had been head of the Soviet security police and minister of the interior, was arrested and executed. His downfall was followed by the taming and cleansing of the security police, by the release of a certain number of prisoners from forced-labor camps, and by the announcement that the rule of law would henceforth be respected.

The struggle for power in the Soviet Union revealed a profound disarray among the Soviet leadership. The liquidation of Beria brought about first the discrediting and then the disorganization of the Soviet secret police, with which the Polish police apparatus was closely linked. In December 1953 a high official of the Polish ministry of public security, Józef Światło, fled to the West. His revelations of the corruption of the party leadership and the bestiality of its secret police were broadcast by Western radio stations in 1954–55, and increased the already spreading uneasiness among the ruling circles. Denied at first by the regime, the revelations eventually compelled the party leadership to launch an extensive shake-up of the secret police. On December 7, 1954, the ministry of public security was abolished and the dreaded Radkiewicz dismissed; the functions of the secret police (*Bezpieka*) were divided between the ministry of the interior and a newly established committee of public security responsible directly to the council of ministers. The most discredited and unpopular figures of the dreaded *Bezpieka* organization were removed, and the vicious practices of the secret police as well as the internal party intrigues made a subject of public discussion.

As a result of these events, the all-pervading terror diminished considerably during 1954 and 1955. The abating of fear brought to the surface the hitherto suppressed political divergencies among many party factions. While numerous maneuverings were going on behind the scene, public pressures for more liberalization proceeded. The regime tried to appease them by means of numerous small concessions, including the quiet release of Gomułka from detention at the end of 1954.[2]

In May 1955, Khrushchev went to Belgrade, where he publicly repudiated Stalin's policy toward Yugoslavia and accepted Tito's program of a national way to Communism-Socialism. This was a development of special importance to Poland in view of the impact of the Soviet-Yugoslav dispute on events in 1948. In February of 1956, the twentieth congress of the Communist party of the Soviet Union, attended by a strong Polish delegation with Bierut at its head, opened in Moscow. At the beginning of the congress a special committee was set up composed of delegates from the parties of the Soviet Union, Italy, Bulgaria, Finland, and Poland. The committee examined the problem of the liquidation of the Polish Communist party in 1938 and concluded that "the dissolution of the Communist Party of Poland was an unfortunate act." "Revolutionary honors" were restored to the party, a significant gesture that was bound to have profound psychological as well as political consequences for the Stalinist leadership of the PUWP.

The congress ended with Khrushchev's speech attacking Stalin's personality cult and his vicious practices. The denunciation put the Stalinist clique then ruling Poland on the spot. A few days later, it was announced in Moscow that Bierut had died on March 12, apparently of a heart attack brought on by Khrushchev's revelations. Bierut's place as first secretary of the central committee was taken by Edward Ochab, a party hand of prewar standing, who was personally installed by Khrushchev in Warsaw.

The twentieth congress was both more meaningful and more dangerous to the PUWP than to any other Communist party outside the Soviet Union. Poland was the only country where Khrushchev's speech was published for the benefit of the party apparatus. Once distributed to party members, the gist of the speech became widely known throughout the country. This had a profound effect on the mood of the country. The speech had not only debunked Stalin, but had also rehabilitated the CPP, the organizational and spiritual parent

Twelfth-century church in Tum

P/A: INTERPRESS PHOTOS, WARSAW

A lake in the Tatra Mountains

Students celebrating Juvenalia in Cracow

Warsaw, 1945

Warsaw, 1975

Ruins of Warsaw ghetto, 1945

Monument to victims of Warsaw ghetto

Łazienki Palace in Warsaw, summer residence of the Polish kings

Automated mining complex at Zabrze

Sixteenth- and seventeenth-century architecture in Kazimierz, on the Vistula

Medieval fortifications in Warsaw

Stefan Cardinal Wyszyński, Primate of Poland

Karol Cardinal Wojtyła, Archbishop of Cracow

Marshal Józef Piłsudski

Władysław Gomułka

Bolesław Bierut

P.A: INTERPRESS PHOTOS. WARSAW

Polish leaders (from l. to r.): Prime Minister Piotr Jaroszewicz, President of Council of State Henryk Jabłoński, party leader Edward Gierek

Tomaszewski's Polish Mime Ballet Theatre

of the PUWP. The discrediting of Stalinism was a risky operation because, for most Poles, Stalinism and Communism were one and the same. The destruction of the Stalinist myth was probably the last straw needed to complete the process of disillusionment of the generation brought up in the aura of the personality cult.

🖋 🖋

Under the impact of the spirit generated by the Moscow congress, events in Poland began to move rapidly. Stalinist textbooks, teachings of Marxism-Leninism, and Socialist realism in the arts were openly criticized. The emboldened people began asking openly whether Stalin alone was responsible for the brutal, dreary, and soulless society created in Poland during the preceding decade. The collapse of this apparently infallible individual led to a collapse of the infallibility of the doctrine, thus eroding the already precarious position of the PUWP. Now the "thaw" became a flood and began to threaten the party's very existence.

In June 1956 the workers of Poznań revolted, marching in the streets and demanding more "bread and freedom" as well as more independence from Soviet control. The uprising was cruelly repressed by the army. Some fifty-four people were killed and several hundred wounded. The revolt represented a most serious challenge to the regime and was a new factor in the annals of Communism. By going out on strike, staging a massive demonstration, and fighting the tanks, the workers of Poznań disregarded the grim precedent of the suppression of a similar affair in Berlin in June 1953. By this courageous act, the workers became a new force to be reckoned with.

The Poznań uprising, together with the series of lesser provincial strikes, riots, and demonstrations that preceded and followed it, revealed the critical position of the party and dramatized the yawning gap separating the party from the people. The very composition of the PUWP indicated that it had become the party of bureaucracy. In the membership the percentage of workers between December 1948 and February 1954 had actually dropped from 53.6 to 48.3 percent, while that of peasants and land workers went from 26.5 to 13.2 percent and the number of white-collar workers grew from 17.6 to 36.4 percent.

The seriousness of the situation was obvious to the party bureaucrats, but they could not unite on a common solution. The partisans of the old Stalinist methods interpreted the uprising as a direct and disastrous result of the "thaw" and felt that further relaxation would mean the final collapse of the regime. The more moderate wing of the party urged further liberalization of the regime and its further modification in ways that would make it more acceptable to the masses of the Polish people, who keenly desired a higher standard of living, end of forcible collectivization, more religious freedom (especially freedom of religious instruction), and, last but not least, a measure of domestic autonomy from the Soviet Union. The mounting ferment among youth gave a further push to the elements within the PUWP that realized the necessity of channeling the discontent to save the existing system from crumbling.[3] To rescue itself, the party not only had to make concessions to the angry people, but to alter its image, had to at least partially rearrange the leadership. In this way the Poznań uprising paved the way for Gomulka's return to power. Among the non-Communist people, in comparison with the ruling establishment, the victim of Stalin's vengeance appeared as a martyr and a hero. By the summer of 1956 he was the party's only hope, its only trump card, and both factions, the "liberals" and the "dogmatists," began to court his favor. After some bickering and behind-the-scenes negotiations it was decided to reinstate Gomulka as first secretary of the central committee. This was achieved at the historic eighth plenum of October 20, 1956. The plenum deliberated under the threat of Soviet military intervention, foreshadowed by a formidable delegation headed by Khrushchev, who suddenly descended on Warsaw accompanied by a team of top military leaders, including Marshal Georgi Zhukov. At the same time the Soviet troops in Poland began to march toward Warsaw, and the Soviet Baltic fleet staged a menacing demonstration off Gdańsk and Gdynia. Khrushchev and his companions put strong pressure on the Poles not to elect Gomulka, even

178

to the point of threatening to return the Oder-Neisse territories to Germany. The Poles withstood the pressure, however, and put Gomułka at the helm.

Once again first secretary, Gomułka made a strong programmatic speech, one of the most significant public pronouncements ever made by a Communist leader. Gomułka mercilessly dissected the Stalinist system in Poland, pointing out that as a result of its practices, many "innocent people were sent to their death. Many others, including Communists, were imprisoned, often for many years, although innocent. Many people were submitted to bestial tortures." He promised a return to legality and a thorough democratization of the ruling party, which "must not govern but merely guide" the state apparatus. He insisted on restoration of "democratic centralism" in inner party life and pledged "to insure adequate control by party bodies over the party apparatus, beginning first of all with the central apparatus." Forcible collectivization was to be discontinued and private initiative given more leeway. In his speech, Gomułka asserted Poland's right to pursue its own road to Socialism and concluded by declaring:

> Socialism is a social system eliminating man's exploitation and oppression by man. . . . The roads to it, as well as the models of socialism, may differ. . . . They are determined by various circumstances of time and place. . . . Only through experience and thorough study of accomplishments of the various countries building socialism can a model of socialism be created that best fits given conditions.[4]

Thus, Gomułka implicitly rejected the universality of the Soviet experience, including the Soviet type of economy planned in all respects by the state, and instead accepted an economy at least partly coordinated by the market forces of supply and demand; the state was to retain merely the commanding heights and general direction of the economy. The party was to continue the process of democratization, but the move was to be channeled not toward social democracy of the Western type but toward a more humanized version of Communism, now to be purified of its worst abuses and made more palatable to the

Polish people by an admixture of patriotic slogans. This was still Communism, but different from its Soviet variety. The central committee firmly supported Gomułka's stand. Poland, stressed the resolution of the eighth plenum, was to be closely linked with the "camp of the Socialist states" and to be in an "unshakable alliance with the Soviet Union," although this alliance must be based "on principles of equality and independence."

During his imprisonment from 1949 to 1956, Gomułka, essentially a practical man and a realistic politician, had obviously submitted the beliefs of his youth to critical scrutiny; but basically his speech was a return to his ideas of eight or even ten years before: a relatively mild, gradual transformation of the country's social and economic structure, and an autonomous Communist Poland as a member of the Socialist camp. Thus, the outcome of the eighth plenum was the triumph of Gomułka's original program of a Polish way to Socialism.

The eighth plenum was followed by a further period of far-reaching changes in various fields of national life, later referred to as "the gains of the Polish October." Marshal Rokossovsky and a large group of Soviet officers were sent back to Moscow, and a friend of Gomułka's, General Marian Spychalski, was appointed commander-in-chief of the Polish armed forces. Censorship was relaxed and travel abroad made more easy. On October 28, Cardinal Wyszyński was freed from house arrest after some two years of detention; this was followed by the release of most ecclesiastics still remaining under arrest. Soon negotiations between the party and the Catholic hierarchy were opened for the purpose of establishing a modus operandi between church and state. Catholic organizations and publications were allowed a larger margin of freedom. At the beginning of November, a joint commission issued a statement outlining the main points of the new church-state arrangement. The statement stressed that the "representatives of the Episcopate expressed full support for the work of the Government aiming at the strengthening and development of People's Poland." In return, religious teaching in schools was to be permitted for children whose parents desired such instruction. Finally, the decree of February 9, 1953, giving the control of

180

church appointments to the government, was abolished. This was the peak of the liberalization process.

The return of Gomułka was greeted with genuine enthusiasm by the overwhelming majority of the Polish people, who expected that further liberalization would follow. In November 1956, Gomułka went to Moscow to have his position formally legitimized by the Kremlin. In his negotiations with the Soviet leaders he was able to extract for his country a considerable measure of internal autonomy in return for compliance with the directives of Soviet foreign and economic policy; the ties with the Warsaw Treaty Organization and the CMEA, as well as the leading role of the PUWP in domestic affairs, were reaffirmed. In return for this support Moscow acknowledged that it had exploited Poland economically and granted an indemnity of 700 million rubles in reparation. But the great expectations of the "thaw" of 1956 were never to materialize. From then on the process of liberalization was soft-pedaled. Poland did, however, manage to salvage a measure of internal autonomy, and after 1956 it was never again to be a mere Soviet colony.

✒ ✒

During the critical October days the Poles amazed the world by abandoning their endemic attitude of insisting on everything or nothing and showed a surprising spirit of compromise. The October 1956 upheaval made it clear that the majority of Poles did not necessarily oppose all the social and economic changes that had taken place since 1944. After ten years or so of vainly waiting for some sort of "liberation" from the West, most Poles gradually became convinced that as long as Poland was an abandoned island surrounded by Soviet-controlled territories, it must assume protective coloring and accept a regime that Moscow would tolerate. At the same time a great majority of Poles hoped to stop the imported revolution at a point that would preserve a certain measure of political and economic pluralism as well as basic freedom and respect for human dignity.

Gomułka was backed by the Poles because he represented the only hope of returning to a system somewhat nearer to democratic Socialism than to Soviet Communism and the only chance of regaining at least a margin of autonomy from the Soviet Union. But the support of the Polish people did not spell support of the party as such. The tacit compromise of October was a kind of social contract with Gomułka, to last as long as he defended Poland's internal autonomy and the people's basic human rights.

One of the secrets of Gomułka's success was the fact that he never went as far as Imre Nagy in Hungary, who had threatened secession from the Soviet camp. The chasm separating the party from the rest of the nation was wide indeed in Poland, but the events of 1956 would not parallel the tragic and bloody upheaval in Hungary the same year. Despite its subservience toward the Kremlin, the Polish party managed to preserve a spark of independence, sometimes carefully camouflaged by outward signs of servility. Characteristically, Poland was the only satellite country that erected no monument to Stalin. Numerous competitions were arranged and many prizes awarded; but each time some pretext would be found not to proceed with the actual construction. Eight years passed, but no monument was built to honor the dead Soviet leader.

Polish agriculture was less collectivized than any other in the satellites. In 1955 the state farms covered only some 13 percent of the land, and all types of rural cooperatives only about 10 percent. There were fewer forced-labor camps than in other Communist countries, and the opposition, on the whole, was treated less brutally. Many writers and artists conformed to the standards laid down by the party, but only a few did so with conviction.

The Polish Armed Forces were never forced to wear Soviet style uniforms or emblems. Moreover, unlike Hungary, Communist Poland never staged a show trial of the leader of the Roman Catholic church; Cardinal Wyszyński was never brought before a court. Finally, Poland, unlike Czechoslovakia, Hungary, or Bulgaria, did not physically liquidate the chief opponents of the Stalinist line. No mock trial of Gomułka or Spychalski was ever staged, despite repeated reminders from Moscow. By this means, the Polish party managed to save from destruction an alternate team of former underground leaders, who automatically gained a certain popularity in the eyes of the public because of their opposition to Stalin and his Polish stooges. This team was invaluable when the party eventually maneuvered itself into a truly "revolutionary situation." Gomułka was lucky indeed that Bierut died when he did, and that Ochab quietly stepped down and even helped in a smooth transfer of power to Gomułka.

Another secret of the bloodless course of the "Polish October" was Gomułka's leadership, his cool head and strong nerves. Unlike Imre Nagy, who was carried away by the patriotic sentiments of his countrymen, Gomułka never lost control of the army and militia and was thus able to tame the wave of anti-Soviet feeling. Gomułka also had the bulk of his party behind him, which the Hungarian leader did not. Both in Poland and in Hungary the struggle for democratic freedom merged with the striving for national independence, but in Poland the party managed to avert catastrophe by giving in to the popular demands in time and temporarily becoming the spokesman for the masses in their resistance to the Soviet encroachments.

The palace revolution that swepted Gomułka back into power was indeed a reformation within the Communist framework, a modest change within the existing system. Gomułka and the Communist minority still in control had no intention of tolerating any serious threat to their party's leading position. That is why Khrushchev, after some hesitation, decided to accept the changes. Nevertheless, the compromise was, under the circumstances, a positive, progressive development that, on the whole, benefited the Polish people.

The "Polish October" was one of the most important political events in Eastern Europe after World War II, second in importance only to Tito's revolt in 1948. In the long term, however, the Polish upheaveal was more significant: it constituted a major turning point in the evolution not only of Poland, but also of Communist Eastern Europe as a whole. For the first time in the history of any Communist party the pressure of public opinion had brought about a change and a significant reform of government. Despite the gradual retrenchment of the party authority during the late 1950s, Poland enjoyed more freedom and internal autonomy than any other member of the Communist camp. Mass terror was discontinued and agriculture decollec-

183

tivized. Socialist realism in the arts was soft-pedaled, if not abandoned altogether. Travel to the West for selected individuals, especially scholars, intellectuals, and specialists in various fields, was now permitted. East-West cultural exchanges were lively, and many Polish scholars and writers visited Western Europe and the United States. A limited number of Western books and periodicals were imported. As for émigré writers, the years between 1957 and 1959 were a short period of grace; for instance, some works of Witold Gombrowicz were reprinted in Poland.

The triumph of Gomułka demonstrated the power of the concept of independence in the minds of the Polish people. The party, in consequence, made an effort to identify independence with adherence to the Socialist camp. Moscow was portrayed as the sole power both willing and able to assure the preservation of the Oder-Neisse frontier, and remaining within the orbit of the Soviet Union was a precondition for the survival not only of the Polish state, but of the Polish people as such. The party also made an effort to link the cause of Poland's independence to the Communist regime's continuation in power. This took place during the preelectoral campaign and *Sejm* (Diet) elections that were conducted on January 20, 1957.

The elections, although not democratic by Western standards, were more than a plebiscite of the Soviet type. Candidates were proposed to local commissions by social, economic, and cultural organizations, and by the two political parties tolerated by the PUWP: the United Peasant party and the Democratic party. There were approximately seven candidates for every four seats in the *Sejm*. Besides the candidates of the three political parties, some prominent Catholics and other non-Communists were put on the ballot. The electoral campaign was actually a national referendum posing two fundamental questions: were the Polish people for or against the Gomułka regime; and were they for or against the newly gained measure of autonomy within the Soviet bloc? The real meaning of the election was dramatized by Gomułka himself, who, on the eve of the polling, warned his countrymen that a failure to support him would result in Poland's disappearance from the map of the world.

The results were more a personal triumph for Gomułka than a victory for the party. The response of the Polish people meant a conditional approval of Gomułka, provided he continued the policy of democratization and domestic autonomy. The election, which provided at least a modicum of choice, was a novelty in Communist-controlled Eastern Europe. The end of 1956 and the beginning of 1957 constituted the high-water mark of the Gomułka regime.

Gomułka now found himself in power enjoying a wide and spontaneous popular support seldom, if ever, enjoyed by a Communist politician. Always painfully aware of the limitations under which he could act, he must have borne in mind Marshal Bulganin's grim warning, made in one of the speeches delivered in Poland in July 1956 while on tour on behalf of Khrushchev: "We cannot close our eyes to the attempts at weakening the international bonds of the socialist camp under the label of so-called 'national peculiarity,' or to the attempts at undermining the power of people's democratic countries under the label of an alleged 'broadening of democracy.' " [5]

That Poland was only half a step away from outright Soviet military intervention and that there were powerful forces favoring such a step was confirmed by Sir William Hayter, the British ambassador to the USSR from 1953 to 1957, who noted in his memoirs that Marshal Georgi Zhukov, while describing his visit to Poland in October 1956, said with an expressive gesture: "We could have crushed them [the Poles] like flies. . . ." [6] Similar threats were made by various members of the Soviet delegation during their visit in Warsaw. An American correspondent reported that during heated discussions Anastas Mikoyan told Polish Prime Minister Józef Cyrankiewicz: "The Soviet Union cannot afford any trouble in Poland. If you start trouble, we will crush it by force, if necessary." [7] Why the Soviets did not follow through on their threats is still something of a mystery. With Hungary and the Middle East in turmoil, they probably had too many more pressing problems on their agenda.

🖎 🖎

With the crisis over, the country settled into a more or less normal existence. The 1957 elections had bestowed on Gomułka's program the conditional approval of the Polish people; but various groups supporting Gomułka interpreted the implications of the October program in different ways. The expectations aroused in various quarters were far too ambitious for Poland, given its precarious geopolitical situation. Gomułka himself obviously understood that the program was the very maximum that could ever be achieved, and it was inevitable that it would be modified in many respects under the pressure of circumstances, one of them being the sullen hostility of the rest of the Communist camp, especially East Germany and Czechoslovakia.

Once in power, Gomułka began to gradually lose the qualities that had made him a popular leader. As long as he was in opposition to the Stalinist system, he had naturally attracted the support of revisionists like Jerzy Andrzejewski, Leszek Kołakowski, Jan Kott, Eligiusz Lasota, and Adam Ważyk, all of them associated with the weekly *Po prostu* (Speaking Frankly), which had supported Gomułka during the crucial October crisis. But once Gomułka was entrenched in office, their restlessness and unorthodoxy came to be regarded as a liability, an obstacle to the gradual process of reestablishing good relations with Moscow and the other Communist countries of Eastern Europe. Their demands for a second stage of the "October revolution" became embarrassing and even intolerable. Consequently, Gomułka tried to dump his rebellious friends, men who were once necessary but who could not now be expected to form part of an orderly government. This process of disengagement from the old allies and soft-pedaling of the old slogans is usually called the "retreat from the October." The process disappointed most people, but particularly the more outspoken and independent intellectuals. Their vociferous protests provoked denunciations, and eventually reprisals. The consolidation of the Gomułka regime was, therefore, accompanied by increasing signs of harshness and rigidity.

Many explanations have been advanced for the reasons why the "fallen angel" of revisionism lost his early boisterousness and flamboyance and turned into a rigid, narrow-minded despot. Some reasons were of a domestic nature, some were motivated by the rapidly changing international scene, and some may be attributed to his failing health and to psychological evolution. As Gomułka grew older,

186

he lost much of his former drive as well as his receptivity to new ideas. He became withdrawn and increasingly dependent on an inner circle of trusted, often sycophantic comrades to keep him advised and informed. Like most authoritarian rulers, he became self-indoctrinated by the obligatory atmosphere of official optimism, and came to distrust those advisers who brought bad news. Moody and capricious, he would often fly into fits of rage.

Another reason for Gomułka's retreat was the unstable economic situation of Poland. The Poznań uprising, the strikes and work stoppages connected with the October coup, followed by the reshaping of economic planning, further dislocated the operations of the Polish economy. In the process of liberalizing certain Stalinist practices, Gomułka loosened the bond of labor discipline that kept the old economic system working. But all of this occurred before the stimulating effects of various labor incentives could be felt.

In the interval, Gomułka undertook numerous piecemeal changes while postponing a fundamental overhauling of the economic system. Several reform programs were outlined by various experts. The most notable were formulated in 1957–58 and 1964–65 by Professor Oscar Lange and a group of able economists around him. In both instances their efforts were thwarted by the hardliners, who warned Gomułka that the decentralization of planning and control over individual enterprises would result in undermining of the party's political power. Against warnings of many of his advisers, he returned to the old, essentially Stalinist, policy of pursuing rapid industrial growth regardless of obstacles and human sacrifices. The economic stagnation that followed was soon reflected in Gomułka's personal loss of prestige and popularity.

In addition to the domestic reasons for the growing rigidity of the regime, were also international pressures. It was hoped that Poland's reassertion of independence vis-à-vis Moscow would be followed by a considerable measure of Western aid, in order to make the Poles less dependent economically on Soviet favors. When, after long negotiations, credit of $95 million was granted in June 1957, Gomułka described it in a speech at Poznań as "rather modest compared with our needs." In February 1958 the United States provided further credit, this time for $98 million. Nearly half the first credit had been allocated to the purchase of American farm surpluses, and three-quarters of the second grant was to be used for the same purpose. Further loans followed during the next few years, but they were spent predominantly for the purchase of farm surpluses. By the summer of 1960, the total amount provided or promised for this purpose amounted to $365 million. The American aid did not compare favorably with the help given by the Soviet Union, East Germany, and Czechoslovakia, and did not essentially diminish Poland's dependence on the COMECON partners. Another reason for Gomułka's caution had to do with the balance of forces within the Soviet camp. By 1957, after the suppression of the Hungarian uprising, Gomułka found himself isolated within the Communist world. The remaining East European countries—except, of course, for Yugoslavia—were either suspicious of him or jealous of his success. It became obvious that Poland would not be permitted to outdistance the other countries of Eastern Europe, either in domestic liberalization or in cultivating links with the West. Had the extreme revisionists prevailed, the party would have been exposed progressively to open controversy with other parties, and Poland might in the end have suffered a fate similar to Hungary's in 1956 or Czechoslovakia's in 1968.

The return to repression was also a result of the power struggle within the party and the balance Gomułka tried to keep between the dogmatists and the revisionists, the latter being represented by a group of able theoreticians, the most brilliant of whom was Leszek Kołakowski, a young professor of philosophy at the University of Warsaw. From the beginning, Gomułka took a middle position. In his speech to the party's tenth plenum (October 5, 1957), he vigorously attacked both the revisionists and the dogmatic Stalinists, using a medical metaphor:

> Influenza, even in its most serious form, cannot be cured by contracting tuberculosis. Dogmatism cannot be cured by revisionism. Revisionist tuberculosis can only strengthen the dogmatic influenza. . . .
> The revisionist wing must be out of the Party. We shall destroy with

188

equal firmness all organized or individual forms of anti-Party activity
launched from a position of dogmatism.[8]

Gomułka obviously calculated that the dogmatists, while constitu-
ting a nuisance, could be contained and manipulated, while the revisionists were dangerous. With their battle-cry "forward toward the
second stage of the Polish October," the revisionists were a menace
to the stability not only of the regime in Poland but also to the Soviet-
Polish relations.[9]

This fear of creeping revisionism had a great deal to do with the
"offensive on the cultural front" launched by the party in 1963. The
two most popular weeklies, *Nowa kultura* (New Culture), and *Przegląd kulturalny* (Cultural Review), were discontinued, and a new
paper, *Kultura,* set up in their place. For years *Kultura* (which bor-
rowed its name from the Polish émigré monthly in Paris) was boycot-
ted by many writers, who saw its creation as an attempt to break up
the solidarity of Communist and non-Communist writers on basic cultural issues. After 1963, personal contact between writers and representatives of the establishment became increasingly rare. As a result,
Gomułka became misinformed about the real situation "on the intellectual sector" and began to impute hostile political motives to any
criticism of the regime coming from writers. He and his henchman,
Zenon Kliszko, tended to treat the more outspoken writers as the
enemy within, as saboteurs of their efforts to unite the nation behind
the party's leadership.

Gomułka's repressive policies soon led to disillusionment and
created a rebellious spirit not only among writers and artists, but
among a broad spectrum of the population as well. The dissatisfaction of the intellectuals was reflected in the "Letter of the 34,"
sent to Cyrankiewicz on March 14, 1964. In this manifesto thirty-
four well-known intellectuals protested against the growing restric-
tions on book publication and the stiffening of censorship, insisting
on "a change in Polish cultural policy in the spirit of the rights
guaranteed by the constitution of the Polish State." In 1960, 7,305
titles were published (including 1,451 titles of belles-lettres), but of

189

the 8,260 books published in 1964, only 1,149 were titles of fiction, poetry, and criticism. Throughout the 1960s dissatisfaction was expressed more and more in the form of bitter criticism and open defiance.

In the summer of 1964, two young Marxist scholars at Warsaw University, Jacek Kuroń and Karol Modzelewski, circulated a ninety-page open letter incisively criticizing the Gomułka regime as stale, bureaucratic, and ineffective. The document also contained recommendations to remodel Poland as a "true socialist state." In November 1964 both authors were expelled from the party for alleged dishonesty and immorality, and imprisoned.[10] The conflict between the regime and the intellectuals escalated when in May 1965 the Warsaw branch of the Writer's Association passed a resolution demanding, among other things, the abolition of censorship.

The tenth anniversary of Gomułka's return to power provided the critics with an opportunity to assail his record. On October 20, Leszek Kołakowski, in a talk to a group of students, drew up a critical balance sheet for the past decade. Kołakowski's speech condemned "repressions, the lack of democracy, the regime's intolerance of opposition and the bureaucratic political system." His analysis was stormily applauded by the audience, which included not only students but also young instructors and professors. In reprisal for the speech, Kołakowski was expelled from the party. Twenty-two writers, members of the PUWP, signed a protest against his expulsion, and by mid-1967, sixteen of these nonconformist writers had also been thrown out of the party.

The battle with the intellectuals, however, was not the only struggle the party waged during the 1960s. A new offensive was also launched against the Catholic church. Gomułka had said to the editor of *Le Monde* in October 1961: "Religion . . . is deeply rooted in a major section of our population. It would be nonsensical for us to try to enforce changes in mentality and beliefs by administrative measures." But from the beginning he never followed this sagacious observation. In September 1958 the government issued a directive forbidding members of religious orders to give instruction in schools

190

unless fully qualified as teachers; the decree also stipulated that schools, as lay institutions, were not permitted to display religious emblems.

The two most grave issues that arose between the Roman Catholic hierarchy and the state after 1956, besides the church property in the western territories, were the questions of taxation and religious education. Early in 1959 the government decreed that the income and property of the clergy, churches, and such religious institutions as monasteries, convents, and seminaries were no longer to enjoy their customary exemption from taxation. In 1961 a law was adopted to abolish all religious instruction in schools, although the church was able to continue with religious instruction through its own network of catechism centers. Another controversy was over birth control. During the crucial year of 1966, when Poland was celebrating the millennium of Christianity, the party declared a boycott of church-sponsored festivities and tried to stage rival celebrations. Their failure resulted in a loss of face and further tarnished the image of the aging and ailing first secretary.

The restrictive policies of Gomułka from 1963 on reflected the increased influence of the right-wing faction of the PUWP, largely former members of the Communist underground movement, the so-called Partisans. The Partisans, headed by Mieczysław Moczar, a ruthless and resourceful former chief of *Bezpieka* in Łódź, emerged in the early sixties as a coherent and dynamic group. Their program, which aimed at broadening mass support of the party, consisted of a mixture of nationalism with a belief in the tough operational methods inherited from wartime days. Largely composed of younger, restless, ambitious members of the party, they were critical of the alleged predominance of Jews in the top echelons of the PUWP. The Partisans soon took over the War Veterans Organization (known in Polish as *ZBOWID*) and broadened its membership by including non-Communist groups and individuals. Moczar, who became minister of internal affairs at the end of 1964, was well aware of the significance of the intellectuals in shaping public opinion. Using his power of patronage, he managed to win over to his side some writers and journalists. By the middle 1960s he had his spokesmen in such weeklies as *Kultura* and *Stolica*. Gomułka, bent on preserving the middle road, and focusing increasingly on his fight against revisionism, began to lean more and more on Moczar's support in party squabbles.

The mounting conflict between the revisionists and the establishment burst into the open in February and March of 1968. The clash was precipitated by the official ban of the Warsaw production of Adam Mickiewicz's drama, *Dziady* (*The Forefather's Eve*). Mickiewicz's classic contains some antitsarist and antiauthoritarian passages that were demonstratively applauded by the audience, composed largely of young people. The government decision to close the play provoked sporadic demonstrations among the students of Warsaw University, followed by an indignant protest on the part of the writers of Warsaw. The conflict came to a climax at the beginning of March, when a wave of protest meetings, sit-ins, and peaceful student demonstrations took place in most institutions of higher learning. The demonstrations, the origins of which are still shrouded in mystery, were ruthlessly suppressed by large-scale police action directed by Moczar's ministry of the interior. The "March events" were taken advantage of by the police, and were followed by numerous reprisals against dissenting students and intellectuals, writers as well as professors (many of Jewish extraction), who were held responsible for the acts of protest, including the demonstrative applauding of Mickiewicz's play.

Thus, by the late 1960s, Gomułka, who came to power in 1956 as the champion of liberalization and national unity, had become an increasingly isolated individual engaged in a bitter struggle against the church, the party revisionists, and the intellectuals. The fight against the latter two groups was intertwined with the anti-Zionist campaign, about which more will be said later. At the same time, Gomułka was facing mounting economic difficulties.

According to Nicholas Bethell, the chief biographer of the first secretary, one of the reasons for his intolerance of any opposition, especially on the part of the revisionists, was a result of his perception of

Poland's position in the world. Bethell stresses Gomułka's constant preoccupation with internal security as well as with the pervading specter of a Russo-German rapprochement at Poland's expense, should the Russians become disappointed with Poland as a stable and loyal ally. The danger was dramatized by the visit of Khrushchev's son-in-law, Alexei Adzhubey, to Bonn early in 1964. Apparently the mission greatly alarmed Gomułka, who feared it might be a prelude to German reunification before Poland's western frontiers were recognized by Bonn. Bethell points out that:

> The whole affair shook the Polish leader horribly. He saw it as a confirmation of his worst fears: the memories of the Stalin-Hitler pact of 1939 must have been vivid in his memory in those days. Again Poland had had a hair-breadth escape from becoming yet again a matter of Russian-German bargain. Gomułka had long ago discarded what he thought were the over-liberal ideas of the Polish "October". . . . But after the experience of 1964 he began to turn into that epitome of conservatives, the man who is frightened of political change. . . . Gomułka's former flexibility, his lack of Marxist dogma, became hardened by his obsession with preserving the integrity of the Polish state, both her existence as a separate political entity and her western frontiers. . . . Gomułka's greatest complaint against his political opponents is that they take Poland's existence for granted, that they act as if Poland were a self-sufficient island. He sees such men as totally unrealistic and does not hesitate to accuse them of being ready to sacrifice Poland's vital interest for the sake of such luxuries as freedom of expression.[11]

Gomułka's preoccupation with Poland's security has to be viewed in perspective, and his stand at the first Cominform conference of September 1947, and his electoral appeal of 1957, have to be borne in mind. This preoccupation continued throughout Gomułka's rule. Soon after his coming to power, Poland launched a plan designed to indirectly enhance the country's security. The scheme was connected with the name of Adam Rapacki, a former Socialist, the only postwar Polish minister of foreign affairs who was a colorful as well as courageous and independently minded personality.

Rapacki was a member of an old Polish family with a long liberal

intellectual tradition and with social-democratic ties. After the unification of the Communist and Socialist parties in 1948, he held
various posts, but his most important role began in 1956, when he
became the minister of foreign affairs. Being a realist, Rapacki
viewed Poland's international position as it was, not as it might be.
He believed, therefore, that all moves in the field of foreign relations
should take as their point of departure the rigid international structure
of the postwar world and the existing balance of forces. Instead of
unrealistic efforts to achieve impossible dreams, the government
should use all avenues to raise the living standard, national culture,
and political education of the Polish people. In this line of reasoning
Rapacki and Gomułka were the successors of the National Democratic leader, Roman Dmowski. In a world divided between two
superpowers, neutralism was an impossibility. The first purpose of
Polish foreign policy, according to Rapacki, should be to contribute
as much as possible to the relaxation of tension between the two
camps, encouraging small steps to bring about international détente.
In a relaxed world there would be a greater role for the smaller states
that must exist and cultivate their own way of life in the shadow of
the superpowers.

Rapacki's ideas provided the philosophical background of the plan
to create a nuclear-free zone in Central Europe, a zone that would
consist of both East and West Germany, Czechoslovakia, and Poland. Its creation would be one of the first and important steps in
relaxing East-West tensions. The Soviet Union agreed to support
Poland's initiative, even though the project had rather different implications for the two countries. Poland, no doubt, hoped that the proposed "disengagement" might give it greater independence in relation to both Russia and West Germany, while for the Soviet Union
the plan would mean an atom-free zone to include West Germany and
a strengthening of its conventional forces compared with those of
NATO.[12] It was because of this change in the balance of conventional forces that the plan was rejected by the United States.

The suppression of the youth protests against the loss of academic rights and cultural freedom, the anti-Zionist campaign, and the participation in the invasion of Czechoslovakia in 1968 were among the most controversial actions of Gomułka's declining years. The principal goal of his strategy during the Czechoslovak crisis was to consolidate the Polish-Soviet alliance. From the beginning, he assumed a convergence of basic interests between Poland and the Soviet Union, for geopolitical and ideological reasons. Close relations with Moscow were the only safeguard of the country's external security and domestic stability, hence, Gomułka's efforts not to exceed permissible limits of internal autonomy but instead to practice coordination within subordination. Throughout the Czechoslovak crisis of 1968, by acting consistently along parallel lines with Moscow, Gomułka tried to reverse the endemic pattern of Russo-Polish mistrust and enmity.

The second factor behind Gomułka's pressure for intervention was his fear that the triumph of the liberals in Czechoslovakia would destabilize the domestic situation in Poland, still suffering from the aftermath of the Zionist purges and the "March events." The downfall of Antonin Nowotny and the emergence of Alexander Dubček were for Gomułka "a signal alarm of a gathering storm." [13] Despite the Czech and West German protestations that the rapprochement between Prague and Bonn was merely an innocent case of economic cooperation, Gomułka remained suspicious of the eventual effects of *Ostpolitik* on Prague. All Czech assurances of loyalty to the Warsaw Pact and COMECON notwithstanding, Gomułka, as a man schooled in Marxist dialectics, must have interpreted Prague's economic opening to the West as the first step in a broader and deeper cooperation between Czechoslovakia and the strongest of the NATO countries. Like Leonid Brezhnev, Gomułka must have viewed Czechoslovakia's evolution as representing not only a danger of revisionist contamination, but also a potential threat to the coherence of the East European Communist system, and especially to the stability of the East German regime, the survival of which was regarded as vital to Poland's integrity and security.

By loyally supporting the Soviet-led military invasion, Gomułka tried to persuade Moscow that it was possible to trust the Poles. This attitude was one of the most constant facets of his policy. The first precedent was set in October 1956, when he prevented a seemingly imminent violent outburst against Soviet domination, pacified the country, reasserted the leading role of the party, and bolstered Poland's ties with the Warsaw pact and COMECON countries. Since 1956 he had stuck to the bargain, limiting Poland's domestic autonomy and guaranteeing its loyalty to the USSR. The second precedent was established in August 1968, when against the pro-Dubček sentiments of his people, he ordered Polish troops to march along with other Warsaw pact partners.

In a conversation with this writer, a Polish historian compared Poland's participation in the Soviet-sponsored intervention with the behavior of the Poles in November 1830. At that time, Nicholas I had ordered the forces of the Polish Kingdom, of which he was constitutional ruler, to mobilize in order to send the Polish army westward as the vanguard of the imperial army to suppress the Belgian revolt. But the Poles had refused to march. This was the beginning of the uprising of 1830–31, which cost the country the loss of its limited but precious autonomy. The insurrections of 1794 and 1830–31, together with the uprising of 1863–64 and the diversionary role played by the Poles during the Russo-Japanese War of 1904–5, had helped create in the Muscovite mind an image of Poles as the most anti-Russian people in Europe, the eternal conspirators, rebels, and traitors to the Slavonic race. Gomułka tried to erase this negative image and create a new picture of Poles as reliable allies.

Thus, Gomułka, while bent on safeguarding what he considered as his country's fundamental interests, lost no opportunity to prove his loyalty to Russia. In this respect he followed in the footsteps of Roman Dmowski and his policy during the period 1904–14. The residue of National Democratic thinking was still rather strong in Poland, and Gomułka knew it: while condemning the "Endeks" for their conservatism and anti-Semitism, he often quoted Dmowski whenever the fundamentals of Russo-Polish relations were discussed.[14]

Another factor which, besides the Czechoslovak crisis, enhanced

Poland's position within the Communist camp was the Sino-Soviet split. Only a generation before, Roman Dmowski had bluntly warned his countrymen against getting involved in a conflict with Russia: "The time may come when those who are now dreaming about partitioning Russia will anxiously ask whether she is strong enough to withstand the pressure of China. . . . this moment may not be very far away." [15] Following again in the footsteps of Dmowski, Gomułka firmly ranged Poland in the pro-Russian camp. Prague's unreliability, as well as the intensification of the quarrel with Peking, had made Warsaw's loyalty valuable to Moscow. After China's defection from the Soviet camp, Poland became the largest and the most important ally of Moscow. Thus, the "Prague Spring" and the Sino-Soviet split catapulted Gomułka to a new position of prominence and prestige. The place previously occupied in the Soviet system by Czechoslovakia had been taken, at least partially, by Poland.

Soviet gratitude to Gomułka was displayed at the fifth congress of the United Polish Workers' party in Warsaw, in November 1968. At the congress, faced by the provincial party *aparat* (largely penetrated by Moczar's Partisans) and with Brezhnev watching the procedure, Gomułka was once again elected first secretary of the central committee.

The climax of Gomułka's career was reached on December 6–8, 1970, when he scored a great personal and political triumph by playing host to West German Chancellor Willy Brandt, who came to Warsaw to put his signature on the Warsaw-Bonn treaty acknowledging the Oder-Neisse line as a legitimate frontier of Poland. The fact that the country's western frontiers had already been guaranteed in the Soviet-West German treaty of September 1970 was deemphasized by official propaganda. Despite this limitation and the fact that Bonn had merely renounced the use of force in seeking to alter the Potsdam frontiers, Gomułka's success could not be denied. He had muddled through the events of 1967–68, the student revolt, and the Czechoslovak crisis. With the legitimizing of the new western boundaries of his country, Gomułka could apparently relax and enjoy his outwardly secure position of power and prestige. He was, however,

197

soon to be overtaken by the events that took place a week later on the Baltic coast.[16]

🙠 🙢

What happened in mid-December 1970 must be viewed against a broad background of events that had taken place in Poland since 1967–68, including the anti-Zionist and anti-intellectual campaigns. The former was a particularly sore spot on the record of Gomułka and the party, which had often invoked proletarian internationalism as one of its battle cries. In order to set it in a historic perspective, one has to remember some basic facts about the "Jewish problem." In 1939, the population of Poland was slightly more than 10 percent Jewish, or about 3,500,000 people. They were concentrated overwhelmingly in urban centers and engaged in trade, handicrafts, industry, and liberal professions. In the early 1930s, the Jews formed some 40 to 50 percent of the membership of the Communist party of Poland; earlier, in the 1920s, the percentage had been even higher.[17] On the other hand, since the party was really a tiny sect, its Jewish component constituted merely a fraction of the total Jewish population. It appears that many Polish Jews saw in Communism an ideology of universal brotherhood, and looked upon the Communist party as an instrument of transplanting to their country the highly idealized Soviet pattern. In a country as anti-Russian and anti-Communist as prewar Poland, the pro-Communist sentiments of many Jews were eagerly exploited by the native anti-Semites, who tended to identify Jewishness with Communism.

Following the Soviet occupation of eastern Poland in September 1939, many Jews fled to the area incorporated into the USSR. Most of the Polish-Jewish Communists, as well as some fellow travelers, eagerly offered their services to Moscow, spending the war years on Soviet soil working with great zeal for the USSR. In 1943, when Stalin took up the idea of extending Soviet power over Eastern Europe, they eagerly collaborated with his plans for a postwar Communist Poland. Among the "Muscovites," as opposed to the "natives," the Jews formed a much larger segment, and their actual influence went far beyond their numerical strength because they had

198

closer contacts with the Kremlin, especially its security organs, and were more skilled in displaying their pro-Soviet sentiments. After the war, when the two groups merged and formed the ruling elite of the Polish People's Republic, these differences and antagonisms continued to linger and were the basis of numerous personal and factional animosities.

Meanwhile, in the German-occupied parts of Poland, Hitler pressed his "final solution" of the Jewish question, and applied an almost equally cruel policy toward the educated elements of the Polish society. Some 6 million Polish citizens were annihilated by the Germans, and half of them were Jews.[18] As a result of the Nazi extermination and a gradual exodus, mostly to Israel (which Poland, unlike the Soviet Union, tolerated from the very beginning), the number of Jews in Poland by 1967 had dropped to some 30,000, or only about 0.1 percent of the population.

The Soviet takeover of Eastern Europe after World War II brought large numbers of Jews to high official positions in many countries, and Poland was no exception. According to an American historian, during that crucial period the Communist-oriented East European Jews played a significant role.

> Just below the summit of power, the party Jews tended to concentrate in certain ministries and functions. They congregated in the foreign ministry and the ministry of foreign trade, because they were almost the only ones whom the party could trust who had the requisite knowledge of foreign languages and high finance. They also flooded into the central committee and the security police, perhaps because they felt safer near the centers of decision-making. In Bucharest, Budapest, and Warsaw virtually every important police official was Jewish. . . . Often these police officials were survivors of Nazi extermination camps, and they did not let mercy or other humanitarian considerations stand in their way when it came to dealing with the class enemy. Indeed, many Jews were publicly associated with the extremist policy followed by the satellite regimes. . . .[19]

The emergence of Israel, and its increasingly pro-Western orientation, brought about a change in the pro-Soviet sentiments of many Jews, and in Stalin's policies toward them. Consequently, the years

🖎 The "Polish October"

1948–49 saw the launching in the USSR of a new phenomenon—an official Communist anti-Semitism presented in the form of anti-Zionism. During the last years of Stalin's regime there was a ruthless purge of most leading Soviet officials and intellectuals of Jewish origin, who were usually described as "rootless cosmopolitans." Parallel with these events, a far-reaching realignment of political forces took place throughout the Soviet orbit. The wave of brutal anti-Zionism gradually filtered down from Russia to Romania, Hungary, and Czechoslovakia, but during the 1950s had no effect in Poland.[20]

In 1955–56, the inner circle of the "Muscovites" abandoned their previous Stalinist attitude and sought to placate the people by small concessions and by paying lip service to more patriotic and liberal-sounding slogans. After the Poznań uprising, these now more moderate elements, often called the "Puławy faction," threw their support to Gomułka and the forces favoring the loosening of the Soviet controls over Poland.

The record of the Polish party and that of Gomułka personally as far as the Jews were concerned was somewhat better than that of other East European parties. Throughout his career Gomułka had many close Jewish co-workers and supporters, and his wife was of Jewish extraction. After the Poznań rising, when Moscow suggested that the Polish party put Minc and Berman on trial as scapegoats responsible for the sorry state of the Polish economy, the Poles refused to do so.[21] Khrushchev repeatedly chided Gomułka, saying that there were too many Jews in his party. A secretary of the Soviet embassy in Warsaw criticized the party for "Judaisation" of the Polish mass media, and urged creation of a national cadre of the PUWP free of Jews.[22] Despite this pressure there was no purge of the Jews, and until 1967 the Jewish members of the PUWP were relatively better off than in any other satellite ruling group with the possible exception of Hungary. The Polish state maintained many Jewish organizations, including the Jewish Historical Institute and the excellent Yiddish Theater of Warsaw, with its great star Ida Kamińska. The split between Gomułka and his Jewish comrades came only with the outbreak of the six-day Arab-Israeli war of June 1967.

200

The start of the war found the Polish mass media engaged in a rather perfunctory discussion of "the growing threat of Israeli aggression," but without the vehemence characteristic of Soviet propaganda. Henry Kamm, the *New York Times* correspondent in Warsaw, reported on June 13, 1967, that the sentiments of the Polish people were running strongly in favor of Israel, and that after the six-day war the Israeli embassy in Warsaw received numerous telegrams of congratulations. The overwhelmingly favorable, often enthusiastic reaction of the Polish public to the Israeli victory surprised and frightened the party leadership and was most embarrassing to Gomułka. The Soviets pressed Gomułka not to tolerate internal dissent and security risks in high positions. Accusing Tel Aviv of an act of aggression, Warsaw broke off diplomatic relations with Israel on June 12, 1967. It is noteworthy that a Catholic deputy, Konstanty Łubieński, had abstained from a resolution (officially reported as unanimous) passed on June 10 by the *Sejm* strongly condemning Israeli aggression.

A week or so after the break in diplomatic relations an intense domestic anti-Zionist campaign was launched by the party. In a speech of June 19, Gomułka issued a solemn warning to those who "applauded the Israeli aggression" and stressed that Poland would not tolerate a fifth column in its midst.[23] Soon, similar speeches were made by other leaders, including the defense minister, Marshal Spychalski. The anti-Zionist drive was dramatically stepped up. By December 1967 the campaign included a purge of high officials who had been compromised by their pro-Israeli stand or were regarded by Moscow as security risks. Some were ethnic Poles sympathetic to Israel, but the majority were Jews.

The stormy year 1967 was followed by a still more turbulent period. The already mentioned antigovernment student demonstrations of March 1968, partly influenced by the "Prague Spring," preceded the hot summer of that year and the launching of the Soviet-sponsored intervention against Czechoslovakia. The mass media immediately stressed that among the leaders of the March demonstrations, the Jews, as it happened, were rather numerous. Moreover,

201

it was stressed that the parents of several demonstrators held important state as well as party posts. These facts were seized upon to point out the existence of a widespread "Zionist-Revisionist plot" eager to push Poland towards an "irresponsible, anti-Soviet adventure" at the time of the Middle Eastern crisis.[24]

While the supporters of the demonstrations accused Moczar of having provoked the disturbances to deal the final blow to his opponents, his people launched the theory of a coup d'état. In the March 24, 1968, issue of *Prawo i Życie*, Kazimierz Kąkol, a mouthpiece for Moczar, argued that the party had been confronted with an attempt at overthrowing the existing leadership. According to the article, unnamed forces were trying to take advantage of the troubles in the international Communist movement to push plans for

> a political earthquake in 1968. . . . A conspiratorial group connected with the Zionist center was trying—under cover of patriotic and democratic slogans—to bring about an increase of demonstrations and street clashes which would raise the very question of the continuation of our rule and its present personnel. . . . We were faced with an attempt to strike at the leadership . . . with an attmpt at—I believe this is the proper phrase—a coup d'etat.[25]

As a result of the "March events," the purge of Jews in Poland's political, economic, and cultural life was intensified. On March 19, 1968, Gomułka, seeing that the whole affair was getting out of hand, delivered a speech in which he tried to tone down the campaign. He classified the Jews in Poland into three groups: first, the Zionists with open allegiance to Israel; second, the "cosmopolitans," with allegiance divided between Israel and Poland; and the third segment, composed of the "most numerous group, the true native sons." He suggested that the first group should feel free to leave Poland, while he advised the second category to "avoid the fields of work in which national affirmation is crucial." Those in the third group got high praise for their loyalty; he urged them to continue their good work. He declined to put the responsibility for the disturbances solely on Zionists, emphasizing that Zionism by itself was not a major threat to

202

Poland. The party's anti-Zionist drive "may have been misunderstood by some in the past," he stressed, condemning both anti-Semitism as well as Zionism as incompatible with the internationally oriented Communist doctrine.

Despite Gomułka's speech, the purge, which had acquired a momentum of its own, continued. Many people of Jewish extraction were removed from top-level party and state positions. Since the victims of the purge were allowed freedom of emigration, a mass exodus of Jews from Poland followed.[26]

Gomułka's anti-Zionist campaign is a bewildering event and cannot be understood in isolation from the broad trends affecting the Soviet imperial system in general. The role of Communists of Jewish descent in the Soviet takeover of Eastern Europe is in itself a puzzling phenomenon worth further study. It should be stressed that while Stalin was ruthlessly suppressing Jewish life and culture in the USSR, and purging individuals of Jewish extraction as "dangerous cosmopolitans" from practically all sensitive posts, he was still using East European Jewish Communists to further his designs in his new satellite empire. One must also bear in mind not only the Polish party's subservience to Moscow, but also the vital intrafactional struggle going on within the PUWP. Besides the previously mentioned clash between the "Muscovites" and the "natives," one should stress that the majority of the Jewish party activists, irrespective of their individual political past, had become after 1958–59 the core of the "liberal" opposition to Gomułka, the faction that pressed for the second stage of the "Polish October." Threatened by the revisionist offensive, Gomułka sought a measure of support among the Partisan faction. He failed to perceive that their anti-Semitic slogans would eventually be turned against him personally and against his essentially middle-of-the-road policy. On the other hand, feeling momentarily more threatened by the revisionists, he concluded a temporary tactical alliance with Moczar but without approving his anti-Semitism.

The ethnic and generational conflicts within the party were also important factors in the struggle. During the 1960s the aspirations of the

203

young *aparatchyki* (mostly ethnic Poles of proletarian or peasant background) for advancement grew more rapidly than the party's ability to promote them. Only an upheaval that would fundamentally shake the existing power structure could open new opportunities to the young, ambitious activists. Any careful observer of the Polish scene during the late 1960s was bound to notice this increasing pressure of the impatient, intolerant, and ruthless young people, eager to get rid of the usually better-educated party members of Jewish origin.

To the rivalry within the party structure one has to add the ambitions of some "native" intellectuals, jealously enhanced by certain echoes of their factional squabbles produced in the West. For more than a decade they had to watch with envy as their revisionist rivals were basking in the international limelight, lionized and cheered by Western leftist circles, while their own Marxist orthodoxy was summarily condemned as neo-Stalinist.

In 1967–68, the hour of the younger activists struck. They saw their opportunity coming, and they exploited it with the cold-blooded ruthlessness that they had been taught to consider a cardinal Bolshevik virtue. In a way, what happened in Poland in 1967–69 was similar to the process of replacement of the old revolutionary cadres of the CPSU that had taken place during the 1930s under Stalin. But unlike the earlier operations in the USSR, Czechoslovakia, Hungary, and Romania, the Polish purge involved no executions or imprisonment.

The changing social and ethnic structure of the party was a reflection of a profound transformation of Polish society after 1945. One of the most important of the socioeconomic changes that have taken place in Poland during the post-World War II years has been the urbanization of the country. It has involved a dramatic shift of the peasants into the cities and their influx into the party. This peasantization of the Polish party is a striking phenomenon. The prewar Communist party of Poland had been largely run by intellectuals of Jewish background. The Polish Workers' party and its successor, the present-day Polish United Workers' party, were at first strongly influenced by the survivals of this prewar Communist elite. But the postwar socioeconomic changes eroded the initially preponderant position of this small group. The events of 1967–68 dealt the final blow to the role of the Jews in the party.

The process has brought about a further "domestication" of the party, or the development of "a domestic perspective," which involved a "frequently unconscious preoccupation with local, domestic Communist objectives, at the expense of broader, international Soviet goals." Although this cannot be identified with national Communism of the Yugoslav type, the similarities are considerable.[27]

The anti-Zionist campaign had far-reaching repercussions. It affected Polish intellectual life, the structure of the party's leadership, and the national economy. Some of the country's leading economists, proponents of the reform, were victims of the purge. The reform preached by people like Professor Włodzimierz Brus was similar to the Hungarian New Economic Model and to the plans discussed in Czechoslovakia in 1968. Brus's suggestions also centered on regulated use of market mechanisms, including application of cost accounting, profit motive, and increased material incentives. Gomułka's opposition was determined. He well understood that economic reform had its inescapable political effects. The local party boss exercised his power the same way the old Tammany Hall man did his: by the simple fact that his word was law. The local chieftain had the final say on houses, rents, jobs, and who got what reward in his bailiwick. Every far-reaching economic reform raised the issue of how far the party could allow the changes to go without losing the political control necessary to rule effectively. One may imagine the following case: a factory manager who, under a new system, has authority to hire and fire, uses this power and fires a man who had obtained his job through the party. Who is to decide then whether the man is to go or to keep his job? In the atmosphere of the post-March 1968 days, Brus's projects were condemned by the party hardliners as a grafting of revisionist, bourgeois ideas on a Socialist economy, ultimately threatening the party's control of the national economy and

205

undermining the foundations of the system. His plans were rejected, and he was forced to emigrate together with other "Zionists." By this means, another attempt at economic reform was torpedoed.[28]

Meanwhile, the economic situation of the country was deteriorating. After 1960 the percentage of national income devoted to consumption continued to decline, while the accumulation of capital was on the increase, from 24.2 percent in 1960, to 28 percent in 1969. These figures were higher than the corresponding percentages in East Germany, Czechoslovakia, and Hungary. The rapid expansion of investments required a substantial increase in imports of industrial machinery and other equipment, and this, in turn, brought about a growing trade deficit. All this took place despite the stepped up export of food, especially meat. Such exports were continued at the expense of the home market, which was increasingly suffering from a faulty policy of inadequate prices paid by the state to cattle and hog breeders, as well as high prices for animal feed. Moreover, the expanded output of capital goods and the resulting shortage of consumer products had an adverse effect on the market equilibrium and intensified the already operating inflationary pressures. In November 1968 another price increase was decreed. All this further depressed the already low standard of living. During 1966–69, the real income of the people grew by 2.4 percent; during 1969–70 no growth was registered, even in the official statistical figures, which the people said resembled bikinis: they revealed the interesting while covering the essential. The economic stagnation deepened the accumulated bitterness, which was bound to erupt sooner or later.

The final showdown was brought about by the events of December 1970, the dramatic and bloody mass demonstrations in the Baltic coast cities of Gdańsk, Gdynia, Sopot, and Szczecin. The immediate cause of the uprising was another series of increases (up to 30 percent) in the prices of food and coffee, and the introduction of new industrial wage scales. The fact that the party undertook such strict measures drastically affecting the lives of every citizen, and coming at such an inappropriate moment (on the eve of Christmas), revealed the unresponsiveness of the leadership to the needs of the masses and the lack of contact between the party and the people.

The revolt bordered on civil war, with workers fighting the police and forming their own workers' committees and militia. The revolt was suppressed only with the support of the armed forces closely collaborating with the security apparatus. According to official publications, forty-five were killed and 1,165 wounded. Despite the bloodshed, the workers won on many scores. They gained a series of impressive economic successes and won an immediate withdrawal of the wage payment system that would have inflicted hardships. What was more significant, they forced Gomułka's resignation as first secretary of the central committee and compelled the party and the government to reshape their upper echelons. Gomułka was replaced by Edward Gierek, the former party boss in Silesia. Thus, the revolt of December 1970 was more than a series of bread riots: it amounted to another Communist reformation of the same caliber as that of 1956. For the second time in the history of postwar Poland, a workers' revolt forced a change of leadership which, without being fundamental, was nevertheless quite significant.[29]

The uprising had another significant aftermath. After the suppression of the revolt in Szczecin the workers of that city scored a telling victory, when, on Sunday, January 24, 1971, they compelled a group of top party leaders to come in person from Warsaw to hear the workers' grievances. The first secretary of the central committee, the prime minister, the minister of the interior, and the commander-in-chief of the armed forces all had to appear before the workers and spend some ten hours, from 4:00 p.m. to 2:00 a.m., negotiating with them in a free and most outspoken dialogue. What was noteworthy was that the party leaders gave in to most of the workers' demands.[30] Similar dialogues lasting some seven hours took place in Gdańsk, Łódź, and Białystok. No other Communist regime had experienced a similar phenomenon, which, at least temporarily, made the "dictatorship of the proletariat" a living reality.

A balance sheet of the fourteen-year Gomułka era is highly complex. In a way it is a story of continuous withdrawal from the achievements of October 1956. Yet, the "gains of October," although greatly eroded, had not been completely destroyed even by 1970. Mass terror as a systematic instrument of power was never restored; Soviet colonial exploitation of the country was mitigated; the peasants retained most of the land, and after 1956, Polish agriculture was on the upswing. Under Gomułka, cultural exchange with the West was never completely interrupted. Limited religious instruction was tolerated, although not without state hindrance and occasional nasty administrative tricks. On the other hand, the program of "democratization" of the party remained largely on paper: the party was ruled autocratically by Gomułka and a group of his henchmen. The attempted changes of the economic model were frustrated, and workers' councils were reduced to the role of harmless, largely decorative, debating circles. Private initiative in economic and social matters was discouraged and even penalized. On the whole, the pledge to better the lot of the common people was subordinated to forcible capital accumulation, the cost of which was largely borne by the working class.

However, the plight of Poland's economy during the 1960s should not overshadow the fact that during the years 1955–57, the Poles spearheaded the movement for economic as well as political reform within the Soviet camp, and that their example was regarded throughout Eastern Europe as a beacon to follow, almost on the same level as the Yugoslav experiment. During those years Poland provided a significant contribution to the reexamination of Marxist political and economic theory. The methods as well as the social objectives of the Stalinist system were openly criticized, its priorities reversed, and new, more humanistic alternatives outlined. Thus, the universality of the Soviet experience was squarely rejected.[31]

In perspective the most important gains of the "Polish October" were, perhaps, in the field of culture. During the late 1950s, Poland enjoyed more freedom and internal autonomy than any other member of the Communist camp. Socialist realism was ridiculed and softpedaled, if not formally abandoned altogether. East-West cultural exchanges were lively, and many Polish scholars and writers visited Western Europe and the United States, and vice versa. The films of Roman Polański and Andrzej Wajda, the music of Witold Lutosławski and Krzysztof Penderecki, the novels of Marek Hłasko and Jerzy Andrzejewski, the poetry of Zbigniew Herbert and Tadeusz Różewicz, the plays of Roman Branstaedter and Sławomir Mrożek, were known widely throughout the world. The new generation of Polish movies especially astonished the West. As Nicholas Bethell put it:

> Perhaps for the first time in her history Poland was, in certain fields, giving the world a cultural lead. The film is the verbal artform that can most easily break the language barrier, and Polish films were blazing a path for Poland into the mainstream of world intellectual attention.[32]

But all this could not be counterbalanced by Gomułka's extreme incompetence in economic matters, which cost the country enormous losses. His economic decisions in December 1970 and the bloody events that followed were a symptom of this growing estrangement from the great majority of the people. Thus, the man who in October 1956 came to power as a national hero, in December 1970 went down in disgrace as a hated and despised enemy of the people.

CHAPTER EIGHT

Gierek's "Renewal"

Among the many problems . . . which the political crisis revealed to the Party and the nation, one is foremost in our mind: how to avoid tragic upheavals in the future?

Władysław Kozdra, first secretary,
session of the PUWP central committee
held on February 6–7, 1971.

✍ THE WHIRLWIND that swept the Baltic cities in December 1970 profoundly frightened the Communist rulers of Poland. It propelled into power a new team led by the former Silesian party boss, Edward Gierek,[1] a man of genuine proletarian background with working-class experience in France and Belgium. More pragmatic than dogmatic, he believed the reasons for the discontent lay in the lack of adequate rewards which would provide the needed incentives for better work, in the neglect of the social and economic needs of the people, and in the gap separating the party from the populace as a whole.

In a radio and television speech on December 20, 1970, Gierek reversed the party's initial condemnation of the revolt and admitted that it was predominantly a manifestation of legitimate grievances of the working class. Three days later, in a speech to the *Sejm,* Gierek and Prime Minister Jaroszewicz pledged more housing, better food supplies, and a revision of the new wage system (including a 7 billion zloty increase for the lowest paid workers). They also rescinded the price increases and promised a two-year freeze on prices. Later on

210

the freeze was extended through 1975. After a few weeks of hesitation and hard bargaining with the workers of the Baltic seacoast, as well as of Łódź and Białystok, Gierek decided on suspension of the new wage scales and the boosting of the minimum pay rates, family allowances, and pensions. Soon, the current economic plans were revised to emphasize agriculture, consumer goods, and housing. The original Five-Year Plan for 1971–75 was redrafted and geared to satisfy the social and economic needs of the people rather than to fulfill quantitative targets. An inexpensive, small car and more houses were promised to Polish consumers.[2] The official negative attitude toward some 200,000 private enterprises in retail trade and services was toned down somewhat. Jobs were to be created for some 1.8 million people in order to provide full employment.[3]

At the same time, the government outlined and put into practice a new agricultural policy. The 10 million farmers who lived on 3.6 million small, private units won significant concessions from the state. Compulsory delivery quotas, which the farmers had to fulfill at artificially low, fixed prices, were abolished, private ownership of land consolidated, and indivisibility of small farms established. At the same time, social security and an all-inclusive free health service were extended to private farmers and their families. Thus, no social class benefited more from Gierek's new agrarian policy than the individual farmers. Besides increased income, he gave them a sense of economic security they had not enjoyed under Gomułka.

While the economic position of workers and farmers was improved, efforts were also undertaken to bolster relations with the disgruntled and sulking intellectuals. In 1971–72 censorship was relaxed somewhat. The party abandoned the policy of suppressing the works of certain writers, particularly Stefan Kisielewski, Antoni Słonimski, Jerzy Andrzejewski, Wiktor Woroszylski, and Paweł Jasienica, although some of their writings continued to be banned. Some writers, like Kisielewski and Słonimski, previously ostracized, were permitted to go abroad. Funds allotted to scholarly research were increased dramatically; by 1975 they amounted to 2.5 percent of the GNP and were scheduled to increase to 4 percent by 1980. Scholars were in-

211

vited to advise the party and the government on various problems, including the economy and education.

In less sensitive, nonpolitical areas, Gierek proved to be liberal. For instance, at the beginning of his rule, as a gesture to appease his rebellious countrymen, Gierek decided to allow the reconstruction of the royal castle in Warsaw. For a long time this had been an ardent wish of the great majority of Poles, both at home and abroad, but the stubborn Gomułka had refused. The issue of the Warsaw castle, as well as Gierek's radio speeches and frequent visits to various provincial centers, were the most significant steps taken by the party in its effort to build bridges to the man-in-the-street and to create a new political climate. Not Communist ideology, but "historic tradition," was stressed in appeals for funds to rebuild the castle.[4]

Unlike his predecessor, Gierek also traveled widely throughout Poland. During 1971 alone he attended 187 various grass-roots meetings. He held conferences with factory committees, listened to workers' grievances, and made himself available for questioning and debate. In his speeches, Gierek avoided the Marxist, abstract style so characteristic of Gomułka, and used instead a more colloquial language. A new daily television program called "Citizen's Tribune" was established, on which different officials answered questions telephoned in by viewers.

But the initial relaxation of censorship was soon followed by a reimposition of some controls. This especially affected more independently minded publications and writings on contemporary history. The jamming of foreign broadcasts was reintroduced, and repeated warnings left no doubt that the party was determined not to tolerate any meaningful cultural plurality. Thus, the end of the Gomułka regime brought only a limited change in the regime's cultural policy.[5]

Gierek's pragmatic economic policy produced some striking short-term successes. The years 1970–74 witnessed a considerable growth of the GNP, as well as in labor productivity, and in the standard of living, especially in the countryside. The progress was rooted in three factors. The first was large-scale imports, especially of consumer goods, as well as the purchase of several hundred foreign licenses, most of them on credit. The second element of Gierek's momentary success was the decision to selectively modernize industry, which was greatly aided by these foreign licenses. The slight decentralization of management of economic enterprises and the granting to individual directors of greater initiative in the running of their factories, to satisfy both export needs and requirements of the domestic market, were minor contributing factors. Thus, the slight shift from a command to a market economy not only did not hamper the growth of investment (as classic Soviet doctrine maintains), but quite the contrary; the mobilization of human energy and the utilization of hitherto dormant reserves resulted in accelerated growth. Last, but not least, a new, more Bukharinist policy toward the small farmer was a major factor behind the marked economic improvement of 1971–74.[6]

The question of how long such stimuli will operate, and whether short-term successes would lead to long-range troubles, are another matter. Fast-growing foreign indebtedness may be a problem in the future unless the credits are utilized speedily and to their full extent. Moreover, while investing heavily in selected branches of industry, Gierek seems to be neglecting to modernize many old ones, which may become a source of serious trouble in the future. These piecemeal moves, like Gierek's political reforms, are all changes within existing patterns. No serious attempt has been made at a fundamental, qualitative change in the existing economic model. Yet, what Poland needs is not patchwork measures, but a thorough reform of its economy.

Although there have been noteworthy gains in industrial and agricultural production, labor productivity, real wages, and national income since 1971, considerable imbalances persist between imports and exports, the tempo with which investments are completed, and earned and distributed income. In 1973, for instance, produced national income rose by 10 percent, while distributed income increased by 13 percent. Moreover, in spite of price freezes on basic food products, the government has not been able to prevent a noticeable rise in the overall prices of consumer goods and services, especially food.[7]

Gierek's "Renewal"

In 1974 imports rose by 33.2 percent over 1973 and exports by only 29.5 percent, with the result that the deficit in the balance of payments increased by 49.5 percent. It seems that some of the difficulties encountered by Polish foreign trade and the deficit may be a result of the economic consequences of the politically motivated drive for a higher standard of living; this has created expectations that are difficult to satisfy. On the other hand, a considerable part of the reason for such a jump in the deficit is that the cost of imports of vital raw materials, capital goods, and sophisticated complete industrial installations reflected the effects of inflation much more keenly than did exportable goods, which consisted mainly of raw materials, foodstuffs, and agricultural produce. In the long run Gierek's program of "renewal" may depend on the strength of his determination to reform the system of management and planning and to make domestic industries produce enough consumer goods and housing to satisfy growing needs.

In the serious balance of payments situation, food and coal are the two most marketable resources Poland possesses, with copper, sulfur, and ships next.[8] It was food that was the main topic of the two-day state farms' cadres conference held in Warsaw on January 27, 1975. Apparently, in the minds of the authorities, the necessity of providing food overshadows the question of the cost of its production. Consequently, doubling the output by 1990 remains the top priority, with a pledge of continued backing for the private farmers. On the other hand, the party has repeatedly stated that its ultimate goal, a socialized agriculture, has not been abandoned, and that it is determined to strive toward this end by all means short of compulsion and administrative pressure. The party's relentless drive toward socialized agriculture is facilitated by the fact that one in three private farms is run by a farmer more than 60 years of age. Nearly three-quarters of a million farmers quit working the land between 1970 and 1973, and as many again are likely to move out in the next few years.[9]

The 1970 rebellion was closely tied with some striking anomalies in Polish-Soviet economic relations. In addition to protesting against

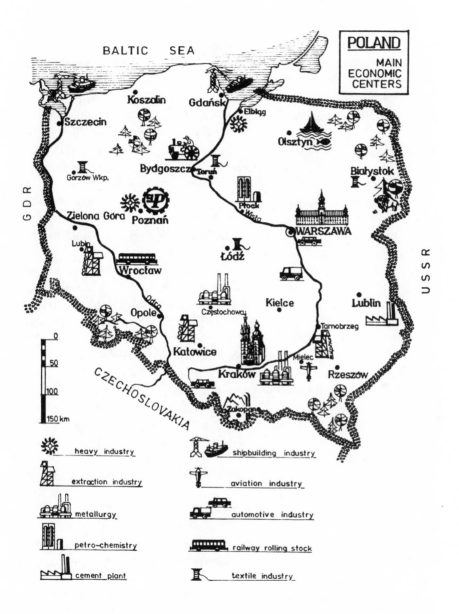

POLAND
MAIN ECONOMIC CENTERS

heavy industry

extraction industry

metallurgy

petro-chemistry

cement plant

shipbuilding industry

aviation industry

automotive industry

railway rolling stock

textile industry

the increase in food prices, the shipbuilding workers manifested their indignation toward the camouflaged exploitation of their country by the powerful eastern neighbor. During the previous two decades Poland had supplied the USSR with some 3 million tons of shipping; in fact, one-fourth of the entire Soviet merchant marine was of Polish construction. The export of ships to the Soviet Union, while keeping the Polish Baltic wharves busy, has actually been disadvantageous— the Poles not only had to build the ships, often being subject to haughty and capricious treatment from arrogant Soviet officials, but also had to fit and maintain the vessels with costly equipment such as radar, which the Poles themselves had to import from the West. In this way the Poles had to spend a large part of their hard currency reserves obtained from their export to non-Communist countries, the export which had been, until recently, generally on the whole favorable to Poland.

One of the ways of obtaining the surplus of hard currency necessary for importing the costly equipment required by the demanding Soviet master was an intensified export of Polish agricultural products. It was this export that exacerbated the shortage of meat, caused essentially by the lowering of prices paid by the state to farmers for hogs. Both these factors, but primarily the first, created acute food shortages and necessitated a rise in food prices. The workers knew about these facts and their indignation was a factor contributing to the outburst. Gierek's protestations in Moscow seem to have had some immediate effect. The negotiations conducted by him in the Soviet capital at the beginning of 1971 brought about not only a loan of $100 million, but also changes in the terms of trade between Poland and the USSR. Soviet credits in foreign currency were given, it seems, as a sort of compensation for past losses suffered by the Poles. Moreover, Gierek apparently obtained "now, fairer prices," as the official communiqué put it, for Polish exports to the Soviet Union. The expression "fairer prices" was in itself an admission that the old rates had not been fair. These were not negligible gains, since they affected some one-third of all Polish exports.

One has to assume that Gierek had also been granted Moscow's

216

blessing for Poland's intensified commercial contracts with the West. If Polish goods, including ships, were to be of high quality, the main source of superior (i.e., Western) technology had to be made more accessible to Polish producers. Since 1971, Poland's trade with the USSR and other Communist countries has decreased, while it has expanded considerably with capitalist countries of the West and with the Third World. Plans for 1971–75 provided for an annual expansion of foreign trade by 11 percent, a tempo faster than the rate of growth of the economy as a whole. Yet Poland's economic dependence on its eastern neighbor is still staggering. From the USSR, Poland receives practically all its oil, 85 percent of its iron ore, 65 percent of its raw cotton, and a large part of its machinery. In addition, Polish commercial aviation is entirely dependent on Soviet supplies.[10]

The global energy crisis also introduced new factors into Polish-Soviet relations. By the end of 1973 the higher oil prices imposed by the Organization of Petroleum Exporting Countries (OPEC) finally hit Poland. Brushing aside objections, Moscow scrapped the earlier five-year trade agreements with the East Europeans and doubled the price of oil from $3 to $6 a barrel. For political reasons the Russians kept the price considerably lower than the world market price, and allowed the East Europeans to buy the oil, as well as other Soviet raw materials, without having to pay hard Western currency. The USSR also agreed to pay updated, higher prices for the manufactured goods their vassals produce, but all these concessions do not fully compensate for the rise in raw material quotations.[11] The higher oil prices and rocketing costs of imports from the inflation-ridden West began affecting Polish price levels, which had been artificially maintained by means of considerable subsidies. Consequently, the Polish people seem certain to face much greater inflation or shortages, or both. This adds another snag to Gierek's economic plans, one of such magnitude that in the long run it was bound to have adverse political repercussions.

Another potentially explosive problem is the increasing difficulty of finding enough jobs for young people entering the labor market. Officially a socialist economy can have no unemployment or depression, just as a Diesel engine can have no spark plug troubles. There is, however, obviously a great amount of underemployment, both in the cities and in the countryside, which is not revealed in statistical publications but is visible to the naked eye. The pace in most Polish factories is often easygoing, and there is no air of hard-driving effort. The problem of what to do with the surplus labor is serious. Mass labor migration, an accepted phenomenon of economic life in Western Europe since the early 1960s, has recently become more common also in the Soviet orbit. The two most industrially advanced countries, East Germany and Czechoslovakia, import the most foreign labor, and Poland, with its considerable surplus of manpower, has been their principal supplier.[12]

Despite the considerable economic advances under Gierek, present conditions still fall short in satisfying popular aspirations, and everyday life in Poland is still difficult. It is said that in order to support a family, a Pole must hold down two full-time jobs and have a deal on the side. The need for housing is acute, and a young couple seeking an apartment with an area of about 400 square feet is likely to have to wait six to eight years. Families of four to five people often live in two or three rooms, sharing a kitchen and toilet facilities with neighbors. A baby carriage may cost as much as a month's salary. The housewife seldom plans a menu in advance, for she cannot be sure that the items she requires will be available at the shops. Waiting in line for groceries is a part of the daily shopping routine.

The first signs of a growing impatience because of food shortages, especially meat, appeared during the early months of 1975. The first official admission of trouble was made on March 6, 1975, when Gierek and Jaroszewicz, speaking to Polish women, took great pains to explain the causes of these shortages and asked for patience and understanding. The problem was judged by the leadership to be serious enough to warrant providing a safety valve in the form of limited public discussion. In its issue of April 5, 1975, the most important party weekly, *Polityka,* published a number of letters from angry readers complaining about the shortage of meat and trying to explain the causes. The letters revealed that the problem became acute as

218

early as mid-January and continued into the summer.[13] The dissatisfaction of the people was based more on disillusionment with the failure to meet the great expectations raised by the new ruling team after December 1970 than with any actual drop in living standards.

✍ ✍

In his policy of "renewal," Gierek also made a conciliatory gesture to appease, at least partially, one of the Roman Catholic hierarchy's more pressing grievances: he promised to restore to the church's ownership 7,000 of the sequestered church buildings, chapels, monasteries, and parish halls in the western territories. But these promises were never fully implemented. Only a fraction of 1,000 churches asked for by Cardinal Wyszyński were allowed to be constructed in various new localities, including the industrial town of Nowa Huta, near Cracow. Nowa Huta, with more than 100,000 inhabitants, had been denied the right for two decades to build its own church, despite considerable popular pressure. There were also numerous cases of refusal to grant similar permission in other localities in almost equal need of appropriate places of worship. Moreover, there were instances of the militia dismantling churches and chapels begun before the formal granting of the promised building permits.

One of the major stumbling blocks to establishing normal diplomatic relations with the Vatican was Warsaw's insistence that the church officially recognize the Oder-Neisse line. The Vatican was unwilling to take this step before the signing of a formal peace treaty. The obstacle was removed by the ratification by the Bonn parliament of the Polish-West German treaty of December 1970, legitimizing the post-World War II frontiers. On June 28, 1972, six Polish bishops were appointed to the dioceses in the western lands acquired from Germany. This step by the Vatican finally legalized the ecclesiastical authority of the Polish church in these territories and thus implicitly recognized the western boundaries of Poland. A significant symptom of the détente between Warsaw and the Vatican was the visit of the Polish foreign minister, Stefan Olszewski, to Pope Paul VI on November 12, 1973. In 1974 a working group of diplomats was established at the Polish embassy in Rome to continue the confidential contacts aiming at a formal accommodation between the Polish People's Republic and the Holy See.

Negotiations have since been opened with the hierarchy to settle other outstanding problems of the state-church relationship, but they have made little progress. The main stumbling block has been the education reform aimed at limiting the family's and the church's influence on youth, while strengthening that of the party. Moreover, the authorities have continued to pursue their line of harassing the remaining courses in religious instruction and of insisting on Marxist instruction for children. Repeated attempts to draft students at Catholic theological seminaries for military service, contrary to the church-state agreement of 1950, have also embittered the atmosphere. On June 18, 1973, the Roman Catholic bishops formally protested the national educational reform as "including elements hostile to religious upbringing," and accused the country's state-run schools of teaching atheistic principles and undermining the religious motivation of children. The hierarchy stressed that the reform, because of the long school day and the consolidated parish schools, will make it more difficult to organize religious education classes. A protest against the regime's discrimination toward Catholics was also raised by Janusz Zabłocki, the vice-chairman of *Znak,* a small parliamentary group of Catholic deputies, in his *Sejm* speech of December 17, 1973.[14]

Despite some limited and hesitant concessions granted to the church in the negotiations with the Vatican, the diametrically contrary objectives of the two rivals were bound to result in difficulties. The Polish hierarchy was apprehensive that in their eagerness to reach an accord, Vatican diplomats might not guarantee the legitimate interests of Polish Catholics. At the 145th National Bishops' Conference, held on November 26–27, 1974, they warned that the normalization of relations between the Vatican and Warsaw would be complete and lasting only if preceded by the normalization of church-state relations within the country. Similarly, the 146th conference, held on January 15–16, 1975, insisted that the citizens' right to free-

220

dom of conscience and religion was among the most basic of human rights, and emphasized the bishops' determination to do everything in their power to keep the church in Poland a protector of these rights.[15]

The Vatican's *Ostpolitik* has persistently tried to bring about some sort of normalization with Warsaw as a stepping stone to its farther-reaching goal of an eventual accommodation with the Soviet Union. This tendency has found its expression in intense behind-the-scenes negotiations and in a series of visits of various Vatican diplomats to Poland. Archbishop Luigi Poggi, since November 1974 the chief Vatican delegate for contacts with the Polish government, visited Poland in February and March 1975. Poggi's mission was not limited to meetings with government officials, but involved close contacts with members of the hierarchy and an extended tour of the country's dioceses, seminaries, and other ecclesiastic and lay institutions. The content of Poggi's official negotiations has been indirectly revealed by the most formidable opponent of normalization at any price, Cardinal Wyszyński. On March 16, 1975, he delivered in Warsaw's St. Michael church a sermon in which he assessed current developments in church-state relations. According to a UPI report from Warsaw on March 16, the cardinal told his congregation that:

> When the representative of the Holy See arrives in Poland, it is not enough to discuss peace between nations and talk about securing people against hunger in the world, which is what we read in the recent communique released by the Polish news agency.

The cardinal warned that true accord would come only if the negotiations focused on the problems of the Polish church and not on broad international issues. He restated firmly that the bishops would reject any agreement that ignored internal problems but would support an accord taking into account a possible alleviation of the problems Catholics faced in Poland. What the bishops wanted was a "religious truce," giving freedom to the church and its followers.[16]

To counter the rumors about the differences of opinion persisting between the Holy See and the Polish hierarchy, Poggi stressed that the normalization of relations with the Vatican would be carried out with the full agreement of the Polish primate, the bishops, and the clergy.[17]

⤢ ⤣

Since the spring of 1971 there has been a marked improvement in Poland's relations with the West, especially with the United States. The turning point was President Richard Nixon's visit in Warsaw on May 31 and June 1, 1972, the first visit by a United States chief executive to Poland. The trip was followed by President Gerald Ford's stopover in Warsaw, Cracow, and Auschwitz on July 28 and 29, 1975, on his way to the Helsinki conference on European security. In both cases the correct, but not demonstrative official receptions stood in contrast to the tumultuous welcomes from the crowds. The presidential visits were followed by a series of political, economic, and cultural agreements intended to bring the two countries closer together. Air and sea connections as well as cultural exchanges were expanded, and a consular agreement concluded. Gierek paid a return visit to the United States in October 1974.

Despite the 1973 war in the Middle East, Polish-U.S. relations continued to improve, largely because of the discovery of a mutual stake in meeting the energy crisis. Increased American attention to conservation of oil and to antipollution measures coincided with a return to coal as a major source of energy, thus opening a United States market for low-sulfur Polish coal. During 1974, Poland became a major exporter of hard coal to America. The United States was also interested in Polish coal-mining techniques, which were said to be considerably more advanced than U.S. methods. As a result of this, trade between the two countries more than doubled. In November 1975, Poland agreed to buy an average of 2.5 million tons of American feed grain annually for the next five years. In 1973 trade with the United States exceeded $500 million and it was expected to reach $2 billion by the end of the decade. Many private American companies have been doing business in Poland, including Universal Oil Products, International Harvester, and Universal Marketing Systems.[18]

Along with the efforts to bolster relations with the West, the party

222

has been trying to improve its image, so badly tarnished by the anti-Zionist campaign of 1967–68. Among the steps taken were an annual official observance of the heroic uprising by the Jews of the Warsaw ghetto in World War II; [19] the granting of funds for a new building to house the Jewish Theater in Warsaw, and for rebuilding the ancient Jewish temple at Tłomackie; and the opening of confidential negotiations for resumption of diplomatic relations with Israel.

While, on the whole, there was a tendency toward improved relations with the West in 1974 and 1975, the newly established and still tenuous relations between Warsaw and Bonn reached a new low during that same period. The thorniest of several issues dividing the countries was the problem of indemnities to the Polish victims of Nazi terror. It was difficult to explain to these Poles why they should be forgotten when indemnities had been promised to Soviet Jews leaving the USSR. [20] In addition, there was the question of the resettlement of ethnic Germans, the problem of credits, an agreement on pension and insurance claims, and Poland's deficit in its trade with West Germany. An agreement on these issues was finally reached in an eight-hour meeting in Helsinki between Edward Gierek and West Germany's chancellor, Helmut Schmidt. Bonn would give the Poles $500 million to satisfy any outstanding pension claims, and a further $400 million trade credit would be granted at low interest rates. The pension-claims agreement marked another gesture of West German atonement for the occupation of Poland and the horrors committed there during World War II. In exchange, Poland agreed to let 120,000–125,000 ethnic Germans emigrate to West Germany over the next four years. [21] Gierek's visit to West Germany marked further improvement of Warsaw's relations with Bonn.

🖋 🖋

In line with trying to improve relations with the non-Communist countries, the Gierek regime has paid considerable attention to some 8 to 10 million Polish émigrés living in the West, mainly in the United States, Canada, Brazil, Great Britain, and France. Unitl 1956 the emigrants had been criticized and ostracized by Warsaw as representing backward and thoroughly reactionary forces. Between 1956 and 1970 the old policy alternated with occasional clumsy and reluctant attempts at making gestures of reconciliation. This attitude was reversed under Gierek. In 1971 a vigorous offensive was launched to regain the confidence and cooperation of Poles living abroad. Considerable sums of money were earmarked for propaganda, and several institutions were created for that purpose. The main goal of this campaign was to win the support of the émigrés for the regime and thus diminish the corroding influence of any remaining centers of opposition still surviving abroad.[22]

The government's change in policy was in itself a tribute to the strength of the Polish diaspora. Gierek understood that the Poles abroad, or "Polonia," as they are collectively called, were a significant force, not only because of their numbers, but also because of their composition. A large part of the intellectual elite did not return to their native country after the war. Included were such prominent writers as Jan Lechoń, Kazimierz Wierzyński, Józef Wittlin, Witold Gombrowicz, Józef Łobodowski, Tadeusz Nowakowski, to mention only a few. Some well-known writers like Czesław Miłosz, Marek Hłasko, and Sławomir Mrożek left Poland and settled abroad. Also, numerous scholars from both the pre- and postwar periods decided to live in exile; in this latter group were Jan Kucharzewski, Oskar Halecki, Henryk Paszkiewicz, Marian Kukiel, Wacław Lednicki, and Wiktor Weintraub. Some 2,000 teach now at institutions of higher learning on the North American continent alone. Some of these scholars are playing a considerable role in academic life as well as in American politics as advisers on national security and foreign affairs (for example, Professor Zbigniew Brzeziński of Columbia University). Important publications like *Wiadomości* in London, *or Kultura* in Paris, penetrate into Poland by various channels and exercise a considerable influence on the minds of the people. There are also Polish desks at such various radio stations as the Voice of America, Radio Free Europe, and the London BBC. Poles abroad thus have a direct affect on the climate of opinion prevailing in Poland—through their writings, broadcasts, personal contacts, and parcels, as well as

224

through the money sent to their families and friends in the old country.

🖎 🖎

In addition to pursuing his broad program of "renewal," Gierek had to deal with the party which was still shot through with the men owing allegiance to his main rival and temporary ally, Mieczysław Moczar. During 1971, Gierek was able to remove Moczar and many of his henchmen from positions of power. The sixth PUWP congress, convened in Warsaw in December 1971, gave sanction to these and other moves. Among the most significant changes, besides the removal of Moczar from the politburo, was the dropping from this top policymaking body of two key people of the Gomułka era: the minister of foreign affairs, Stefan Jędrychowski, and Józef Cyrankiewicz; the latter had been prime minister almost without interruption from 1948 until 1970. Although a highly skillful politician, Cyrankiewicz had discredited himself once more during the 1970 upheavals by delivering a militant antistrike speech, similar to the one he had made against the Poznań workers in June 1956. Cyrankiewicz was now removed not only from the politburo, but also from chairmanship of the state council, where he was replaced by Professor Henryk Jabłonski, a historian from the University of Warsaw.[23] Within a year after the December 1970 upheaval, Gierek had considerably bolstered his position in the top echelons of the party. Despite this, his hold on the lower and middle levels of the PUWP was not as secure because of the lingering influence of Moczar's Partisans. A further reshaping of the party was intertwined with the two-step administrative reform, which was also indirectly connected with Gierek's struggle to restructure the party. The first far-reaching reshaping of the administrative structure that took place on January 1, 1973, was the introduction of consolidated rural communes (*gminy zbiorowe*). It involved the merging of over 4,300 rural administrative entities into some 2,350 larger units; this change, while eliminating much red tape and parochialism, also enabled the party to exercise greater control over the rural communes.[24]

225

ᕲ Gierek's "Renewal"

The second stage of the administrative reform reduced the existing three tiers of the territorial administration to two by eliminating the middle level, or the 314 districts (*powiaty*) roughly corresponding to American counties. Most of the executive functions of the districts were taken over by the lower of the two remaining tiers—i.e., the communes (*gminy*) and towns, while their control prerogatives of the former districts passed to the higher level, i.e., the provinces, or voivodships (*województwa*). The existing twenty-two voivodship units (seventeen voivodships and five independent cities) were split into forty-nine units, of which forty-six were classified as voivodships and three as city voivodships. In the latter category were Warsaw Metropolitan, Cracow Municipal, and Łódź Municipal. Such important urban centers as Poznań and Wrocław lost their independent status. Under the new system each province consisted of fifty to sixty basic units, communes, or towns. Poland's administrative structure was thus simplified, with the country divided into forty-nine provinces and 2,365 communes. To help implement the reform, a party-government team was established, and the existing ministry of area planning and environmental protection was transformed into the ministry of local administration, area planning, and environmental protection.

Gierek was well aware that the elimination of over 300 counties and the unseating of many district chieftains linked by bonds of comradeship with other local officials was bound to cause a great deal of dissatisfaction. About 13 percent of local administrators lost their jobs. To coat this bitter pill, Gierek and Premier Jaroszewicz promised to absorb the deposed officials into the newly created voivodships or into other government bodies.

Despite official rhetoric to the contrary, there was definite political motivation behind the reform. It offered the opportunity to remove many of Moczar's sympathizers from positions of authority, and it enabled the regime to rid itself of many older party members who had been promoted to responsible administrative positions mainly as a result of their political connections, and who were now obviously unfit to serve with a modicum of competence. These old party func-

226

tionaries caused many problems for the new leadership, which was bent on modernization and efficiency. With a growing number of younger and better-trained individuals who satisfied the requirements of both efficiency and ideology, Gierek decided to get rid of the deadwood or to shift them to positions where they would do less harm. With the quick implementation of the two-stage administrative reform, Gierek was able to curb the local government and party machine, recentralize national authority, and further consolidate his own position in power.[25]

Gierek also made a valiant effort to tighten the ideological training of his party cadres. After the sixth party congress of 1971, a new three-step system of general party training, mandatory for every PUWP member, was given special attention. The same year the Higher School of Social Sciences, abolished by Gomułka in 1968, was reestablished and expanded. In 1973, Gierek merged the country's five youth organizations into a new group called the Federation of the Socialist Unions of Polish Youth. The purpose of the federation was to tighten the party supervision of the hitherto quite separate youth organizations. Thus, in the era of détente and of potentially easier flow of people and ideas (interpreted by the Communist world as that of "ideological confrontation" with Western capitalistic ideas!), Gierek stressed a better organizational grip on the key institutions of the country.

🖋 🖋

Although Gierek has pursued a more pragmatic policy than his predecessor, he realizes that good relations between Poland and the Soviet Union are of paramount importance to the very existence of the Polish People's Republic and its ruling group. On the other hand, the Soviet Union, after the Czechoslovakian experience of 1968, has been careful to refrain from too open an intervention in Polish affairs.

Gierek's pragmatic approach has led him toward economic, technocratic, and organizational solutions that will not endanger the foundations of the system. The emphasis on modernization and institu-

227

tion-building has been paralleled by an effort to consolidate the party and to restore its sagging discipline and ideological motivation. This he has accomplished basically through an alteration in the style of leadership, through updating the existing system and satisfying minor grievances.

But the path is rent by two conflicting and perhaps irreconcilable requirements: to placate the powerful protector, and to keep the continuing specter of domestic dissatisfaction to manageable proportions. The pressure on the party from below has been mounting steadily and the progressive erosion of the official ideology continues. And as this occurs, the suspicion of the Soviet Union will be aroused only further.

Many Poles seems skeptical about the long-term prospects for reform and about the willingness of Moscow to implement the Helsinki declaration of 1975, and to allow such liberal reforms as free flow of information or the right to travel. According to William Rademakers, *Time* magazine's chief European correspondent:

> In contrast to the enthusiasm of their leaders, the vast majority of Eastern Europeans appear to be either indifferent or cynical about the Security Conference. At worst, they regard it as an extension of the 1945 Yalta Conference which delivered Eastern European into the Soviet sphere. At best, they acknowledge that it puts some pressure on Communist regimes to relax travel restrictions, gives easier access to Western information, and perhaps slightly widens the room for maneuver between the Soviet and East European brands of Communism. There are no longer any illusions in Eastern Europe about crusades for freedom. These were shattered by Soviet tanks in East Berlin in 1953, in Budapest in 1956, and in Prague in 1968. That is why the documents to be signed in Helsinki are creating so little interest among the peoples of Eastern Europe. In the absence of any hope for political freedom, they have turned to the pursuit of materialistic goals: a summer cottage, a Japanese stereo set or—the greatest of all Communist status symbols—a new car.[26]

No lasting changes in Poland's domestic structure are possible as long as the country remains within the Soviet sphere. And any attempt to alter the status quo, let alone leave this orbit, would be suicidal, as proved in the cases of Hungary and Czechoslovakia. Thus, Gierek walks the tightrope between the Kremlin and his own people, and the nation's international and domestic policies are inexorably bound together. Poland under Gierek approaches the last quarter of the twentieth century in a mixed mood of scepticism, cynicism, and hope. With the experiences of the past, including the post-1956 era, the people of Poland remain apprehensive and suspicious.

The latter part of 1975 and the first half of 1976 were marked by two significant controversies that both ended with the tactical withdrawals by the regime: the constitutional issue and the problem of food pricing. The guidelines published in September 1975 for the approaching seventh party congress in December stated that the 1952 constitution should be amended in order to acknowledge the PUWP's leading role in state affairs:

> The historic fact that the Polish People's Republic is a socialist country, in which the power belongs to the working people of towns and villages and the leading force is the Polish United Workers' Party, must be confirmed in the Constitution.[27]

The guidelines suggested the insertion into the constitution of language that would stress Poland's "unshakable bond with the Soviet Union." They also proposed the existence of a link between fulfillment of duties in the task of "Socialist construction" and exercising of basic civil rights by the citizens of People's Poland.

The project met with stiff and widespread opposition, especially on the part of Polish intellectuals, various groups of whom protested the proposed changes. The signatories of numerous letters and petitions submitted to state authorities opposed the alteration as incompatible with the spirit of the Helsinki conference and called instead on the authorities to guarantee all citizens the full pursuit of such fundamental human rights as freedom of conscience and religion, of work, of

229

expression and information, of scholarly research and learning. The nationwide protest against the constitutional changes proposed by the party was soon joined by the Catholic hierarchy. On several occasions, Cardinal Wyszyński voiced the bishops' serious apprehensions over the alterations of the constitution, the consequences of which, it was feared, would turn out to be far-reaching, and came out with a request that the regime put into actual practice the civil rights granted by the 1952 constitution to all citizens irrespective of religion, philosophy, or party affiliation.

In view of the widespread opposition, the government took a cautious line. On February 10, 1976, at the final session of its term of office, the *Sejm* adopted only minor amendments to the 1952 constitution. The amendments contained such provisions as the definition of People's Poland as a "Socialist" state, with the PUWP as "the leading political force in society in the construction of Socialism," and a reaffirmation of the alliance with the USSR.[28] In effect, while the two basic points, the Socialist character of the state and its reliance on the Soviet Union for political support and defense, have remained in force, the government camouflaged them in a cocoon of generalities. Such provisions as a possible denial of civil rights to those failing to fulfill their duties toward the state, were essentially rewritten. Finally, important concessions were added canceling the severe legal punishments previously incurred by persons abusing their civil rights in a way harmful to the state.

Another crisis was precipitated by the announcement of steep rises in food prices, especially of meat, which unleashed a series of strikes and riots in various industrial centers of the country, especially in Radom in central Poland. The riots were suppressed and severe sentences were imposed on thirteen persons identified with the most turbulent actions, while another 53 people were punished for lesser offenses. But the government, mindful of similar events in December 1970, hurriedly withdrew the proposed price rises. Nevertheless, the persisting shortages of food compelled the regime to introduce a program of sugar rationing.[29]

The reaction of the government to both crises testifies to its acute awareness of the latent hostility of public opinion to any further tightening of the political controls or lowering of the standard of living. It is worthwhile stressing that, for the second time in six years, the Polish party and government have withdrawn announced price increases when confronted with the violent reaction of the people.

The food situation is pregnant with all sorts of unpleasant consequences. The basic problem is that the Poles had become accustomed to relatively inexpensive food, and the government failed to prepare the ground for the higher prices forced on it by the necessity of paying higher prices to the main suppliers, the private farmers. Most state network prices had not changed since the late 1960s, and the state has had to subsidize food prices to the tune of $5 billion a year. The present situation is extremely volatile, and much of Poland's future depends on how well the Gierek regime is able to cope with the problem of food prices.

231

CHAPTER NINE

The Polish Paradox

Poland is a very touching, proud little country. They have something in common with the Spaniards, a certain noble pride. A bit stupid, some practical people might say. They will go a thousand strong against an army of a million, fighting with forks and spoons and I don't know what. . . . They are the only ones who opposed Hitler from first to last.

Arthur Rubinstein

There are certain things in this world that are at once intensely loved and intensely hated. They are naturally things of a strong character and either very good or very bad. They generally give a great deal of trouble to everybody; and a special sort of trouble to those who try to destroy them. But they give most trouble of all to those who try to ignore them. . . . This curious case is perhaps best illustrated by examples. One example of it is Ireland. Another example is Poland.

G. K. Chesterton

✍ FOR POLAND, the twentieth century has been a period of dramatic, revolutionary changes, many of them traumatic. After a bloody, four-year war, which passed over the country like a bulldozer, the Polish people regained their political independence. The brief and exhilarating period of reunification and rebuilding was followed by the hideous destruction of World War II. Nearly six years of the Nazi New Order meant humiliating enslavement and the threat of physical extinction. Between 1939 and 1945 every fifth citizen of the second Polish republic lost his life one way or another, most dying in German concentration camps. The end of the war did not fulfill many of

232

the expectations the Polish people had nurtured during the horrible years of Hitler's rule. The liberation, Soviet style, was followed by the Stalinist experiment, with its harsh and crude attempts at political and spiritual indoctrination enforced by terror. The trials of the first postwar decade were interrupted by the "thaw" of 1955–57. The close succession of upheavals and shocks, the disappointment in the great expectations kindled by Gomułka's rise to power, and promises of a genuinely Polish road to Socialism have left the great majority of Poles deeply shaken and disillusioned.

The people of Poland are far from happy in the role of vassals in a vassal state, a condition created by World War II. They are profoundly critical about the manner in which the hegemonical role of Soviet Russia has been imposed and carried out. It remains to be seen how the Helsinki conference of July and August 1975, with its confirmation of the Soviet sphere of influence in east-central Europe, will affect Poland in the long run. The dependence of the ruling party on Moscow is generally considered by the broad masses of the Polish people as excessive; it is believed that the obsequiousness of the PUWP is merely encouraging further Soviet encroachments on Polish sovereignty by means of constant behind-the-scenes intervention even in minor details of the country's internal affairs, for instance, in the area of book and periodical censorship. Here one should add the widespread conviction that Moscow, despite the changes that have taken place since 1956, still much too often takes undue advantage of its political ascendancy and exploits Poland economically. The memories of the early postwar years, when Poland had to deliver coal to the USSR for a few dollars per ton while the world price was at least ten times higher, still linger. Even now the imposition of unfair terms of trade and the nonobservance of assumed contractual obligations by the Soviet side are quite frequent. The already mentioned case of Polish ships is merely one example of this camouflaged exploitation. All this is enforced by all means available to a ruthless and greedy superpower that militarily and politically dominates its sphere of influence. A great majority of the Polish people realize the hopelessness of the present situation. Yet they believe that, in the long run, any meaningful, lasting relationship with the Soviet Union should be based on voluntary agreements deriving from mutual self-interest.[1]

Another criticism of the Communist regime pertains to the condescending attitude of the minority in power, "the owners of People's Poland," as a popular saying goes, toward the non-Communist majority. The people object to the party's high-handed methods of exercising power while disregarding the existing law, the constitution notwithstanding. Also, the erratic and often arbitrary practices of the public administration and its less-public organs are profoundly resented. The events of 1956, 1970, and 1975 are the most striking manifestations of this smoldering wrath.

The PUWP exercises power with the rationale that for ideological and geopolitical reasons, the country should have its domestic as well as foreign policies closely coordinated with those of the Soviet Union. While the geopolitical motive is being reluctantly accepted by a number of Poles who see no alternative to this alignment, the ideological premises of this policy are squarely rejected by most people.

Agreeing with basic tenets of what is currently called the "Socialist Construction," many Poles have been critical of the way the reshaping of the socioeconomic and cultural patterns of the country has been conducted by the ruling party. There is, however, evidence that the Polish people are trying hard to adjust themselves to a situation they cannot alter. The events of 1956, the example of Czechoslovakia in 1968, the December days of 1970, the policy of détente that culminated in the Helsinki conference, all have reaffirmed two basic convictions: first, that the pressure of public opinion can bring about only limited changes, and second, that Poles can count only on themselves, since the West is not going to lift a finger on Poland's behalf. Despite the repeated and profound disappointments with the West, the Polish unrequited love for things Western persists. This lingering sentiment is now, however, more and more tainted with somber political realism, philosophic skepticism, and even bitter cynicism. The realization that the Poles will have to rely only on themselves increasingly permeates the country's political climate.

234

Having to bear their role as vassals of Moscow, the Poles have set themselves to improve their situation within the Soviet sphere, as far as possible, both by reasserting their cultural autonomy and by exploiting the modest margin of freedom still available to them. Since the launching of the Rapacki plan in 1957, Warsaw diplomacy has tried to exploit the narrow field of maneuver available to it in foreign relations by working for cooperation among European states, irrespective of ideological orientation. Despite the repeated rejection of the Rapacki plan by the West, the Poles have attempted to expand their contacts with various countries, including the United States, France, Britain, Belgium, the Netherlands, Italy, and even Spain. The significant improvement in relations between Warsaw and Bonn since 1970, despite periodic ups and downs, has contributed to the emergence of a somewhat more relaxed climate in Central and Eastern Europe.[2]

By working hard to reduce East-West tensions in Europe, the Poles have been trying to overcome the barriers separating them from the outside world. By this means, they have sought access to Western markets and technology, both of which they need to modernize their economy. They also believe that détente should first be brought about in a less sensitive field, namely that of culture, where power considerations are not predominant. Poles have achieved some modest successes with cultural exchanges. Many Polish scientists, technicians, scholars, and artists have been allowed to accept Western scholarships or invitations to visit Western countries every year, and other specialists have received grants or contracts from Western governments or organizations such as the United Nations for study or work in other countries.[3] No other country from the Soviet sphere has permitted so many of its scholars to travel to the West.

Since 1945, Poland has functioned as a segment of a closely knit system of Communist states dominated by Moscow. The impact of Soviet Russia on Poland has undoubtedly been far-reaching. Yet empires are never one-way affairs, and the Soviet imperial system is not an exception. Polish influence on the USSR has been limited by the overwhelming military and economic dependence of Poland on its

235

protector and by the endemic Soviet mistrust of everything foreign, but it has not been as negligible as may appear on the surface. Every year a considerable number of Soviet scholars and students, artists and technicians, as well as ordinary tourists, come to visit Poland. They are almost invariably amazed at the unexpectedly large degree of freedom enjoyed by the Poles—a striking comparison with their own domestic conditions. The Soviet visitors also admire the high academic standards of Polish scholarship as well as the free range of Polish art and literature. They also envy, and resent, the relative abundance of consumer goods.

There is much evidence that the Soviet dissenters have been considerably impressed by the "Polish October" of 1956 and by the events of December 1970. The fact that the émigré Literary Institute in Paris was first to publish abroad the works of the Soviet dissenters Yuri Daniel and Andrei Sinyavsky is not without significance. During a visit to the USSR in 1960, the author was surprised by the number of Soviet intellectuals who were learning Polish in order to be able to read their western neighbor's books and periodicals, which were so much more outspoken than domestic counterparts. For them the Polish publications embody much of what they miss in their own, and are also more accessible than the largely forbidden Western items. What effect this restricted cultural osmosis, and the protracted stay of the Soviet soldiers on Polish soil, will have on the domestic evolution of the USSR will only be determined in the future.

Thus, despite the tragedies and disappointments that the Polish people have suffered since 1939, the balance sheet by the mid-1970s is not entirely negative. In spite of the continuing Soviet overlordship and the imposed dictatorial rule of the Communist party, there are some positive points that should not be overlooked. The most important phenomenon is the very physical survival of the Polish people. There are now more than 35 million Poles living in their homeland, more than at any time in previous history. Poland today is also a more viable state than before the war, with better shaped frontiers and a more balanced social and ethnic structure. Industrialization has also made great strides in the postwar period. The country now produces about three times more coal and ten times more steel than in 1939, and has emerged as the third largest sulfur producer in the world. The industrialization of Poland is also reflected in the country's foreign trade. Before the war raw materials, fuels (mainly coal), and agricultural products constituted over 90 percent of Polish exports, but these items made up less than half of the country's exports in 1970. Capital goods, which played practically no role before the war, now account for a large share of Poland's exports.[4] On the other hand, Poland's per capita volume of foreign trade is very low, only slightly ahead of the USSR, one of the most self-sufficient countries in the world. Moreover, the country is almost entirely dependent on the import of oil and iron ore from the USSR.

Poland's social structure in the mid-1970s was that of a fairly developed industrial country. Despite the harshness accompanying the process of industrialization, the workers, now the key social stratum of the country, are proud of the new mines and factories. Many of them believe that, at the cost of acute privation, they are laying the foundations for future prosperity. But the workers are also the most defiant group in Polish society. In 1956, 1970, and 1976 they revealed their toughness in fighting stubbornly for their rights, and in all three instances forced considerable policy changes on the party leadership. These triumphs have given the Polish working class a new sense of importance.[5]

Another reason for the increasing self-confidence of the Polish working class has been the growth of urban population, expanding at a rate of 140,000 to 150,000 a year. There have been three main sources of this increase: the migration from villages to cities; the elevation of some villages to the status of cities and their incorporation into neighboring urban centers; and a high birth rate in cities during the 1940s and 1950s. For instance, in the period from 1951 to 1958, the urban population increased 1,726,000 by births, 1,708,000 by administrative changes, and 786,000 by the migration of rural population. In 1953 the urban birth rate was 19.8 percent. During the 1960s and 1970s, however, the situation changed radically (in Warsaw and Łódź, an increase was recorded of only 1.0 percent and 0.7

percent, respectively). On the other hand, in certain years the percentage of migrants from rural communities to cities was higher than the national birthrate.[6]

After industrialization and urbanization, the spread of education was the most significant change of the postwar years. By the mid-1970s, nearly four times as many pupils were attending secondary and academic schools as were attending prior to 1939. It is true that before the war the best of these schools could boast of much higher standards than corresponding institutions in present-day Poland; yet one must admit that the often brilliant prewar academic institutions catered primarily to a restricted group of mostly well-to-do young people, who came largely from the families of the intelligentsia, and that the influx of working-class students was far too small. Although educational opportunities are still unequally distributed, and social stratification still persists, the situation is less abnormal than it was prior to 1939. The educational law of 1961, which went into effect in 1963 and provided for the prolongation of the seven-year primary school course to eight years, is a step in the right direction.

In addition to the spread of general education, there occurred an expansion in the number of technical and vocational schools; some, for example the Film Academy of Łódź, are widely respected throughout the professional world. Also, the faculties of the University of Cracow and of Nicholas Copernicus University of Toruń, which train specialists in restoration of works of art, have a high reputation the world over. Polish sociologists and historians are generally regarded as the most competent and independently minded in the Communist world. In the field of mathematical logic the Poles have maintained the high position they had occupied before the war. This educational progress has to be counterbalanced by an undeniable lowering of academic standards, by the heavy admixture of crude Communist indoctrination, and by a stubborn persistence of rigid social stratification.[7] The indoctrination, however, does not seem to have taken hold, even among most young Communists.

Another interesting phenomenon of the last three decades has been the spread of physical culture and the emergence of Poland as a major

238

sports power. During the Olympic Games in Rome (1960), Tokyo (1964), Mexico City (1968), and Munich (1972), Polish sportsmen were among winners in such competitions as track and field, boxing, cycling, skiing, fencing, and soccer. Since 1948, Poland has won 125 Olympic medals. The winning of the gold medal in soccer in Munich in 1972 and the third place in the World Soccer Cup in 1974, after victories over such giants as Italy, Argentina, and Brazil, has consolidated Poland's leading position in this most popular of all sports among Europeans. The Montreal Olympic Games of 1976 gave Poland 25 medals, which placed it sixth on the list of participants, just behind West Germany and Japan.

The questions immediately arise: to what extent has the party been given credit or blame for the merits and shortcomings of the process of transformation of the Polish society? To what extent has the self-image of the party, being solely responsible for the modernization of Poland, been accepted by the non-Communist people? To what degree did the party's program filter down to the masses? The fact that the party enjoys a monopoly of political power and, for all practical purposes, control of all mass media except the church pulpits, makes any definite answers problematic. In private conversations one hears a great deal about the harsh and so often inefficient methods used by the Communists to achieve their objectives. The events of 1956, 1970, and 1976 may be a better answer than any public opinion poll.

One of the most striking features and puzzling paradoxes of contemporary Poland is the paramount position of the Roman Catholic church. This phenomenon is no novelty in Polish history. The church has been playing a prominent role in Poland since the early Middle Ages, and the country's turbulent history has tended to reinforce its position. The church actively supported the national struggle against the Muslim Tatars and Turks as well as against the Orthodox Muscovites and Lutheran Swedes. The fact that two out of three partition powers, Russia and Prussia, were non-Catholic further bolstered the significance of the church. By the nineteenth century it had become a key national institution. The second Polish republic could not fail to pay tribute to the historical significance of the church: the constitution

239

of 1921, while granting religious tolerance, referred to the Roman Catholic church as occupying the preeminent position in the state among legally equal religions.

During World War II the clergy behaved in an exemplary manner. Some 1,200 priests perished in German concentration camps. One of them, Father Maksymilian Kolbe, was canonized a saint. The outcome of war saddled an overwhelmingly Roman Catholic and believing society with an atheistic government. One aspect of the Polish paradox is that, despite some three decades of Communist rule, Poland, next to Ireland, remains the most fervently religious country of Europe, far more so than Spain or Italy. There are nearly twice as many secular and regular priests in Poland now than there were prior to 1939, and the seminaries are filled with candidates for priesthood.[8] The overwhelming strength of the church in Poland made even the Communist regime respect certain basic rights of the believer. The church in Poland still enjoys many rights not granted to either the Orthodox church in the Soviet Union or to other churches of the Communist orbit. The Catholics of Poland have, for instance, their own university in Lublin, the only private institution of higher learning in the Communist world.

The Polish regime is careful not to exceed the limits of administrative pressure and turn to open persecution. Despite pressure and harassment, the Roman Catholic character of Poland has not been affected by three decades of Communist rule. Again, paradoxically enough, in many cases, especially among the educated people, the hitherto traditional, emotional, and rather ritualistic religiosity of the people has been deepened by a more mature, intellectual approach to religious life. The significance of religion in present-day Poland lies in the fact that the church provides a large part of the population with a system of values that form an alternative to Communism. As Velizar Savic, a Yugoslav journalist and former correspondent of the Belgrade daily, *Politika,* put it: "A large majority of the Poles consider their Catholicism a patriotic affirmation." [9]

Yet, the Polish hierarchy has encountered various problems. The Roman Catholic intelligentsia of the country is split into two hostile camps: those loyal to the hierarchy and Rome, and those who attempt to reconcile their Catholicism with Marxism and tend to cooperate with the regime in many fields. The latter group is led by Bolesław Piasecki, a former leader of a prewar Fascist movement then called Falanga. Now he heads the proregime organization called Pax. To this group one may also add a handful of progovernment "priest-patriots," and the Catholic welfare organization Caritas.

The prudent conservatism of the Polish church, firmly led by its primate, Stefan Cardinal Wyszyński, has often been criticized by progressive Catholics, but has been largely vindicated and has found understanding among the Roman Curia. The Vatican has accepted the cardinal's leadership as well as the slow tempo of implementation of the Vatican II reforms as fitting the situation of the Polish church, engaged in a protracted and intricate struggle. The fact that Polish Catholicism is flourishing is responsible for its increasing impact on the church as a whole. Despite the splits and internal quarrels, despite the undeniable process of laicization of the intelligentsia, along with the growing number of divorces and abortions, the pulse of Catholic intellectual life beats now more quickly and vigorously than ever.[10] Every year a considerable number of Polish missionaries go to the countries of Asia and Africa to work there on behalf of the universal church, and this has also contributed to the growing prestige of Polish Catholicism.

Probably the best periodicals in Poland are the Catholic weekly, *Tygodnik Powszechny,* and the monthlies *Znak* and *Więź.* Hampered and harassed by the authorities, these papers have some of the most interesting thinkers and writers in contemporary Poland and exercise an influence far beyond their limited circulation.[11] The Catholic University of Lublin, which before the war was a second-rate academic institution, has considerably bolstered its standards and is now a first-rate center of learning, despite constant discrimination and shortage of funds.

Poland has one of the youngest populations in the world. Well over 50 percent of its inhabitants are under the age of 30. This means that most people do not remember World War II and its horrors and are looking more and more to the future. Nevertheless, the young generation has a keen sense of historical continuity. This is reflected not only in the attachment to religious values, but also in a recent increase in interest in historical novels, movies, and theater. The decision to reconstruct the royal castle in Warsaw unleased an unprecedented wave of enthusiasm and generosity.[12]

What are the aspirations of the young generation of Poles now in their twenties? The most comprehensive polls so far were those carried out in 1974 by the University of Warsaw and by the Center for Public Opinion Research of the Polish radio and television system. To the question, ''What do you most desire in life?,'' the majority of young people answered love, friendship, and satisfaction from a job selected in accordance with one's wishes. All of these, to the amazement of those conducting the survey, were placed ahead of material gains. Most young people declared themselves to be believers of the Catholic doctrine.[13]

In a country so long deprived of its political sovereignty, the arts have traditionally played a special, largely compensatory role. Since the eighteenth century, artists and intellectuals, especially great poets, have served many social as well as individual needs which in other countries are filled by scholars and statesmen. That is why the Poles bury their most distinguished poets in the royal castle of Wawel, next to their kings: Adam Mickiewicz and Juliusz Słowacki lie near Casimir the Great and John III Sobieski. Probably in no other country, except perhaps Serbia and Russia, has poetry played such a vital role. On the other hand, the preoccupation with national issues until recently has kept Polish art largely a part of a specifically provincial Polish environment, at best an art expressing national messianic longings, with little relevance to, or understanding by, the outside world. This was the lot of the great Romantic poetry, which was exuberant and brilliant, but on the whole esoteric, exotic, and too strictly confined to purely Polish issues.

Art grows out of national culture, but great art must transcend it.

242

Such attempts are striking in higher levels of Polish artistic creativity since the war. Besides waging the policy of extermination, the Germans for six years suppressed all artistic creativity. The unparalleled suffering of the Polish people during World War II, and the traumas that they shared often on equal terms with Jews, seem to have opened new sources of artistic inspiration. Soon after the end of the German occupation, the country witnessed an elemental outburst of artistic creativity. A natural desire for individual self-expression, held back for years, was overwhelming. It was as if the Poles were shouting: "Look at us! We have survived! We exist! We create again!" The intensity of intellectual life during the years 1945–48 was astonishing and surprised many foreign observers.[14] Despite the advent of Stalinism and its harsh attempts to impose Socialist realism, the artistic rebirth of the Polish arts made remarkable progress. Suppressed at the peak of the Stalinist period, during the years 1949–53, Polish arts revived during the "thaw" of 1955–56. Ever since, they have been characterized by a passionate avant-gardism strangely intertwined with attachment to native tradition.

This book deals with Poland's evolution during the twentieth century only in the most general terms; it can not do justice to all trends and personalities, especially in the literary and artistic field. What has been attempted here is merely an impressionistic, and hence selective, analysis of those figures that have affected national life in an especially strong manner.

Perhaps the most original and creative personality in Polish art is Jerzy Grotowski, the creator and promoter of the austere "theater of the poor." Grotowski, who found the Polish Laboratory Theater in 1959 in Opole, soon moved to Wrocław, which he helped turn into Poland's theatrical capital. He runs not a conventional performing company, but a laboratory devoted to experimentation with theatrical techniques. While largely dispensing with scenery and costumes, he concentrates on rigorous training of his actors, as well as on imaginative, innovative directorship. Through his performance he tries to involve the spectator and make him a participant in a mystical ritual.

Grotowski introduced to Poland a highly original concept of repertoire of composite plays made up of fragments by various authors. He has produced a series of spectacles that since the 1965–66 season have scored triumphs on numerous stages of the world, including the United States. His pioneering work has put him beside such re- formers of theater as Craig, Meyerhold, Reinhardt, and Stanislavsky. An American critic did not hesitate to call Grotowski "the most radi- cal creative force in modern theater." [15]

Witkiewicz's role in Polish cultural life has already been discussed in the chapter dealing with the interwar period. Two more contempo- rary writers are now competing with him for prominence and the scope of impact on intellectual life outside their native country. They are Witold Gombrowicz and Sławomir Mrożek. Gombrowicz started his literary career in the 1930s with his novel *Ferdydurke* (1937); even before the war he was recognized as a leading figure of the Polish avant-garde. Abroad when the war began in 1939, he went to live in Argentina, where he supported himself by working in a bank. There, he continued to write novels, essays, and plays, as well as his provocative diary. In 1957, during the "thaw," his collected works were published in Poland. Shortly afterward they began to be trans- lated into French and then into other languages, and soon his plays found their way to the stage. In 1964, Gombrowicz settled in France, and he died there in 1969. Two of his plays, *Yvonne, Princess of Burgundy* (1935) and *The Marriage* (1946), were written before any major French theater of the absurd had appeared. After moving to France, he wrote only one play, *Operetta* (1966).

Gombrowicz's rapid rise to fame is probably accounted for by his highly original, surrealistic, almost absurdist treatment of such sub- jects as distorted social forms, the multiplicity of psychological roles played by each person, and the superiority of pliable youth over os- sified old age. Gombrowicz often wrote about adolescence, which he saw as a mass of contradictions. When young people enter the adult world they are molded to fit preexisting norms. According to Gom- browicz, men are constantly adapting to what is expected of them, for even if they rebel they merely fall into another conventional pattern. Life is viewed by him as a set of interacting impositions and deformations.

Poland's most famous living dramatic writer and satirist, Sławomir Mrożek, is another master of the pure absurd. He was born in 1930, and after a spectacular rise to fame at an early age, during the "thaw" of the 1950s, he left Poland in 1968 and has lived abroad ever since. In his numerous plays (*The Policeman, The Turkey, Tango,* or *Charlie*), Mrożek uses deadpan irony to probe searchingly the incongruities of contemporary life. His sense of humor with a gadfly sting stretches from goodnatured remarks about shortcomings of human nature, to sarcastic, acerbic witticisms about graft, bribery, and inefficiency of the party bosses and governmental bureaucracy that stifle the life of the country. Mrożek believes that humor immunizes against both the harshness of everyday life and the historic reminiscences so full of bitter, tragic memories. His technique is frankly absurdist, which he believes fits the nature of the epoch. Mrożek's plays, like those of Witkiewicz and Gombrowicz, have been performed all over the world, but especially in Western Europe. In the United States they have been staged mainly by experimental and university theaters.[16]

The period since 1955–56 has abounded in political satire and social criticism, as well as in works of a philosophic nature that incorporated satire as a tool. One of the writers who straddled the frontier between scholarship and satire has been the versatile Leszek Kołakowski. Kołakowski, a maverick as well as a humanist, philosopher, and essayist, has combined the serious study of ideas with lighter writing and theatrical plays. Discarding his early Stalinist upbringing, he has boldly stood in opposition to the dictatorship of a minority party in social and political life, and especially in the fields of art, science, and philosophy. This was the meaning of his book, *The Priest and the Jester: Toward a Marxist Humanism* (1958). Kołakowski distinguishes between two kinds of men: priests and jesters. The priests are those members of the establishment, be they Communists or capitalists, who are wedded to the status quo and who reaffirm its values in a dogmatic, authoritarian way. They are usually serious, pompous, and humorless. They accept no criticism of their doctrines and manner of exercising power. The jesters are those who move in a society "without belonging to it" and who "doubt all that appears self-evident." Kołakowski declared himself "in favor of the philosophy of the jester, that is for an attitude of skeptical vigilance in face of any absolute," any established authority. According to Kołakowski, the basic issue in the debate between the official Communist theoreticians and their critics has not been so much the nature of the economy (whether it be private or state-owned) as the democratic character of its political and social institutions and respect for the morally autonomous personality.

In addition to several philosophic essays, Kołakowski is the author of the controversial play *Entrance and Exit*, which spoofs the incompetence of authoritarian regimes. His book of parables, *Keys to Heaven*, used an apparently innocent biblical setting to suggest that the destiny of man, if it is to be changed at all, must be changed by man himself by means of moral and not merely technological progress. The case of Kołakowski, originally an enthusiastic party member, seems to confirm the correctness of the saying by the country's foremost satirist, S. J. Lec, that "in a regime of thought control one has to multiply thoughts to the point where there aren't enough policemen to control them."

Another man who has profoundly affected the performing arts in general, and music in particular, is Krzysztof Penderecki. Penderecki started his meteoric musical career in the 1950s as a typical child of the avant-garde, bent on shocking and scandalizing the traditionalists. In the early 1960s he drew the attention of the musical world with his *Threnody in Memory of the Victims of Hiroshima*, a work full of tonal novelties like whispers, murmers, rappings, and haunting vibrating hums, imitating the ominous drone of approaching airplanes. Quickly the *Threnody* became one of the most frequently performed of all advanced orchestral works. Soon, however, abandoning his early modernism, he branched off in a new direction and proceeded to make a bold synthesis of modernity and tradition. The remarkable results are widely recognized by musical critics as well as by the public at large.

The rejuvenation of contemporary music has been achieved by Penderecki through two basic means. First of all, he has incorporated modern techniques of instrumental and choral articulation into the traditional form of the religious oratorio. Second, he took his startling musical compositions out of the conventional concert halls and placed them into the church. There, his sight-and-sound spectacles have found their ideal esthetic background, with its spaciousness, acoustic resonance, and vast possibilities in the deployment of large choruses and various instrumental groups. Since the early performance outside his native country of his *Passion and Death of Our Lord Jesus Christ According to St. Luke,* in the Münster cathedral in West Germany in March 1966, the works of Penderecki have made a triumphant procession throughout some of the most famous churches and concert halls of the world.[17] Within a decade or so, by uniting the new musical techniques with the timeless and universal content of religious emotions, Penderecki brought about a revolution in modern music.

Almost equally fascinating and admired throughout the musical world is Witold Lutosławski. His music adheres to more traditional forms than that of Penderecki, yet Lutosławski also uses many contemporary techniques and sonorities. He is especially known for his *Concerto for Orchestra, Funeral Music* (dedicated to the Hungarian composer Béla Bartok), *Vencian Games, Three Poems of Henri Michaud,* and *Le Livre pour Orchestre.* The latter composition earned him the coveted Ravel Prize. In March 1975, Lutosławski was elected an honorary member of the American Academy of Arts and Sciences, a distinction previously awarded to Paderewski.

🖎 🖋

Another striking phenomenon of the postwar period has been the influence that Polish contemporary arts and letters have exercised on the Germans, especially those from the Federal Republic. In the past the Germans have tried to reduce the concept of European civilization to its Germanic-Roman dimensions, presenting Slavic cultures as alien to Western traditions; but following World War II the trend was dramatically reversed. After having denied that Poles had any culture at all, and after having made a brutal attempt at destroying it during the years 1939–45, many Germans suddenly discovered the subtle, seductive lure of Polish artistic genius. Since the 1950s, German translators, impresarios, and publishers have done perhaps more than any other single group to introduce and interpret Polish arts and literature to Western eyes. Between 1945 and 1970, 502 works of Polish authors were published in West Germany, and 322 in East Germany. Some Polish authors were published in larger editions in West Germany than in Poland. For instance, the collected works of Gombrowicz appeared in the Federal Republic even before they were printed in Warsaw.[18] This was achieved largely through the efforts of a group of able, dedicated translators, headed by the indefatigable Karl Dedecius, a German born and educated in Poland, and endowed with a remarkably perceptive and sympathetic understanding of the intricacies of the Polish pysche. Polish music, theater, and painting have also gathered many devoted admirers in both Germanies, but especially in the Federal Republic. As Dedecius put it: "For the last two decades or so Germany witnessed an almost uninterrupted festival of Polish arts."

Contacts and exchanges between Polish and West German scholars have also been developing steadily and seem to be yielding results. Karl Moersch, a minister of state in the West German foreign office, told the Bundestag in December 1974 that Poland accounted for what was termed an "exceptionally large share" of the Federal Republic's total exchanges of scholars "in all disciplines, including the humanities." [19] Probably the most effective Polish-West German scholarly cooperation takes place at the University of Bonn under the aegis of Professor Hans-Adolf Jacobsen, director of the university's seminar for political science.[20] Another group interested in scholarly exchange of views are the lawyers of the two countries. Several professors from various West German universities—including Rudolf Bernard, director of the Heidelberg Max Planck Institute—traveled to

Warsaw in September 1974 to take part in a colloquium organized by the Legal Sciences Institute of the Polish Academy of Sciences. More than a dozen legal experts, along with several high-ranking officials from the Warsaw foreign ministry, met to discuss what was defined as "problems of mutual interest for legal science and practice." [21]

The feverish intensity of Poland's cultural life has been a phenomenon observed by many foreigners. "From poetry to achitecture, pantomime to the theater of pure experiment, the Poles are working with an intensity, an originality, and a pure joy that I, as a solitary observer, have not seen anywhere else in Europe," writes a British observer who traveled through the country during the worst years of the Gomułka era.[22] Poland's cultural vitality is a puzzling phenomenon, the full explanation of which is beyond the scope of this general outline. A young, gifted American painter from Boston, Francis Murray Forbes, who went to Poland at the close of 1972, summarized in a letter to this author his observations on the intricacies of that country's artistic scene:

> Poland does not yet possess a mass society such as we have in the U.S. and as is coming into being rapidly in Western Europe. . . . Poland suffers from extremely clear evils: I should say the two greatest are foreign oppression, tyranny and want. . . . But these evils ironically create certain balancing virtues. Denied the rewards of a material world the Pole looks to the spirit, denied national freedom he longs for liberty. These conditions are strangely enough good conditions for the arts, provided the tyranny is not efficient enough to throttle the imagination, nor the want harsh enough to stupefy the soul. The artist exists in a harsh world, but he is surrounded by others who through tragic necessity also inhabit a world of the spirit. He need not fight the absorbent tentacles of mass mediocrity, nor struggle along in the desert of mass prosperity to express the individual. His battle is shared to an extent by all Poles and he also has the company of other artists, who in Poland still form an intelligentsia: actors, writers, painters, architects—they all belong to a special class in Poland; they are not part of the mass, they know each other, they have good training, in short they are still an elite. In the West, they are just another detail in the "brownian movement of egalitarian particles." The Polish tempera-

ment in the arts combines extreme individualism and daring, a thirst for the *avant garde* and a respect for tradition. That is why today the Poles have so much to offer to the West in the field of artistic creativity.

≫ ≪

The revival of Polish culture after the ravages of World War II has been a work of the intelligentsia, an amalgam of old and new social elements, with the prewar stratum still predominating. According to Jan Szczepański, a leading sociologist, the most characteristic features of the old Polish intelligentsia, largely of gentry origin, have been attachment to the ideas of freedom, intellectual tolerance, strong emphasis on a peculiar, romantic concept of honor, and contempt for the mere "money-making" ideal. With this are connected certain negative values that inevitably flow from a world view shaped more by the romantic poets and thinkers of the nineteenth century than by practical politicians and other sober-minded men of action: a certain dreamlike lack of political realism, and an aristocratic attitude toward economic problems, resulting in the failure to appreciate businesslike methods.

During the 1940s, '50s, and '60s, while promoting its "cultural revolution," the party had to accept the services of the intelligentsia and attracted some of its members into the ruling elite without necessarily absorbing them ideologically. Meanwhile, the ranks of the new intelligentsia have been diluted by the influx of individuals of worker and peasant origin, who by now form its majority. To what extent the traditional model of the Polish intelligentsia has been successfully altered is open to question. Szczepański claims that from "broad nonprofessional amateurish, dilettante, cultivated intellectualism," the new intelligentsia has been gradually shifting to a scientific, technically minded professionalism. According to the observations of other sociologists, however, the old model has proved harder to crack than the Communist social engineers had anticipated. It seems that many attempts to revolutionize national culture have had only limited success. Closer examination of the artistic and intellectual scene seems to indicate that Poland is still a country dominated, perhaps more than any other state in Eastern Europe, by the ethos of the old intelligentsia. It seems that the party has largely failed in its efforts to redirect the thinking of the new arrivals to the educated class toward Marxist ideals: the old gentry patterns and values have proven overwhelmingly attractive to the new intelligentsia, and even to certain strata of the party.[23]

Yet, the tempo of social mobility in Poland is high and is bound to affect the intelligentsia sooner or later. Whatever its ethos, the prestige of the cultural intelligentsia is very high in present-day Poland, higher than in most Western countries. (The three highest rated occupations in 1971 were found to be university professor, doctor, and teacher, while cabinet minister was ranked in the eighth place.)

Academic education in Poland serves a variety of purposes. It helps to legitimize one's social advancement, to enhance the social status of newly promoted members of the intelligentsia, and to perpetuate many of the old divisions along traditional class lines. Although vocational training usually requires less schooling than academic training, and although many people with trade school certificates, for instance miners, earn more than those who hold academic diplomas, the struggle to enter institutions of higher learning continues to be very intense. Thus the measure of class and social status is not income, but education.[24]

🖋 🖋

The Polish historian Ioachim Lelewel noticed around the middle of the last century the striking analogy between the evolutions of Poland and Spain. In his book, *La terre d'Europe,* the Spanish writer Salvador de Madariaga broadened this parallel and compared Poland to Spain and Ireland. The analogy may be somewhat overdrawn, yet it is illuminating in some respects. The parallel is especially revealing in the cases of Spain and Poland. While the former is situated on the western extremity of Europe, facing Africa, the latter lies on its eastern limits and faces Asia. Both nations were shaped in the struggle against the Muslims: the Spaniards against the Arabs, the Poles

251

against the Tatars and the Turks. In both cases the price for the protracted defense of Western Christendom, the struggle that absorbed a large proportion of Spanish and Polish national energies, resulted in economic backwardness as well as in cultural retardation in comparison with the leading countries of Western and Central Europe. Both in Spain and Poland Gothic churches and palaces were built until the beginning of the sixteenth century, and baroque structures were erected in the eighteenth century.

In the Spanish, Polish, and Irish civilizations Roman Catholicism is a quintessential element. Both in Spain and in Poland the Catholic Counterreformation left deeper marks than in any other European country. In both lands, the arch-Catholic religious order, the Jesuits, left deep traces on people's culture and education. Both nations have an exalted sense of honor and suffer from an exaggerated sensitivity. Both are fatalistic and tend to have a cavalier attitude toward death. Nowhere else but in Spain and Poland does dance play such a crucial role, not only in local folklore, but in the totality of both countries' civilization. Both countries have preserved a highly ritualistic, ceremonial, old-fashioned gallantry toward women.

No lesser analogies exist between Poland and Ireland. With the Irish the Poles share a zealous, traditional, ritualistic Roman Catholicism, with its strong devotion to the Holy Virgin, an expression of a latent matriarchal tendency. The Poles and the Irish display their sorrows, and share an exhibitionistic, masochistic enjoyment of sufferings inflicted on them by foreign rule. As a consequence of foreign rule and economic exploitation both countries became, by the second part of the nineteenth century, nations of emigrants, with the largest segments of their diaspora located in the United States.

Poland, like Ireland, is a set of contradictions and even absurdities, often reminding one of an Alice-in-Wonderland world, where a drink is the best way to personal contact, where human relationships mean everything, and where a man's word has the weightlessness of outer space. Both the Irish and the Poles have a deep respect for artists, especially poets. Both have a peculiar, whimsical, often cynical and rowdy sense of humor. They both share proclivities toward capricious moods, highly critical, often negative spirits, bellicosity, and a love for singing and strong drink, apparently as an outlet for their frustrations. About the Poles, as about the Irish, one may say: "Where there is one man, there is agreement. Where there are two men, you have an argument. If you have three people, you have a riot." When, during the Battle of Britain, Winston Churchill asked Doctor Paul Rosenstein-Rodan, a native of Poland, then a professor at the London School of Economics, what the Poles are like, Rosenstein-Rodan answered: "They are like the Irish, only more so." A British writer, J. B. Priestley, who in 1972 revisited Poland, gave the following general characterization of contemporary Poles: "They are more alive than most people, less inclined to turn themselves into zombies and robots . . . They are very brave,tenacious, quite clever, and at the same time slightly daft and refreshingly unpredictable." [25]

Contemporary Poland is a set of puzzling paradoxes and a maze of incongruities. Many of these contradictions are a result of the basic incompatibility between the collectivist and totalitarian Communist system imported from the East, and the essentially individualistic Poles more responsive to incentive than to disciplinarian measures and abstract slogans. The striking contrasts of Polish life under Communism are visible everywhere. In economic life, spasmodic outbursts of energy are frequently followed by fits of lethargic apathy. Outstanding achievements in some fields of activity often go side by side with appalling slapdash inefficiency; catering services and tourism are exasperating examples of indolence and neglect. Exquisitely restored old churches and palaces stand next door to dilapidated houses. As a foreign observer put it to the author: "What can you do with a country where mathematical logic thrives next to the theater of the absurd?"

🖋 🖋

Every nation is, consciously or unconsciously, inspired by an idea that is central to its mentality, an idea that is a guiding principle of its history. Both geographically and culturally Poland cannot be understood except as a transition area between the Western Atlantic world and the Eurasian continental mass forming the heartland of the USSR. While Polish civilization includes both Western as well as Asian elements, the Poles have for centuries identified themselves much more with the West than with the East, with Rome and not Byzantium or Moscow. Since the Tatar invasion of the thirteenth century, the Poles have been convinced that they are a living bulwark of Western Christendom (*Antemurale Christianitatis*). This conviction was deepened during the sixteenth and the seventeenth centuries as a result of the wars against the Turks and the Muscovites, and romanticized and fixed in the popular Polish mind by many nineteenth-century writers, poets, and painters.

Threatened by what they considered "Asiatic forces" and eager to strengthen their ties with the West, the Poles came to regard everything from the East with suspicion. The tsarist domination of the bulk of Poland, lasting some four or five generations, only deepened this endemic mistrust. The Bolshevik upheaval in Russia, and the war of 1919–20, with its splendid last-minute victory at the gates of Warsaw, bolstered the Polish belief in the allegedly providential role assigned to them by destiny. The trials and tragedies of World War II, the repeated disappointments with the West, the establishment of a Communist regime with the tacit blessing of the Western allies, all these have made the Poles reexamine their traditional role as the bulwark of Christendom and grope for a new identity. Without abandoning their cultural identification with the West, they are painfully trying to accommodate themselves to the new situation while fiercely sticking to their national heritage.[26]

Three decades in the Soviet sphere have not yet shaken the continuity of historic tradition or Poland's Western orientation. The idea, fixed in the popular imagination and bolstered by the church, the arts, and literature, is too deeply rooted to be destroyed. Will the Poles be able to adjust themselves to the role with which World War II and the Western policy of détente has saddled them, without having their distinct historic identity eroded? This is one of the vital questions facing the country at the close of the twentieth century.[27]

Notes

1. ROOTS OF THE PRESENT

1. William Woods, *Poland: Eagle in the East* (New York: Hill and Wang, 1968), p. 219.

2. For a recent one-volume treatment of Polish history by a team of Warsaw-based scholars, see Aleksander Gieysztor et al., *History of Poland* (Warsaw: PWN—Polish Scientific Publishers, 1968); for more traditional approaches, see Oskar Halecki, *History of Poland* (New York: Roy Publishers, 1963); and a two-volume symposium by a group of British and Polish scholars, W. F. Reddaway, ed., *Cambridge History of Poland* (Cambridge: Cambridge University Press, 1941–50). Roman Dyboski's *Poland in World Civilization* (New York: J. M. Barrett, 1950) and Wacław Lednicki's *Life and Culture of Poland* (New York: Roy Publishers, 1944) provide useful background reading.

3. For a detailed study of the Polish-Lithuanian union, see Oskar Halecki, *Dzieje Unii Jagiellonskiej* (A History of the Jagellonian Union), 2 vols. (Cracow: Akademia Umiejetnosci, 1919–20). For a Lithuanian interpretation, see C. R. Jurgela, *History of the Lithuanian Nation* (New York: Lithuanian Historical Institute, 1948), pp. 122–52.

4. For a detailed study of the early Polish political theories and doctrines, see Stanislaus F. Bełch, *Paulus Vladimiri and His Doctrine Concerning International Law and Politics,* 2 vols. (The Hague: Mouton, 1965).

5. Knowledge of foreign languages was considerable among the cultural elite of sixteenth-century Poland-Lithuania. The French historian de Thou, who met some of the Polish delegates who came to Paris in 1573 to offer the crowns of the commonwealth to Henri de Valois, was astonished at the high level of their culture. "What was most noticeable was their facility of expressing in Latin, French, German, and Italian; these four languages were as familiar to them as the language of their own country. The Poles spoke our language with such purity that they would have been considered men brought up on the shores of the Seine and of the Loire. . . ."

6. For a series of essays on various aspects of Polish legal systems, see W. J. Wagner et al., *Polish Law Throughout the Ages: One Thousand Years of Legal Thought in Poland* (Stanford: Hoover Institution Press, 1970).

255

Notes

7. Wiktor Weintraub, "Tolerance and Intolerance in Old Poland," *Canadian Slavic Papers* 13 (Spring 1971); see also J. Tazbir, *A State' Without Stakes* (New York: Kosciuszko Foundation, 1974). It is not an accident that until World War II and the extermination of Polish Jews by Hitler, the percentage of Jews in Poland was higher than in any other country in the world, and it was at Wilno (Vilnius) that a flourishing center of Judaic studies existed until World War II; see also Bernard D. Weinryb, *The Jews of Poland: A Social and Economic History of the Jewish Community in Poland from 1100 to 1800* (Philadelphia: Jewish Publication Society of America, 1973), pp. 52–53, 143–44, 174–75, 199–204. Weinryb writes: "The religious freedom of non-Catholics in Poland, as in many other Catholic states before the French revolution, was limited. As a multinational and multidenominational state since the fourteenth century, Poland did not follow the extreme principle of intolerance according to which the majority imposes its faith upon the minority (*Cuius regio eius religio:* He whose state it is, his is the religion). Poland adhered largely to another trend of the pre-modern state whereby members of minority groups had the right to follow their own religion and customs: autonomy. The Polish state generally gave minorities the right to organize as religious groups and to a certain extent even protected their freedom to exercise their respective religions, even supervising their autonomous organizations" (p. 134).

8. Charles H. Haskins and Robert H. Lord, *Some Problems of the Peace Conference* (Cambridge: Harvard University Press, 1920), pp. 160–67. Many historians argue that it was the ethnically mixed nature of the Polish-Lithuanian commonwealth that was largely responsible for its cultural flowering. ". . . [I]ntermixture of nations, so generally felt as misfortune, this source of wars, friction and unrest, has been in reality one of the basic conditions for the national development of the different peoples, a cause of sustained intellectual fertilization begetting innumerable cultural values. The many-colored map of nationalities has sense when one considers the intellectual benefits derived from the mingling of peoples. It is not purity of race, national homogeneity in any one territory, which has advanced culture in the European Middle East, but rather the blending of two or rather several peoples. The development of the nations of Central and Eastern Europe attests that in the cosmopolitan character of a State, province or town lay the best chance for the national advancement of all its inhabitants" (Walter Kolarz, *Myth and Reality in Eastern Europe* [London: Drummond, 1946], p. 41).

9. A German scholar, Professor Gotthold Rhode of the University of Mainz, thus evaluates the Polish-Lithuanian commonwealth: "There were few countries in Europe practicing a tolerance in both religious and ethnical-national matters similar to that of the Polish-Lithuanian Union of the sixteenth and early seventeenth centuries. No less than six languages (Latin, Polish, German, Russian, Hebrew, Armenian) were recognized for use in official documents, and four Christian confessions lived in a nearly perfect coexistence with Judaism and Islam until the

Counter-Reformation began its struggle against Protestant and Orthodox denominations. The memory of this peaceful coexistence was still alive in times of Russian suppression in the nineteenth century" (David S. Collier and Kurt Glaser, eds., *Berlin and the Future of Eastern Europe* [Chicago: Regnery, 1963], pp. 80–81).

10. There are two phenomena supporting this thesis: 1) the constant flight of peasants from the territories controlled by Muscovy to Poland-Lithuania, and 2) the relatively small number of Polish peasant uprisings, as compared with the constant, elemental, and vicious Muscovite peasant rebellions, such as those of Stenka Razin and Ymelian Pugachov. Only the Cossack uprisings of the seventeenth century could be roughly compared with the Muscovite peasant rebellion. Yet, the Cossack problem was not only a social issue because here ethnic and religious factors combined with the social ones: it was a struggle of Greek Orthodox, Ukrainian peasants against largely Roman Catholic, Polish landlords. The main slogan of the Cossack leader was: "Down with [Polish] lords, Jews [their economic agents], and Jesuits [the main instruments and promoters of the religious union]."

11. Despite long and involved debates over what extent the Polish constitution was a major contributing factor to the downfall of the Polish-Lithuanian commonwealth, it is worth recalling the opinion of the leading American expert on the subject: "The constitution of the Republic in its later years was so nearly unique in Europe that there was—and still is—a widespread tendency to regard it as something *sui generis,* as an entirely original creation of a misguided and fantastic people. In reality it was only an exaggerated and one-sided development of a type of political organization once almost universal on the Continent, that of what the Germans call the *monarchisch-ständische Staat* or the *Ständestaat.* Nearly all of the supposed peculiarities of the Polish constitution can be traced to principles and tendencies inherent in the *Ständestaat;* almost all of them find analogies in other countries in the same stage of development" (Robert H. Lord, *The Second Partition of Poland* [Cambridge: Harvard University Press, 1915], p. 7).

12. The saddle of a seventeenth-century squire, Karol Fredro, who was not a great magnate, had 133 rubies, twelve emeralds and several hundred pearls. Fortunes were spent on costly foreign wines, especially from Hungary and Moldavia.

13. In 1701, taking advantage of Poland's involvement in the Northern War, the elector of Brandenburg crowned himself king in Prussia. But since Poland, by the treaty of 1657, had retained a hereditary title to East Prussia failing the electoral line of the Hohenzollerns, his assumption of the royal title was not recognized by Poland until 1764, and then under military pressure.

14. The early period of Poland's political subservience to Muscovy-Russia was a period of considerable ascendancy of Polish culture, and with the annexation of Kiev in 1667, Polish influences began penetrating the Muscovite realm. Peter the Great, for instance, was taught Polish as well as German in his childhood. The former students of the theological academy of Kiev were instrumental in Peter's attempt to

257

modernize the Muscovite Orthodox church. The Latin theater of the Jesuit schools on the eastern fringes of Poland-Lithuania had profound impact on the beginnings of Russian theater.

15. It is noteworthy that practically all the schemes of reform and reconstruction, so abundantly presented to the public toward the end of the century, had already been formulated during the corrupt reign of Augustus III (1733–63). Among the outstanding forerunners of reform one should mention the exiled rival of August the Strong, King Stanisław Leszczyński, who spent most of his active life in France ruling the duchy of Lorraine on behalf of his son-in-law, Louis XV. Leszczyński articulated his suggestions in a book written in Polish and published at Nancy in 1737. A French edition appeared in 1749 under the title *La Voix Libre du Citoyen ou Observations sur le Government de Pologne*. In it, he discussed the reforms necessary to reestablish order and prosperity in his native country by strengthening the power of the crown and the abolition of serfdom. His emphasis on agriculture as the most important of all occupations and the source of all wealth makes him a forerunner of the Physiocrats. The first works of Quesnay appeared in 1766, some twenty-three years after Leszczyński's book.

16. Tadeusz Kościuszko (born in 1746) was an officer of the Polish engineering corps who in 1776 volunteered to join the U.S. forces. With the rank of colonel he entered the Continental Army and served as the chief engineer of the Southern Army. Highly valued by George Washington as a "gentleman of science and merit," he was rewarded by Congress after the war with the rank of brigadier general and became a member of the Society of the Cincinnati. In 1784, Kościuszko returned to his native country and in 1789 joined the expanding army with the rank of major general. He distinguished himself during the campaign of 1792, gaining an international reputation both for his military and civil virtues. A stanch republican and democrat, he was imbued with the ideals of the American Revolution and soon became known all over Europe as the "general-philosopher." On August 26, 1792, the French legislative assembly granted him the honorary title "Citizen of the French Republic," an honor he shared with George Washington. In his testament he left his entire fortune for emancipation and education of black slaves. Another Polish volunteer of the American War of Independence was Brigadier General Kazimierz (Casimir) Pułaski, who was the first to organize large units of cavalry, and hence is often called father of the U.S. cavalry. He was killed at the battle of Savannah, Georgia, in October 1779.

17. It is questionable whether the policy of Catherine, as suggested by the Russian historian Sergey Soloviev in his *History of the Downfall of Poland,* was aimed primarily at the liberation of the Russian Orthodox population of the commonwealth in order to complete the work of unification of the eastern Slavic nations. The historical rights of Muscovy-Russia to the Kievan inheritance were certainly not the chief motives of Catherine's action. By the end of the eighteenth century the western

branches of the east Slavic group had so long maintained a separate existence so different from that of the Muscovites that they had developed into types distinctly unlike that represented by the Great Russian branch. The present Ukrainian and Byelorussian nations were thus already in the making. The only traditional element that was not completely forgotten during the course of the eighteenth century was the Orthodox faith, the sole bond that still united the Muscovites with the majority of the Byelorussian and Ukrainian population of the eastern part of the commonwealth.

2. IN SEARCH OF THE LOST INDEPENDENCE

1. Here the liberal Lamartine did not differ much from the arch-conservative Metternich, who expressed his opinion about the Polish question in the following words: "Polonism is only a formula, the sound of a word underneath which hides a revolution in its most glaring form: it is not a small part of a revolution, but a revolution itself. Polonism does not declare war on the monarchies which possess Polish territory: it declares war on all the common foundations which form the basis of society." Quoted in Józef Feldman's chapter, "The Polish Provinces of Austria and Prussia after 1851," in W. F. Reddaway, ed., *Cambridge History of Poland* (Cambridge: Cambridge University Press, 1941–50), 2: 338. The First International was founded in 1864 following a meeting protesting the suppression of the Polish uprising.

2. For a general background work on Poland's national rebirth after the partitions, see William J. Rose, *The Rise of Polish Democracy* (London: G. Bell and Sons, 1944); Marian Kukiel, *Dzieje Polski porozbiorowe* (A History of Post-Partition Poland) (London: B. Swiderski, 1961); for an anthology of Polish political writings, see Marian Kridl, Józef Wittlin, and Władysław Malinowski, eds., *The Democratic Heritage of Poland* (London: Polish Labour Group, 1944). For a recent history of Poland in the post-partition period, see Piotr Wandycz, *The Lands of Partitioned Poland, 1795–1918* (Seattle: University of Washington Press, 1974).

3. For a discussion of the issue, see Stefan Kieniewicz, *Emancipation of the Polish Peasantry* (Chicago: University of Chicago Press, 1969).

4. Aleksander Świętochowski, "My i wy" (We and You), *Przegląd tygodniowy* (The Weekly Review) 44 (1871). For a recent attempt at analyzing the concept, see Stanislaus A. Blejwas, "The Origins and Practice of 'Organic Work' in Poland: 1795–1863," *The Polish Review* (Autumn 1970). The dichotomy between organic work, or the more realistic trend in Polish politics, and political romanticism has been analyzed by Adam Bromke in his book *Poland's Politics: Idealism vs. Realism* (Cambridge: Harvard University Press, 1967).

5. For a broad examination of modern Polish political trends, see William Feldman, *Dzieje polskiej myśli politycznej* (A History of Polish Political Thought) (Warsaw: Instytut badania najnowszej historii Polski, 1933).

6. For a discussion in English of Galician autonomy, see the chapter by Stanisław

259

⚏ Notes

Estreicher, "Galicia in the Period of Autonomy and Self-Government," in *Cambridge History of Poland*, vol. 2. For the presentation of the issue against a broad background of the monarchy's internal problems, see Joseph Redlich, *Das Oesterreichische Staats- und Reichsproblem* (Leipzig: P. Reinhold, n.d.), 2: 619ff. For the status of the Ukrainians in autonomous Galicia, see Volodymyr Kubijovycz, ed., *Ukraine: A Concise Encyclopedia* (Toronto: University of Toronto Press, 1963), pp. 721–24.

7. Rose, *The Rise of Polish Democracy*, p. 116.

8. As a British historian observed: "The Poles kept faithfully to their side of the bargain struck in 1873, completely abjuring irridentism of international conspiracy. . . . They even abandoned their old boycott of the Austrian State service, which, on the contrary, they now entered on such a scale as to evoke complaints from the Germans of their excessive influence over Austrian affairs. Badeni, Dunajewski and Gołuchowski are examples of Poles who in fact in their days largely directed the fortunes of the Monarch" (C. A. Macartney, *The Hapsburg Empire, 1790–1918* [New York: Macmillan, 1969], p. 464). For a sharp criticism of the economic policy of the conservative circles, see Stanisław Szczepanowski, *Nędza Galicyi* (Poverty of Galicia) (Lwów, 1888), pp. 139–42, 176–78.

9. For a monograph describing the struggle of Poles against the germanizing attempts of Berlin, see Richard W. Tims, *Germanizing Prussian Poland* (New York: Columbia University Press, 1941). For a recent treatment of the issue, see a series of articles in *The Polish Review* (Winter 1972).

10. For a background of the Polish-German struggle for the lands lost to Poland in the fourteenth century, see William J. Rose, *The Drama of Upper Silesia* (Brattleboro, Vt.: Stephen Daye Press, 1935).

11. Rose, *The Rise of Polish Democracy*, p. 68.

12. Sergei Stepniak-Krawczynsky [Stepnyak-Kravchinski], *The Russian Storm-Cloud: Or Russia in Her Relations to Neighboring Countries* (London, 1886), pp. 10–11. For a background work on the Polish working class movement, see Feliks Gross, *The Polish Worker: A Study of a Social Stratum* (New York: Roy Publishers, 1945); see also Stefan Kieniewicz, "The Formation of Mass Political Parties. Nationalism and Socialism (1885–1904)," in Aleksander Gieysztor, et al., *History of Poland* (Warsaw: PWN—Polish Scientific Publishers, 1968).

13. Piłsudski expressed eloquently his political credo of those days in an essay, "How I Became a Socialist," in D. R. Gillie, ed., *Memoirs of a Polish Revolutionary and Soldier* (London: Faber and Faber, 1931).

14. Witold Kula, *Historia gospodarcza Polski, 1864–1918* (Economic History of Poland, 1864–1918) (Warsaw: Państwowe wydawnictwa naukowe, 1947), p. 54.

15. For a sociological study of Polish peasantry, see William I. Thomas and Florian Znaniecki, *The Polish Peasant in Europe and America*, 2 vols. (Chicago: University of Chicago Press, 1958).

16. For the origins of the Polish Populist movement, see Peter Brock's two essays, "The Early Years of the Polish Peasant Party: 1895–1907," *Journal of Central European Affairs* (Oct. 1954), and "Bolesław Wysłouch, Founder of the Polish Peasant Party," *The Slavonic and East European Review* (Dec. 1951). See also Krzysztof Dunin-Wąsowicz, *Dzieje stronnictwa ludowego w Galicii* (A History of the Populist Movement in Galicia) (Warsaw: Ludowa spółdzielnia wydawnicza, 1956). In his essay on Wysłouch, Brock stresses his radical position regarding the demarcation of frontiers between ethnographic Poland and its neighbors: "This was no theoretical problem in Galicia," points out Brock. He adds: "In the west, Upper Silesia and Mazuria, neglected for centuries by the *szlachta,* should in Wysłouch's view return to Poland. In the east, the frontiers before 1772 had meant a partition of the Ukraine as unjust as the partition of Poland by her neighbors. The frontiers, therefore, should run roughly along the line drawn by the San and the Bug. L'vov is left significantly on the Ukrainian side. For, according to Wysłouch, 'democrats in Ruthenia must be Ruthenians, in Latvia Latvians, etc. They must take into consideration the language of the people among whom they work, they must take on the local colour of that nationality . . . a Polish democratic party has its *raison d'être* only on purely Polish territory . . . basing ourselves on the principle of nationality, and condemning the violation of our own national rights, we equally condemn similar violations of the rights of neighbouring nationalities made by our Polish gentry.' " Brock also stresses that the Polish Peasant party, founded in 1895, was the earliest in date among the east-central European Populist movements; the Czech Agrarian party was founded in 1896, the Bulgarian Agrarian Union in 1899, the Croatian Peasant party in 1904.

17. For a presentation of Dmowski's ideas, see his *Polityka polska i odbudowanie państwa* (Warsaw: Perzyński, 1926). For the only comprehensive biography of the National Democratic leader, see Andrzej Micewski, *Roman Dmowski* (Warsaw: Verum, 1971). For a competent presentation of Dmowski's ideas in English, see Bromke, *Poland's Politics.*

18. Bernard Pares, *History of Russia* (London, 1941), p. 411.

19. The kingdom was among the most economically developed parts of the empire, paid more taxes per capita than the rest of the state, and was making a yearly contribution of 150 million roubles to the imperial treasury (Kula, *Historia,* pp. 48–52).

20. ". . . for parliamentary ability the most notable group in the Duma was that of Poles led by Roman Dmowski" (Pares, *History of Russia,* p. 441). Nevertheless, as the leader of the National Democrats admitted: "From St. Petersburg I could not bring a single gain for my country . . ." (Dmowski, *Polityka polska,* p. 54).

21. For a background work on Polish scholarship and arts, see Stanisław Kot, *Five Centuries of Polish Learning* (London: The Shakespeare Head Press, 1941), and Roman Dyboski, *Poland in World Civilization,* ed. Ludwik Krzyżanowski (New

Notes

York: Barrett, 1950). For Petrażycki's psychological theory of law, see G. Langrod's and M. Vaughan's essay in W. J. Wagner, ed., *Polish Law Through the Ages: One Thousand Years of Legal Thought in Poland* (Stanford: Hoover Institution Press, 1970).

3. THE POLISH PHOENIX

1. It is better known in its French version, *La Question Polonaise,* tr. V. Gasztovt (Paris: A. Colin, 1909).

2. In Piłsudski's group the idea of transforming the Hapsburg empire in a federal trialist sense was rather strong. Piłsudski's main diplomatic agent, Michał Sokolnicki, said in a conversation with a French publicist, Pierre Bernus: "Sooner or later . . . there will be formed [in east-central Europe] some supernational, federal association of peoples." The Hapsburg monarchy, added Sokolnicki, was not ideal, but in that part of Europe, "there was nothing better" (Michał Sokolnicki, *Rok Czternasty* [Year 1914] [London: Gryf Publications, 1961], p. 116). These ideas did not quite correspond to those of Piłsudski, who always regarded a temporary link of Poland with the Hapsburg empire as a stepping stone toward independence.

3. Victor M. Chernov, *Pered Burei* (Before the Storm) (New York: Chekhov Publication House, 1953), pp. 296–97.

4. For Dmowski's view of his activity, see his *Polityka polska i odbudowanie państwa* (Polish Policy) (Warsaw: Perzyński, 1926), originally a memorandum submitted to the British foreign secretary, Lord Balfour.

5. Perhaps the best analysis of Piłsudski's tactics during World War I is found in the last chapter of Anatol Muhlstein's *Le Maréchal Piłsudski, 1867–1919* (Paris: Plon, 1939).

6. The romantic atmosphere conducive to hero worship as well as to Nietzschean contempt for popular support, proper to Piłsudski's followers, is best reflected in an essay entitled "The Dream of a Sword," by Stefan Żeromski. The essay is a glorification of an underground revolutionary fight of an heroic, isolated, and alienated individual, misunderstood and forgotten by his nation: "You crept out in the darkness of the autumn night with the wild wind moaning and the rain beating, while we, the twenty million of us, slept in our bedrooms, in our nooks, and attics, and underground holes, sunk in the deep slumber of slaves. You crept out like a thief, naked to the waist, on your back the dismantled parts of a printing press. You were stuffed with leaflets proclaiming the freedom of body and spirit. In your left fist you clasped a torch with which you sought the guard in the darkness, and in your right you gripped a revolver cocked to fire. Thus you crossed the frontier rivers, thus you entered the country, barefoot, bleeding. That very night independence was brought to this land of miserable souls, harassed by foreign soldiers. . . . You brought with you the last remnants of the Polish creed out of the crumbling tombs of the exiles . . ." (quoted by M. Kreidl et al., eds., *The Democratic Heritage of Poland* [London: Polish Labour Group, 1944], p. 219).

262

7. For an outline of the German policy toward Poland, see Werner Conze, *Polnische Nation und Deutsche Politik im Ersten Weltkriege* (Cologne and Gratz: Boehlau, 1958).

8. For a basic work on the subject, see Tytus Komarnicki, *The Rebirth of the Polish Republic* (London: Heinemann, 1957).

9. A German scholar thus summarized Piłsudski's role in the process of restoring Poland's independence: "Piłsudski's historical achievement lay not so much in his faith in Poland's own strength as in his accurate prognosis of the course of the war, a prognosis which enabled him instinctively to choose the right policy. Dmowski on the other hand made a decisive contribution by founding the National Committee, with which he took over the idea of Polish independence at the very moment when its previous exponent, Piłsudski, voluntarily left the political scene. Thus whatever claims may have been made, it was not thanks to any individual statesman in the ranks of the Poles, the Central Powers, the Entente or Russia that the way was cleared for Polish independence. The work was accomplished by the complex and intricate interplay of a number of different political forces" (Hans Roos, *A History of Modern Poland* [New York: Knopf, 1966], p. 46).

10. For an outline of the party's history, see M. K. Dziewanowski, *The Communist Party of Poland: An Outline of History* (Cambridge: Harvard University Press, 1959).

11. Rosa Luxemburg viewed all schemes for emancipation of Poland as nonsensical. In her doctoral dissertation, written in Zürich in 1898, she wrote: "Even the extremist fancy of a cafe politician cannot imagine today how the independence of Poland could emerge from a war between the German Empire and Russia." Quoted in W. F. Reddaway, ed., *The Cambridge History of Poland* (Cambridge: Cambridge University Press, 1941–50), 2: 400.

12. For the Polish issue at Versailles, see "Poland" in Charles M. Haskins and Robert H. Lord, eds., *Some Problems of the Peace Conference* (Cambridge: Harvard University Press, 1920). See also *Akty i dokumenty dotyczące sprawy granic Polski na Konferencji Pokojowej w Paryżu 1918–1919, zebrane i wydane przez Sekretariat Jenerainy Delegacij Polskiej* (Acts and Documents Pertaining to the Problem of Poland's Frontiers at the Peace Conference in Paris 1918–1919, collected and published by the Polish Peace Conference, Paris, 1920); Natalia Gąsiorowską, ed., *Materaby archiwalne do stosunków polsko-radzieckich* (The Archive Materials Pertaining to Polish-Soviet Relations), vols. 2 and 3 (Warsaw: Książka i Wiedza, 1961). See also Roman Dmowski, *Polityka polska,* and Stanisław Kozicki, *Sprawa granic Polski* (The Problem of Poland's Frontiers) (Warsaw, 1921).

13. For a recent scholarly treatment of Polish-Soviet relations during this period, see Piotr S. Wandycz, *Soviet-Polish Relations, 1917–1921* (Cambridge: Harvard University Press, 1969).

14. For an analysis of Piłsudski's federalist views, see A. Tarnowski, *Two Polish Attempts to Bring about a Central-East European Organization* (London, 1943), and

Notes

M. K. Dziewanowski, *A European Federalist: Joseph Piłsudski and Eastern Europe, 1918–1922* (Stanford: Stanford University Press, 1969). For a recent treatment of the Polish-Soviet War of 1919–20, see Norman Davies, *White Eagle, Red Star: The Polish-Soviet War, 1919–20* (New York: St. Martin's Press, 1972). The book makes a significant contribution to the history of the war. It presents the conflict in a broad diplomatic context, connecting it with the major trends in Polish and Soviet policies, including the NEP and socialism in one country. The book also disproves the persistent legend of General Weygand's major role in the battle of Warsaw. Davies proves beyond any doubt that the war was not a marginal event, either politically or militarily, stressing the largely overlooked fact that the contest was the only major war lost by Soviet Russia, and that it decided the fate of east-central Europe for nearly twenty years.

15. For Stalin's letter to Lenin of June 12, 1920, concerning Soviet plans about eastern Europe, see V. I. Lenin, *Oeuvres Complètes, L'Arnée, 1920* (Moscow: State Publishing House, 1955), p. 340. For Lenin's attitude and hopes connected with the war of 1920, see Stanley W. Page, *Lenin and World Revolution* (New York: New York University Press, 1959), pp. 154–76.

16. For a recent evaluation of the treaty of Riga, see Wandycz, *Soviet-Polish Relations*, pp. 250–78, 283–84, 286–87. See also Stanisław Grabski, *The Polish-Soviet Frontier* (London, 1943), p. 19; for a typical Soviet evaluation, see Fedor G. Zuev, *Mezdunarodnyi imperializm organizator napadenia panskoi Polshi na Sovetskuiu Rossiu, 1919–1920* (International Capitalism as Organizer of the Landlord's Poland in the Soviet Union, 1919–1920) (Moscow: State Publishing House, 1954).

17. Wandycz, *Soviet-Polish Relations*, p. 285. Although most National Democrats welcomed the treaty of Riga, there was a great deal of regret about the loss of the Polish "cultural sphere" of influence in eastern Europe. A National Democratic politician thus deplored the Polish losses resulting from the treaty of Riga: "Foreign statesmen and diplomats, accustomed to the terminology in use for so long under the Tsars, could consider every square mile beyond the Bug incorporated in Poland as an intrusion upon Russia. Thoughtful Poles did not fail to realize that Poland was recovering but a fraction of what had been hers for centuries, and what had been wrested from her by Russia in the three successive acts of partition. In the vast areas now renounced and abandoned, Polish culture, language, institutions, and customs had not only been accepted in the past, but had largely grown up, developed and formed part of the native background. If that state of things had changed in the last 130 years, it was not due to inevitable developments, but to a ruthless and consistent policy aimed at uprooting and destroying every vestige of Polish life and tradition. Even so, more than a million Poles dwelt outside the new border, the way of life there still differed widely from the Russian, Catholicism was widespread and respected, Polish influence was by no means dead, as the share of members of that nationality in representative bodies had recently shown; in thousands of homes Polish

264

culture reigned supreme, and Polish interests in economic terms were very substantial. Under existing conditions, all these important assets had not only to be politically renounced, but definitely written off as irretrievably lost to the nation" (Adam Żółtowski, *Border of Europe* [London: Hollis and Carter, 1950], p. 214).

18. The present-day attitude of the two former rivals for leadership of eastern Europe is best characterized by a British historian: "The present-day, the Polish-Soviet War is still an embarrassment in the two countries where it is best remembered. The leaders of People's Poland and of the Soviet Union quite naturally recoil from memories which threaten to disturb the even tenor of their comradely relations. They are rightly concerned lest a headstrong nation such as the Poles should be misled into comparing their present condition with the supposedly golden independence of fifty years ago. The Soviet government does not want to be reminded of the time when a former Tsarist province refused to join the Soviet club and inflicted the only unredeemed defeat in the Red Army's history" (Davies, *White Eagle, Red Star,* pp. 277–78).

4. EXPERIMENT IN INDEPENDENCE

1. Howard of Penrith (Sir Esmé Howard), *Theater of Life,* 2 vols. (London: Hutchinson, 1936), 2: 320.

2. For short surveys of Polish economic development, see Ferdynand Zweig, *Poland Between Two Wars* (London: Secker and Warburg, 1944); and Jack J. Taylor, *The Economic Development of Poland, 1919–1950* (Ithaca, N.Y.: Cornell University Press, 1952).

3. "Broadly speaking, one may distinguish two types of anti-Semitism: an 'objective' or a 'realistic' type and a 'subjective' or an 'unrealistic' one—to use the terms in the technical, 'value neutral' sense in which they were used by George Simmel in his *Sociology of Conflict.* A manifestation of hostility toward the Jews may be called 'objective' if it is born of a genuine conflict of interests between the Jews and their host people as a whole or some segment of it. A classic illustration of an objective form of anti-Semitism is the Jew-hatred prevailing in Eastern and Central Europe between the two World Wars. In the twentieth century, in Poland, Rumania, and Hungary, the indigenous petit bourgeois classes of merchants and traders, emerging relatively late in history, found themselves competing with a large proportion of the Jewish population that had hitherto performed the intermediary functions in the economy. Economic rivalry bred enmity, which fused with religious prejudices into an intense hatred permeating the moral, intellectual, and political lives of the respective countries" (Erich Goldhagen, "Pragmatism, Function and Belief in Nazi Anti-Semitism," *Midstream* [Dec. 1972]).

4. Describing a conference of the Federation of Polish Jews in Great Britain, held in July 1933 in London, with the objective of assessing the situation that had arisen in Germany, a Jewish paper reported a speech by its president, Mr. Nahum Sokolow,

who said: "The Polish Republic was as liberal and hospitable as it was possible to be in the present circumstances, and he would like to give expression on that occasion to the appreciation of the Jewish people of the attitude of the Polish government to the Jews. . . . The Chief Rabbi [of Britain] said that for centuries Poland had no more loyal friend than the Jews. . . . And the reason was not far to seek" ("Federation of Polish Jews, Well-attended Conference," *The Jewish Chronicle* [London], July 21, 1933, p. 12).

5. For a scholarly discussion of the coup, see Joseph Rothschild, *Piłsudski's Coup d'Etat* (New York: Columbia University Press, 1966).

6. An observer of the Polish political scene writes about Piłsudski's political methods: "His alternative to undiluted parliamentary democracy failed partly because of its anachronistic character. The methods of parliamentary control which Giolitti had employed in Italy before 1914, or which Taaffe had used in Austria, could no longer easily be applied after the revolutionary upheavals of World War I. Moreover, Piłsudski and his associates had little idea of what it meant to cooperate with even a weak and subservient parliament. Their political training had been concentrated in conspiratorial technique, and they had little understanding of the nature of parliamentary debate, or of the function of parliamentary criticism of the Government. In addition, the contempt which Piłsudski came to hold for all politicians made difficult the achievement of smooth relations with the Sejm" (Antony Polonsky, *Politics in Independent Poland, 1921–1939: The Crisis of Constitutional Government* [Oxford: Clarendon Press, 1972], p. 511).

7. When Marshal Piłsudski died on May 13, 1936, the *New York Times* correspondent in Warsaw reported on May 15: "All classes share in this sorrow. There is no radical division whatever, for Marshal Piłsudski is mourned by Jews as much as by Christians." On May 15, the same paper reported that a message of condolence sent by the American Jewish Committee to Stanisław Patek, the Polish ambassador in Washington, stressed: "We specially recognize his [Piłsudski's] firm opposition to all chauvinistic movements seeking to sow discord among the various elements composing the population of Poland. . . ." On May 20, the *New York Times* reported on p. 8 that "Jewish boys born this month in Rovno, Poland, will be named Joseph for the late Marshal Piłsudski, the rabbinate of Rovno decided today. The city has a Jewish population of 50,000." It is worthwhile remembering that it was Piłsudski who decided to grant Polish citizenship to over 600,000 Jewish refugees who sought shelter in Poland from the Russian pogroms during the civil war of 1918–21. No wonder, therefore, that Joseph Rothschild (*Piłsudski's Coup d'Etat,* p. 236) concluded that the Jews of Poland had "high regard for Piłsudski." Another scholarly observer of Polish politics of the period writes that "The Government strongly supported Jewish aspirations in Palestine, and entered into close contact with international Zionist organizations, the World Zionist Organization of Chaim Weizmann, the Jewish Agency, and the Revisionists led by Vladimir Jabotinsky" (Polonsky, *Politics in Independent Poland,* p. 468).

8. According to two Communist historians, in 1933 the Communist party of Poland, including its autonomous Ukrainian and Byelorussian sections, numbered only 17,800 members (Hanna and Tadeusz Jędruszak, *Ostatnie lata Drugiej Rzeczpospolitej, 1935–1939* [The Last Years of the Second Republic, 1935–1939] [Warsaw: Książka i Wiedza, 1970], p. 24).

9. For a scholarly examination of this crucial period, see Bohdan Budurowycz, *Polish-Soviet Relations, 1932–1939* (New York: Columbia University Press, 1963).

10. For a useful background to the diplomatic relations between the two countries, see Piotr S. Wandycz, *France and Her Eastern Allies, 1919–1925: French-Czechoslovak-Polish Relations from the Paris Peace Conference to Locarno* (Minneapolis: University Press of Minnesota, 1962).

11. For a discussion of this controversial aspect of Piłsudski's foreign policy, see Anna M. Cienciała, "The Significance of the Declaration of Non-Aggression of January 26, 1934, in Polish-German and International Relations: A Reappraisal," *East European Quarterly* (March 1967). "The Polish-German Declaration of non-aggression signed on January 26, 1934 [concludes the author], should not be seen as the beginning of a weakening of the French system of alliances or of collective security, but as a reflection of the weakness of both, and of Poland's quest for security in the light of these circumstances of her specific problems with Germany, and Soviet Russia."

12. Joseph Beck, *Dernier raport: politique polonaise, 1926–1939* (Neuchâtel: Editions de la Baconniere, 1951), p. 110. Leon Noël, in his memoirs, *L'aggression allemande contre la Pologne* (Paris, 1940), gives his version of the conversation which is in basic agreement with Beck's version. While in Warsaw, on February 29, 1936, Göring said that in 1933 France "hatte uns zerschmettern können" (could have crushed us) (Jan Szembek, *Diariusz i Teki, 1935–1945* [London: Polski Osrodek Naukowy, 1965], 2: 92). Piłsudski's controversial and as yet insufficiently documented efforts to launch a preventive war against Nazi Germany have been summarized by Professor Wacław Jędrzejewicz in *Polish Review* (Winter 1966). In this respect see also the evaluation of a German historian, Hans Roos, *Polen und Europa* (Tübingen: Mohr, 1957), pp. 65, 82; John W. Wheeler-Bennett, *Munich: Prologue to Tragedy* (London: Macmillan, 1948), p. 282; V. P. Potemkin, *Istoria Diplomatii* (A History of Diplomacy) (Moscow: State Social Economic Publications, 1945), 3: 471; L. B. Namier, *Diplomatic Prelude, 1938–1939* (London: Macmillan, 1948), pp. 15, 97 n. 3; and Alexander Werth, *The Last Days of Paris* (London: Hamilton, 1940), pp. 218–19.

13. The former British foreign secretary, Anthony Eden, first Earl of Avon, in the second volume of his memoirs, *Facing the Dictators, 1923–1938* (Boston: Houghton Mifflin, 1962), p. 187, thus evaluates Beck's policy: "It seemed to me that Beck was over-confident of his country's position. It might be that a policy such as he was following with so much adroitness would be possible for a strong power with two neighbors of approximately equal strength, or for an island power. I doubted whether

Poland had the resources to carry it through.'' For an overall evaluation of Poland's foreign policy on the eve of World War II, see Anna M. Cieńciała, *Poland and the Western Powers, 1938–1939* (Toronto: University of Toronto Press, 1968).

14. "Record of a Conversation at Geneva between Mr. MacDonald, Sir J. Simon, and M. Beneš, March 18, 1933," in *Documents on British Foreign Policy, 1919–1939,* 2d series, vol. 4, *1932–1933,* ed. E. L. Woodward and Rohan Butler (London: Royal Institute of International Affairs, 1950), pp. 520–21. For Polish-Czechoslovak relations, see W. J. Rose, "Czechs and Poles as Neighbors," *Journal of Central European Affairs* 2 (1951); see also Z. J. Gąsiorowski, "Polish-Czechoslovak Relations," *Slavonic Review* 35 (1956); Jerzy Kozeński, *Czechosłowacja w polskiej polityce zagranicznej w latach 1932–1939* (Czechoslovakia in Polish Foreign Policy During 1932–1939) (Poznań: Instytut Zachodni, 1964). In 1918, Dmowski suggested to Masaryk a Polish-Czechoslovak federation. See Thomas G. Masaryk, *The Making of a State* (New York: F. A. Stocke and Co., 1927), p. 251.

15. Robert Coulondre, *De Stalin à Hitler* (Paris: Hachette, 1950), pp. 263–64.

16. For a set of primary sources illustrating the ups and downs of relations between Warsaw and Moscow, see *Documents on Polish-Soviet Relations, 1939–1945* (hereinafter referred to as *Documents*), 2 vols. (London: The General W. Sikorski Institute, 1961–67), 1: 1–41, which gives basic documents relating to the period prior to September 1, 1939.

17. *Polish White Book: Documents Concerning Polish-German and Polish-Soviet Relations, 1933–1939* (London: Hutchinson, 1939), no. 165; and *Documents,* 1: nos. 19–22, appendix 3. For a discussion of the diplomatic maneuvers preceding World War II by a Western historian well-acquainted with the East European scene, see Lewis B. Namier, *Diplomatic Prelude, 1938–39* (London: Macmillan, 1948); for a contemporary Polish interpretation, see Henryk Batowski, *Agonia pokoju i początek wojny* (The Agony of Peace and the Beginning of the War) (Poznań: Wydawnictwo Poznańskie, 1969).

18. Polonsky, *Politics in Independent Poland,* pp. 478–79.

19. Martin Gilbert and Richard Scott, *The Appeasers* (Boston: Houghton Mifflin, 1963), p. 328. For documents concerning Polish-British relations during the summer of 1939, up to September 3, see *Documents on British Foreign Policy, 1919–1939,* 3d series, vol. 7 (London: Royal Institute on International Affairs, 1954). For an analysis of the September 1939 campaign based exclusively on German sources, see R. M. Kennedy, *The German Campaign in Poland* (Washington, D.C.: Department of the Army, 1956); for a Polish view, *Polskie siły zbrojne w Drugiej Wojnie Światowej* (Polish Armed Forces in World War II), vol. 1 (London: The General W. Sikorski Institute, 1951).

20. For a challenging reexamination of the Polish campaign of September 1939, see Nicholas Bethell, *The War That Hitler Won* (London: Allen Lane, The Penguin

Press, 1972), and John Kimche, *The Unfought Battle* (London: Weidenfeld and Nicholson, 1968). ''The Polish Government was . . . neither consulted nor told in precise language that there would be no military relief for them in the West should it be 'attacked first' '' (Kimche, p. 72). ''The French had lied to the Poles and assured them that they would start a counteroffensive against Germany if Poland were attacked'' (Kimche, p. 73). ''The British and French General Staffs have to share a grave responsibility with their own governments in failing to launch the battle that might have won and decided the second world war in September 1939'' (Kimche, p. 145). See also Gilbert and Scott, *The Appeasers,* ch. 22. Whether the British guarantees to Poland were given in order to deter Hitler from attacking Poland, or, quite the contrary, to provoke him and channel his energies toward the east, is a controversial question that may be decided only after full opening of British archives to scholarly research. There are, however, some indications that the latter opinion may have some justification; in this respect, see the Earl of Birkenhead, *The Life of Lord Halifax* (London: Hamilton, 1965), p. 437.

21. Interbellum Poland was a leading country as far as social insurance was concerned. ''Taking all thirty countries together, twenty have compulsory sickness insurance, twenty-four have some form of contributory pensions, eight have unemployment insurance. Three countries only, among the thirty—New Zealand, Bulgaria, and Poland—make provision against all three risks of sickness, old age and unemployment. That is to say, three countries only aim at covering all the principal forms of social insecurity as fully as Britain'' (Sir William Beveridge, *Social Insurance and Allied Services* [New York: Macmillan, 1942], appendix F, p. 289).

22. For a brief discussion of Polish achievements in art, literature, and scholarship, see Roman Dyboski, *Poland in World Civilization* (New York: J. M. Barrett, 1950), chs. 8, 9.

23. For a symposium devoted to Witkiewicz and his impact on contemporary culture, see *The Polish Review* 1 and 2 (1973). For interesting observations on Witkiewicz and his work, see Czesław Miłosz, *The Captive Mind* (New York: Random House, Vintage Books, 1955). According to two American scholars: ''During the interwar years, the Polish theater . . . both technologically and artistically equalled that to be seen anywhere in the world'' (Oscar G. Brockett and Robert R. Findlay, *Century of Innovation: A History of European and American Theater and Drama, 1870–1970* (Englewood Cliffs, N.J.: Prentice-Hall, 1972), p. 440; for an analysis of Witkiewicz's work, see Brockett and Findlay, pp. 440–42.

24. A Polish-born sociologist teaching at an English university thus characterizes the socioeconomic structure of pre-World War II Poland: ''Until 1939, the correlated factors of birth and wealth characterized the ruling class—comprising the aristocracy, the bourgeoisie and the upper strata of the intelligentsia. This privileged group cumulated political power, social prestige and economic wealth (still predominantly agrarian). On all these dimensions the deprivation of other groups was corre-

spondingly great'' (Michalina Vaughan, ''Poland,'' in Margaret S. Archer and Salvador Giner, eds., *Contemporary Europe: Class, Status and Power* [London: Weidenfeld and Nicholson, 1971], pp. 348–49).

5. THE TIME OF TRIAL

1. For a comprehensive and well-documented study of the subject, see Czesław Madajczyk, *Polityka Trzeciej Rzeszy w okupowanej Polsce* (The Third Reich's Policy in Occupied Poland), 2 vols. (Warsaw: Państwowe wydawnictwa naukowe, 1970); for a German scholarly treatment, see Martin Broszat, *National-sozialistische Polenpolitik: 1939–1945* (Frankfurt-am-Main: Deutsche Verlagsanstalt, 1965).

2. The uprising in the Warsaw ghetto was assisted by the Polish underground movement. An eyewitness report, received by the World Jewish Congress from Jewish sources in Poland, states: ''Many Poles were arrested, suspected of complicity in the preparations for the uprising in the ghetto and of planning to help the Jewish fighters. . . . Large transports of arms had secretly been brought into the ghetto some time earlier when the task of watching the ghetto was assigned to the Polish police who cooperated in preparing for the uprising. Bombs, machine-guns and anti-tank cannon hidden under potatoes had been brought in on hundreds of trucks sent in by the secret Polish military organization. . . . Many young Poles volunteered to fight in the ghetto'' (''The Battle of the Warsaw Ghetto,'' from *The Extermination of 500,000 Jews in the Warsaw Ghetto* [New York: published by the American Council of Warsaw Jews and American Friends of Polish Jews, 1944]; reprinted in Nathan Ausubel, ed., *A Treasury of Jewish Folklore: Stories, Traditions, Legends, Humor, Wisdom and Folk Songs of the Jewish People* (New York: Crown, 1948), pp. 245, 247, 248). Polish-Jewish relations under the Nazi rule have been a subject of numerous controversies; for the background of these relations, see Philip Friedman, ed., *Martyrs and Fighters* (New York: Praeger, 1954); Joseph Tennenbaum, *Underground: The Story of a People* (New York, 1952); Philip Friedman, *Their Brothers' Keepers* (New York: Crown, 1957); Kazimierz Iranek-Osmecki, *He Who Saves One Life* (New York: Crown, 1971); Władysław Bartoszewski and Zofia Lewin, *The Samaritans: Heroes of the Holocaust* (New York: Twayne, 1971); Władysław Bartoszewski, *The Blood Shed Unites Us* (Warsaw: Interpress, 1970); and S. Wroński and M. Zwolakowa, eds., *Polacy i Żydzi, 1939–1945* (Poles and Jews, 1939–1945) (Warsaw: Książka i Wiedza, 1971). The Israeli Institute of National Memory, which plants trees to commemorate each Gentile who risked his life to save a Jew from the Holocaust, planted more trees for such Poles than for any other nationality. The Poles have almost as many trees as all other nations put together.

3. Quoted by Stanisław Piotrowski, ed. and trans., *Hans Frank's Diary*, 2d ed. (Warsaw: Państwowe Wydawn, 1961), 1: 1. Dr. Frank replied on February 6, 1940, to a question asked by Kleiss, a correspondent of the *Völkische Beobachter*, about the difference between the Czech and Moravian Protectorate and the Government

General: "I can give you a vivid definition of the difference. In Prague large red posters were put up stating that that day seven Czechs had been shot. I said to myself then, if I wanted to put up posters for every seven Poles that have been shot, the Polish forests would not suffice to produce the paper for the announcements!" Quoted by Stanisław Piotrowski in his "Confessions of a Goethe Admirer," *Poland Illustrated Magazine* (Warsaw) (Oct. 1972).

4. The question whether a rump Polish state was to be reestablished after the campaign had been left open in the protocol. For a discussion of the issue, see Adam Ulam, *Expansion and Coexistence: A History of Soviet Foreign Policy, 1917–1967* (New York: Praeger, 1968), pp. 282–84.

5. For an outline of the history of the Polish underground movement, see three books by its leaders: Tadeusz Bór-Komorowski, *The Secret Army* (London: Macmillan, 1951); Stefan Korboński, *W imieniu Rzeczypospolitej* (In the Name of the Polish Republic) (London: Świderski, 1964); and *Polskie Państwo Podziemne* (The Polish Underground State) (Paris: Instytut Literacki, 1975), by the same author. For a history of the Home Army, see *Polskie siły zbrojne w Drugiej Wojnie Światowej* (Polish Armed Forces in the Second World War), vol. 3 (London: The General W. Sikorski Institute, 1950), and Tadeusz Pełczynski et al., eds., *Armia Krajowa w Dokumentach, 1939–1945* (The Home Army in Documents, 1939–1945), 2 vols. (London: Studium Polski-Podziemnej, 1970–74). See also Jan Karski, *Story of a Secret State* (Boston: Houghton Mifflin, 1944), a readable book by one of the underground couriers.

6. For a set of primary sources on the subject of Polish-Soviet relations, see *Documents on Polish Soviet Relations, 1939–1945* (hereinafter referred to as *Documents*), 2 vols. (London: The General W. Sikorski Institute, 1961–67), 1: 108ff; see also Władysław Anders, *Bez ostatniego rozdziału* (Without the Last Chapter) (London: Macmillan, 1949), and Jósef Czapski, *Terre inhumaine* (Paris: Editions Self, 1949).

7. Louise W. Holborn, ed., *War and Peace Aims of the United Nations: September 1, 1939–December 31, 1942* (Boston: World Peace Foundation, 1943), pp. 466–67, 470–71.

8. For the documents marking various stages and phases of the defense of the Riga boundary, see *Documents,* 1: 100, 109, 113–14, 119–22, 312–17, 469–72, 502, and ibid., 2: 406. See also Stanisław Kot, *Conversations with the Kremlin* (Oxford: Oxford University Press, 1963), and Edward J. Rożek, *Allied Wartime Diplomacy: A Pattern in Poland* (New York: Wiley, 1958), pp. 52, 59, 65, 187, 193–95, 259–60, 439–40. For a semiofficial presentation of the territorial program of the Polish government in London, see Adam Pragier, *Polish Peace Aims* (London: Max Lore, 1944), pp. 47–59.

9. Sarah Meiklejohn Terry, "Sikorski Reconsidered: An Inquiry Into the Origin of the Oder-Neisse Boundary, 1939–1943" (Ph.D. diss., Harvard University, 1974).

271

🖎 Notes

For the only comprehensive biography of the most important wartime Polish statesman, see Marian Kukiel, *Generał Sikorski: Żołnierz i mąż stanu Polski walczącej* (General Sikorski: Soldier and Statesman of Fighting Poland) (London: Instytut Polski, 1970).

The most important of the émigré heralds of Sikorski's Western school of thought was the *Biuletyn Zachodnio-Słowiański* (West Slavonic Bulletin), published in Edinburgh; nine issues appeared between September 1940 and June 1942. See also Antoni Błoński, *Wracamy nad Odrę: Historyczne, geograficzne i etnograficzne podstawy zachodnich granic Polski* (We are returning to the Oder and Neisse: Historic, Geographic and Ethnographic Foundations of Poland's Western Frontier) (London: Biuletyn Zachodnio-Słowiański, 1942); Henryk Bagiński, *Polska i Bałtyk: Zagadnienie dostępu Polski do morza* (Poland and the Baltic: the Problem of Poland's Access to the Baltic) (Edinburgh: Oliver and Boyd, 1942); Tadeusz Sulimirski, *Poland and Germany: Past and Future* (London and Edinburgh: Biuletyn Zachodnio-Słowiański, 1942); and Henryk Bagiński, *Gospodarcze uzasadnienie zadań terytorialnych dorzecza Odry* (Economic Reasons for Poland's Demand for the Oder Basin) (London: Biuletyn Zachodnio-Słowiański, 1943.

Even some postwar official Communist publications admit that: ''The demand for the Oder and Lusatian Neisse [was] very popular in the press and publications of the London camp until 1942 . . .'' (Marian Orzechowski, ''Koncepcja granic zachodnich w programie i działalności Polskiej Partii Robotniczej i lweicy rewolucyjnej na emigracji'' [The Western Frontiers Concept of the Polish Workers' Party and the Revolutionary Left in Exile], *Sobótka,* no. 2a [1962]: 8–46). The idea to establish the western frontier of Poland may be traced to various groups, largely from the National Democratic movement and to the Association of Poles in Germany, and to people like Dr. Jan Kaczmarek, Stefan Murek, Edmund Osmańczyk, and others.

10. For a discussion of the issue during its crucial phases, see two works by Herbert Feis, *Churchill, Roosevelt, Stalin: The War They Waged and the Peace They Sought* (Princeton: Princeton University Press, 1957), pp. 28–41, 191–97, 283–302, 373–90, 518–24; and *Between War and Peace: The Potsdam Conference* (Princeton: Princeton University Press, 1967), pp. 31–36, 203–34, 259–71. For a recent treatment of the subject, see Diane S. Clemens, *Yalta* (New York: Oxford University Press, 1970), pp. 9–10, 173–215, a study sympathetic to the Soviet point of view. For the defense of the Riga settlement by the Polish government-in-exile, see *Polish-Soviet Relations, 1918–1943: Official Documents,* pt. 2 (Washington: Polish Embassy, 1944), and *Les Relations Polono-Allemandes et Polono-Sovietiques,* pt. 2 (Paris: Republique de Pologne, 1940). For the problem of the future Polish-German frontier as planned by the émigré circles, see Jósef M. Winiewicz, *The Polish-German Frontier* (London: W. Hodge, 1944); Marian Seyda, *Pół wieku walki o granicę polsko-niemiecką* (Half a Century of Struggle for a Polish-German Frontier) (London, 1946). See also Józef Lipski, Edward Raczyński, *W sojuszniczym Londynie: dziennik Ambasadora Edwarda Raczyńskiego, 1939–1945* (In the Allied London:

272

Diary of Ambassador Edward Raczynski) (London: Polish Research Center, 1960); Leon Mitkiewicz, *Z Gen. Sikorskim na obczyźnie* (With General Sikorski in Exile) (Paris: Instytut Literacki, 1968). For the plans of a Polish-Czechoslovak partnership, see Piotr S. Wandycz, *Czechoslovak-Polish Confederation and the Great Powers, 1940–43* (Bloomington, Ind.: University of Indiana Press, 1956). In addition to the Wandycz study, see an article by a former secretary to President Beneš: Eduard Taborsky, "A Polish-Czechoslovak Confederation: A Story of the First Soviet Veto," *Journal of Central European Affairs* (Jan. 1950).

11. Jan Ciechanowski, *Defeat in Victory* (Garden City, N.Y.: Doubleday, 1947), pp. 93–94. See Edward J. Rożek, *Allied Wartime Diplomacy*, p. 431, for an exposition of an almost identical point of view by a former high-ranking member of the Churchill government.

12. See the "Note from Minister Raczyński to Mr. Eden, Concerning Anglo-Soviet Negotiations," *Documents*, 1: 332–35; for a set of sources illustrating the struggle of the Polish government in London for Poland's right to independence and reactions to it in British public opinion, see Wacław Jędrzejewicz, *Poland in the British Parliament, 1939–1945*, 3 vols. (New York: The Joseph Pilsudski Institute, 1946–59).

13. For a set of documents on the subject, see a selection of sources published by the Polish United Workers' party, *W dziesiątą rocznicę powstania PPR: materiały i dokumenty* (On the Tenth Anniversary of the Foundation of the PPR: Materials and Documents) (Warsaw: Instytut Historii Partii, 1952); see also Władysław Gomułka, *W walce o demokrację ludową* (In the Struggle for People's Democracy), 2 vols. (Warsaw: Książka, 1947). Initially, uncertain about the issue of the war and the domestic struggle for power, the Communists were contemplating a possible compromise with the London government. For instance, Gomułka said in a January 1962 speech that the underground Polish Workers' party had "not excluded the possibility that he [Sikorski] would head the government after the liberation of Poland" (Włodzimierz Józef Kowalski, *Walka dyplomatyczna o miejsce Polski w Europie, 1939–1945* [Diplomatic Struggle for Poland's Place in Europe, 1939–1945] [Warsaw: Książka i Wiedza, 1970], pp. 336–37).

14. While on the Communist side the literature on the subject of the Katyń Forest massacre is rather scarce, on the Western side from a host of books one should mention first of all the well-documented works: Władysław Anders, ed., *Zbrodnia katynska w świetle dokumentów* (The Katyń Crime in the Light of Documents) (London, 1962), and Janusz Zawodny, *Death in the Forest* (South Bend, Ind.: University of Notre Dame Press, 1972).

15. The first unit to be formed by the Union of Polish Patriots in Russia was the Kościuszko infantry division. As early as October 12–13, 1943, it took part in the battle of Lenino, in Byelorussia.

16. The literature on the Warsaw uprising is very large, but little of it is available in English. Among the Polish works one should mention Aleksander Skarżyński,

273

≈ Notes

Polityczne przyczyny Powstania Warszawskiego (Political Causes of the Warsaw Uprising) (Warsaw: Piw, 1964). See also a book by the last chief of the Polish wartime underground, Stefan Korboński, *Fighting Warsaw* (New York: Minerva Press, 1956), and Józef Garliński, *Politycy i żołnierze* (Politicians and Soldiers) (London: Polska Fundacja Kulturalna, 1971); Jan M. Ciechanowski, *Powstanie Warszawskie* (The Warsaw Uprising) (London: Odnowa, 1971); for a German treatment, see Hanns von Krannhals, *Der Warschauer Aufstand—1944* (Frankfurt-am-Main: Bernard und Graefe Verlag, 1962).

17. Arthur Bliss-Lane, *I Saw Poland Betrayed; an Ambassador Reports to the American People* (Indianapolis: Bobbs-Merrill, 1948), p. 177.

18. Bór-Komorowski, *Secret Army*, pp. 201, 203.

19. Quoted by Bliss-Lane, *Poland Betrayed*, p. 203.

20. George F. Kennan, *Russia and the West Under Lenin and Stalin* (Boston: Little, Brown, 1961), p. 365. For a reexamination of the events after a quarter of a century, see Andrzej Korboński, "The Warsaw Uprising Revisited," *Survey* (Summer 1970).

21. Jan M. Ciechanowski, *Powstanie Warszawskie*, pp. 380–81; for the Communist point of view see the works of Gomułka's friend, Zenon Kliszko, *Z problemów historii PPR* (From the Problems of PPR's History) (Warsaw: Książka i Wiedza, 1958), and *Powstanie Warszawski* (The Warsaw Uprising) (Warsaw: Książka i Wiedza, 1967).

22. Stanisław Kirkor's testimony based on Professor Grabski's unpublished memoirs in *Zeszyty historyczne* (Historical Folders), nos. 18 and 22 (Paris, 1970 and 1972); see also Raczyński, *W sojuszniczym Londynie*, p. 235. One has to agree with Sarah Terry, who wrote: "The fact that after June 22, 1941, the Poles and Russians were fighting on the same side would do nothing to change the inherent imbalance between Poland's assets and Moscow's anxieties and ambitions. Soviet policy would continue to be shaped less by what the Poles did or did not do than by the pressures exerted and opportunities afforded by the broader political and military situation" (Terry, "Sikorski Reconsidered," p. 208).

23. For a discussion of the treaty, see Zbigniew Brzezinski, *The Soviet Bloc: Unity and Conflict* (New York: Praeger, 1961), p. 108.

24. Feis, *Churchill, Roosevelt, Stalin*, p. 255; Ulam, *Expansion and Coexistence*, pp. 367–74.

25. Winston S. Churchill, *The Second World War*, 6 vols. (Boston: Houghton Mifflin, 1948–53), 4: 438.

26. For an account of the arrest of the sixteen leaders, see a work by one of them: Zbigniew Stypułkowski, *Invitation to Moscow* (New York: Walker, 1962).

27. According to an official Polish publication: *Straty wojenne Polski w latach 1939–1945* (Poland's War Losses, 1939–1945) (Poznań-Warsaw: Instytut Zachodni, 1960), pp. 38, 47.

28. For a detailed discussion of the "Enigma," see Frederick W. Winterbotham,

The Ultra Secret (New York: Harper & Row, 1975). For an outline of activity of the Polish intelligence network in France known as F2, see a paper given by its head, Leon Sliwiński, on October 24, 1975, in Paris at the conference entitled "Poland and France at the Resistance War of 1939–1945."

6. THE POLISH PEOPLE'S REPUBLIC: 1945–1956

1. Probably the best books on the period treated in this chapter are the works of Professor Richard Hiscocks, *Poland: Bridge for the Abyss?* (New York: Oxford University Press, 1963), and Richard F. Staar, *Poland, 1944–1962* (Baton Rouge: Louisiana State University Press, 1962). See also William Woods, *Poland: Eagle of the East* (New York: Hill and Wang, 1968); and M. K. Dziewanowski, *The Communist Party of Poland* (Cambridge: Harvard University Press, 1959), chs. 10–16.

2. As an émigré author has recently stressed, there is a definite connection between the loss of the Eastern Marshes and the acquisition of the "recovered territories" in the west: the Oder-Neisse lands and a segment of East Prussia were given to the Poles as compensation for the loss of territories acquired as a result of the treaty of Riga. Thus, he argues, the Riga settlement did ultimately play a positive role, since the lands acquired at Riga constituted a pawn by means of which the Polish people have regained the smaller but economically more valuable western lands (Tadeusz Piszczkowski, *Odbudowanie Polski, 1914–1921* [The Rebuilding of Poland, 1914–1921] [London: Orbis, 1969], pp. 230–31). For a discussion of the problem, see Anthony Z. Kruszewski, *The Oder-Neisse Boundary and Poland's Modernization* (New York: Praeger, 1972). Khrushchev revealed Soviet motives behind Stalin's support of the Polish claims to the western territories by saying: "The Oder-Neisse Line was advantageous for both Poland and the Soviet Union. We knew that sooner or later Poland would be a socialist country and our ally. Many of us felt, myself included, that some day Poland would be part of one great country or socialist commonwealth of nations. Therefore we were glad to have the Polish-German border moved as far west as possible" (Strobe Talbott, ed., *Khrushchev Remembers,* 2 vols. [Boston: Little, Brown, 1970, 1974], 2: 158). Khrushchev also confirmed that the Polish Communists did ask that Lwów be returned to Poland (pp. 163–65).

3. During the early stages of the reconstruction, the assistance given by the United Nations Relief and Rehabilitation Administration (UNRRA) played a major part. UNRRA's aid between 1945 and 1947 provided Poland with 2.2 million tons of supplies valued at $476.3 million. This assistance ended in 1947 (*UNRRA Operational Analysis Paper,* no. 45, "The Impact of UNRRA on the Polish Economy" [Washington, D.C., 1947]).

4. Stanisław Mikołajczyk, *The Rape of Poland: The Pattern of Soviet Aggression* (New York: Whittlesey House, 1948), p. 100.

5. See Drobner's article in the Socialist daily, *Naprzód* (Forward) (March 11, 1947).

6. Ann L. Strong, *I Saw the New Poland* (Boston: Little, Brown, 1946), p. 59.

7. Between 1935 and 1939, Józef Cyrankiewicz was secretary of the Cracow District Committee of the old Polish Socialist party (PPS). In 1939 he joined Socialist resistance groups. Arrested by the Germans in 1941, Cyrankiewicz was sent to a concentration camp, where he was converted by his Communist fellow prisoners to the idea of a "united front." Kazimierz Rusinek was also active in the PPS before the war, in the Seamen's and Dockers' Union of Gdynia. During the 1939 campaign, Rusinek, too, was taken prisoner by the Germans and sent to various concentration camps, where he came under the influence of the Communists. After the war Rusinek returned to Warsaw and placed himself at the disposal of the provisional government. Soon afterward he was appointed secretary-general of the Polish trade unions.

8. For a short history of the ups and downs of the peasant movement, see Andrzej Korboński, *Politics of Socialist Agriculture in Poland: 1945–1960* (New York: Columbia University Press, 1964), ch. 4.

9. Quoted by Zbigniew Brzezinski, *The Soviet Bloc: Unity and Conflict* (New York: Praeger, 1961), p. 337; see also Włodzimierz Sokorski, *Polacy pod Lenino* (Poles at Lenino) (Warsaw: Książka i Wiedza, 1971).

10. James F. Byrnes, *Speaking Frankly* (New York: Harper, 1947), p. 33. Analyzing President Roosevelt's attitude toward the area west of the prewar USSR, one American scholar concludes: "Roosevelt did attach two conditions to his willingness to grant Stalin's security needs. . . . First, the Russian leader would have to be discreet in establishing control over neighboring countries, operating under the facade of democratic procedures wherever possible. This requirement reflected Roosevelt's concern over public opinion in the United States; having been led by Administration rhetoric to expect literal fulfillment of the Four Freedoms and the Atlantic Charter, Americans would not tolerate too blatant a violation of those principles. Second, the Kremlin would have to abandon further attempts to spread communism outside the Soviet Union" (John Lewis Gaddis, "Was the Truman Doctrine a Real Turning Point?," *Foreign Affairs* [Jan. 1974]: 388).

11. For comments of the U.S. ambassador in Warsaw, see Arthur Bliss-Lane, *Poland Betrayed*, p. 279.

12. Jack J. Taylor, *The Economic Development of Poland, 1919–1950* (Ithaca, N.Y.: Cornell University Press, 1952), p. 92. The extent of state ownership in Poland may be illustrated by the following figures. The value of state property in buildings, railroads, communications, industry, estates, forests, fiscal monopolies, banking shares, etc., was estimated on January 1, 1927, at 16.4 billion zloty, while the entire national wealth was estimated at 137.5 billion zloty. The state owned 93 percent of all the railroads, 100 percent of the commercial aviation companies, 100 percent of the airplane industry, the larger part of the chemical industry, and 95 percent of the merchant marine, and the postal, radio, telegraph, and telephone systems. Three-eighths of the forests belonged to the state. In industry the state controlled 99

276

percent of the salt mines, 100 percent of the potash industry, 70 percent of the iron production, 30 percent of the coal output, 20 percent of the oil refineries, and 50 percent of the metal industry (Ferdynand Zweig, *Poland Between Two Wars* [London: Secker and Warburg, 1944], pp. 108–9).

13. By 1950, the share of private firms in industry and handicrafts had dropped to 6 percent (as compared to 21 percent in 1946) and that of private trade had fallen to 15 percent (78 percent in 1946). By 1947, the socialist sector accounted for 99.5 percent of total industrial output. For a discussion of the problem, see John H. Montias, *Central Planning in Poland* (New Haven: Yale University Press, 1952).

14. Renata Siemieńska, *Nowę życie w nowym mieście* (A New Life in a New Town) (Warsaw: Wiedza Powszechna, 1969), p. 18.

15. There are two standard biographies of Gomułka, one by Nicholas Bethell, *Gomułka: His Poland, His Communism* (New York: Holt, Rinehart & Winston, 1969), and a biography in Polish, written by an Indian scholar, Peter Raina, entitled *Władysław Gomułka* (London: Polish Book Fund, 1969).

16. Quoted by Robert Hugo Bass and Elisabeth Marbury, eds., *The Soviet-Yugoslav Controversy, 1949–1958: a Documentary Record* (New York: East Europe Institute, 1959), p. 15. Although not published at the time, this statement of Gomułka and other details of the June plenum were later brought out at the central committee session at the end of August and reported in the Polish Workers' party theoretical organ, *Nowe drogi* (Sept.–Oct. 1948).

17. *Nowe drogi* (Nov. 1949).

18. For the agrarian reform, see Korboński, *Socialist Agriculture,* ch. 3.

19. Jean Malara and Lucienne Rey, *La Pologne d'une occupation à l'autre: 1944–52* (Paris: Editions du Fuseau, 1952), pp. 158–60.

7. The "Polish October" and the Era of Gomułka: 1956–1970

1. The "Polish October" and its aftermath have a large literature. Among useful background works one should mention those of Flora Lewis, *A Case History of Hope: The Story of Poland's Peaceful Revolution* (Garden City, N.Y.: Doubleday, 1958), and Konrad Syrop, *Spring in October* (New York: Praeger, 1957). See also Frank Gibney, *The Frozen Revolution* (New York: Farrar Straus, 1959); S. L. Shneiderman, *The Warsaw Heresy* (New York: Horizon Press, 1959); Nicholas Bethell, *Gomułka: His Poland, His Communism* (New York: Holt, Rinehart & Winston, 1969); and Peter Raina, *Władysław Gomułka* (London: Polish Book Fund, 1969). For further analysis of the events, see Richard F. Staar, *Poland, 1944–1962* (Baton Rouge: Louisiana State University Press, 1962); M. K. Dziewanowski, *The Communist Party of Poland* (Cambridge: Harvard University Press, 1959), pp. 267–80; and Zbigniew Brzezinski, *The Soviet Bloc: Unity and Conflict* (New York: Praeger, 1961), pp. 333–39. For a selection of documents, see the publication by the Literary Institute, *6 latu temu* (Paris: Instytut Literacki, 1962).

✒ Notes

2. The question of how Gomułka survived without being brought to trial during the wave of purges that were carried out in Eastern Europe is still a mystery. The executions of Laszlo Rajk and Traicho Kostov in 1949 were followed by the trial and execution in 1952 of Rudolf Slansky and ten of his colleagues on charges of treason and Zionism. Less publicized trials followed in East Germany and Romania during 1952 and 1954.

3. For an interesting interpretation of the events by a participant, Witold Jedlicki, see "Chamy i Żydy" (The Bumpkins and the Jews), *Kultura* (Paris) (1962). The author is a former Communist close to the liberal Puławy faction, which originally held most of the politburo posts during the crucial period from 1945 to 1956. The thesis that the "Polish October" was a hoax played by the Puławy faction and ultimately a Soviet victory has not been fully substantiated by the author. Nevertheless, the article is stimulating because it stresses the role of the faction in arousing Polish public opinion and attempting to manipulate it in an anti-Soviet direction.

4. For the text of the speech, see *Trybuna ludu* (October 21, 1956); for various interpretations, see Richard Hiscocks, *Poland: Bridge for the Abyss?* (New York: Oxford University Press, 1963), pp. 115–19, Bethell, *Gomułka,* pp. 213–16, and Dziewanowski, *Communist Party of Poland,* pp. 276–78.

5. Quoted by Syrop, *Spring in October,* pp. 61–74.

6. Sir William Hayter, *The Kremlin and the Embassy* (New York: Macmillan, 1966), p. 112.

7. Lewis, *Case History,* p. 217.

8. Władysław Gomułka, *Przemówienia, 1957–58* (Speeches, 1957–58) (Warsaw: Książka i Wiedza, 1959), p. 36.

9. For confirmation of this point of view, see Gomułka's reminiscences in the Tel Aviv *Nowiny-Kurier* (News Courier) (May 4, 1973).

10. *List otwarty do Partii* (An Open Letter to the Party) (Paris: Instytut Literacki, 1966).

11. Bethell, *Gomułka,* p. 240. Bethell's opinion has been confirmed by Gomułka's reminiscences published in *Nowiny-Kurier* (May 11, 1973).

12. For a broader background of the Rapacki plan, see Mieczysław Maneli, *War of the Vanquished: A Polish Diplomat in Vietnam* (New York: Harper & Row, 1971), pp. 5–8.

13. This expression he used in his reminiscences as published in *Nowiny-Kurier* (June 1, 1973).

14. For an attempt to draw a parallel between Dmowski's and Gomułka's policies of cooperation with Russia, see Adam Bromke, *Poland's Politics: Idealism vs. Reality* (Cambridge: Harvard University Press, 1967).

15. Roman Dmowski, *Świat powojenny a Polska* (The Postwar World and Poland) (Warsaw: Niklewicz, 1931), p. 186.

16. For documents pertaining to the treaties of 1970, see Keesing's Research

278

Report, *Germany and Eastern Europe since 1945* (New York: Charles Scribner's Sons, 1973), pp. 260–98; for a dual Polish-German view of the treaty of December 1970, see Adam Bromke and Harold von Rickhoff, "The Polish West German Treaty," *East Europe* (Feb. 1971); see also Hansjakob Stehle, *Nachbaren im Osten* (Frankfurt-am-Main: S. Fischer, 1971), pp. 255ff.

17. R. V. Burks, *The Dynamics of Communism in Eastern Europe* (Princeton: Princeton University Press, 1961), p. 160. "The influence of Jews on party life, moreover, was generally greater than the percentages would suggest. Jewish activists were probably better educated than the average, and more likely to achieve the level of leading cadre" (ibid., p. 161).

18. For the German policy of extermination of the Jews, see Czesław Madajczyk, *Polityka Trzeciej Rzeszy w okupowanej Polsce* (The Third Reich's Policy in Occupied Poland), 2 vols. (Warsaw: Państwowe wydawnictwa naukowe, 1970), especially vol. 2, chs. 31–36. See also Władysław Bartoszewski, *The Blood Shed Unites Us* (Warsaw: Interpress, 1970); two books by Michał Borwicz, *L'Insurrection de Ghetto de Varsovie* (Paris: Julliard, 1966), and *Vies inderdites* (Paris: Casterman, 1969); and S. Wroński and M. Zwolakowa, eds., *Polacy i Żydzi, 1939–1945* (Poles and Jews, 1939–1945) (Warsaw: Książka i Wiedza, 1971).

19. Burks, *Dynamics of Communism,* p. 166.

20. "Early in 1949, the Hungarian and Rumanian governments, on whose territories 90 percent of surviving East European Jewry was domiciled, outlawed Zionist organizations and deported Zionist missions. Local Zionist leaders were secretly tried and given long prison terms. Israeli diplomats were accused of espionage and expelled. In September, 1949, on the occasion of the trial of Laszlo Rajk, the leader of the nationalist wing in the Hungarian party, almost the entire body of Hungarian Jewish Communists who had spent the war years in Switzerland was executed. In the summer of 1952, three top drawer Rumanian Communists of Jewish origin—Pauker, Georgescu and Luca—were purged. In December, 1952, the *eminence grise* of the Czech party, Rudolf Slansky, was placed in the dock, along with a dozen other Jewish leading cadres. Slansky and his fellow accused were condemned in December 1952" (ibid., pp. 167–68).

21. For an interesting analysis of the situation in Poland in 1953 to 1955, see Witold Jedlicki, "Chamy i Żydy."

22. For a testimony of the Soviet pressure on the Polish party concerning its Jewish membership, see Georges Mond, "A Conversation in Warsaw," *Problems of Communism* (May–June 1964).

23. *Radio Free Europe Situation Reports* (June 22, 1967).

24. *Trybuna ludu* (People's Tribune) (March 20, 1968). Gomułka's British biographer, Nicholas Bethell, shows sympathetic understanding of Gomułka's difficulties in 1967–68 without subscribing to his views or excusing some of his obnoxious methods. Nevertheless, the author stressed that "Gomułka is no anti-Semite" and

279

that he "was dragged along by events, by a situation he did not control." He tried "to limit the anti-Zionist campaign" (*Gomułka,* p. 261). His speech of March 19, 1968, had this very purpose (ibid., p. 36). In his reminiscences, Gomułka admitted that the anti-Zionist campaign was unleashed on the insistence of Moscow: the Soviet government wanted Warsaw to curb the pro-Israeli manifestations in Poland as inadmissible and harmful to the Soviet-Polish friendship (*Nowiny-Kurier* [May 18, 1973]). For a reappraisal of Gomułka's rule, see Adam Bromke, "Beyond the Gomułka Era," *Foreign Affairs* (April 1971).

25. For an analysis of the March 1968 events in Poland, see Stanisław Staroń, "Political Developments in Poland: The Party Reacts to Challenge," *Orbis* (Winter 1970); A. Ross Johnson, "Poland: End of an Era?," *Problems of Communism* (Jan.–Feb. 1970); and Jan Nowak's article in *East Europe* (June 1968). Nowak, head of the Polish section of Radio Free Europe, argues that it was Moczar who, by brandishing the danger of a Zionist plot, tried-to overthrow Gomułka. The Stalinist faction of Polish Communists operating in Albania, while sharply critical of the Gomułka regime, interpreted the March crisis in a way similar to that of Kąkol. "The March events in Poland in 1968 cannot be boiled down to the problem of Mickiewicz's *The Forefathers Eve,* the students or the intelligentsia: it was a political struggle for return to the leadership of the PUWP of the [formerly] eliminated 'Leftist Faction of the Polish October,' the faction which pressed for the 'second stage' of the counter-revolution in Poland" (*W walce o zwycięstwo* [In the Struggle for Victory] [Warsaw, July 1974], p. 12). The pamphlet was most certainly printed not in Warsaw, but in Albania. While writing this chapter, the author also consulted a book-length manuscript of Dr. Peter Raina, an eyewitness, now of the Free University of Berlin, entitled "Polish Intellectuals in Revolt Against Neostalinism, March, 1968."

26. According to various estimates 8,000 to 9,000 Jews left Poland during the years 1967–68; some 10,000 to 15,000 Jews still remain in Poland. Approximately 3,000 of them are organized in 18 religious congregations, but they have not a single rabbi. The Jews in Poland have their Historical Institute, their periodical, *Folks Sztyme,* which prints 3,000 copies, as well as their theater in Warsaw (James Feron, *New York Times Magazine* [April 15, 1973], and *News From Poland,* Radio Free Europe, May 16, 1973).

27. Brzezinski, *The Soviet Bloc,* p. 52.

28. For a scholarly discussion of the issue, see Michael Gamarnikov's "Poland Returns to Economic Reform," *East Europe* (Nov.–Dec. 1969). During the Gomułka era, economic reform was, as the author put it, "a convenient political football in . . . perennial factional infighting"; see also the same author's *Economic Reforms in Eastern Europe* (Detroit: Wayne State University Press, 1968), especially ch. 2 and the epilogue.

29. For a collection of documents pertaining to the December 1970 events, see

Dokumenty: Poznań 1956—Grudzień 1970 (Documents: Poznań 1956—December 1970) (Paris: Instytut Literacki, 1971).

30. *Głos szczeciński* (Voice of Szczecin) (Jan. 26, 1971); see also Ewa Wacowski, ed., *Rewolta szczecińska i jej znaczenie* (The Szczecin Revolt and Its Significance) (Paris: Instytut Literacki, 1971). A Polish sociologist thus summarizes the main causes of discontent among workers: "The Communist establishment by pushing forward toward industrialization, egalitarianism (at least in some fields), and by generating great expectations as regards the general improvement of working class conditions, prepared the ground for dissatisfaction. There is too great a discrepancy between the growing aspirations of workers and the reality of low wages, limited opportunity for promotion, poor working conditions, and ineffective management. What happened in December 1970 was the outcome of these growing contradictions" (Alexander J. Matejko, "Why Polish Workers are Restless," *East Europe* [July–Aug. 1972]).

31. For a discussion of Poland's contribution to the loosening of the Soviet bloc, see Andrzej Brzeski, "Poland as a Catalyst of Change in the Communist Economic System," *The Polish Review* (Spring 1971). For a thorough post mortem of the Gomułka system by his comrades, see "The Eighth Plenum of the Central Committee of the Polish United Workers' Party, 6–7 February 1971," *Nowe drogi* (New Roads) (special issue, 1971).

32. Bethell, *Gomułka,* p. 244. For a critical evaluation of the Gomułka era by a Polish Marxist who was a former close co-worker of the first secretary, see W. Bieńkowski, *Socjologia klęski* (Sociology of Disaster) (Paris: Instytut Literacki, 1971); for a scholarly analysis by a Polish-Canadian, see Adam Bromke, "Beyond the Gomułka Era," *Foreign Affairs* (April 1971).

8. GIEREK'S "RENEWAL"

1. For a recent treatment of events since December 1970, see Adam Bromke and Michael Garmanikow, "Poland under Gierek," *Problems of Communism* (Sept.–Oct. 1972), and Harald Laeuen, *Polen nach dem Sturz Gomułkas* (Stuttgart, 1972); see also a special issue of *Canadian Slavic Papers—Revue Canadienne des Slavistes,* nos. 1 and 2 (1973). Gierek, the son of a miner, was born on January 6, 1913, in the district of Będzin in Russian Poland, near the German border. His father died in an accident when Edward was only ten years old, and soon after that the family emigrated to northern France, where he began work in a mine at the age of thirteen. According to the official party version, in 1931 he joined the Communist party of France. As an organizer of a miners' strike in Pas de Calais, he was arrested and expelled from France in 1934, whereupon he was sent to Poland and drafted into the army. In 1937, Gierek emigrated to Limburg, in northern Belgium, where he worked again as a miner and at the same time took part in the work of the local Communist party cell. He returned to Poland only in 1948 and first worked as secretary of the

281

Silesian district of the Polish United Workers' party. In 1954 he obtained the diploma of a mining engineer at the Cracow Mining Academy. In May 1956 he was appointed secretary of the central committee and, after Gomułka's return, entered the politburo. From 1957 until December 1970, Gierek was also first secretary of the party organization in the Katowice district. In this capacity he made Upper Silesia a model region, "a Polish Katanga," enjoying a standard of living much higher than the rest of the country. It is noteworthy that Gierek speaks better French than Russian and is the first party leader to speak a Western language. Mieczysław Maneli, a former comrade, now an émigré in the United States writes: "Edward Gierek is an old-fashioned Communist, but without fanaticism or zealousness. His Marxism is encumbered by few dogmas. It is almost pragmatic. He believes profoundly in the leading role that history conferred upon Communist parties and lives by the maxim that a government should be strong and rule unshakeably (sic)" (Mieczysław Maneli, "Poland's New Artful Dodger," *New York Times,* Jan. 16, 1971).

2. The small car is a new version of the Fiat 500, which is being produced in two new factories in Tychy and Bielsko-Biała. The car is, however, too expensive for most Poles. To drain excess purchasing power, the Polish authorities promised to sell some 25,000 one-family houses and some 30,000 small dwellings belonging to the state to private owners. For those who prefer to build their own one-family house, the state is to provide credits up to 100,000 zloties, or 75 to 80 percent of the construction costs. See Andrzej Stasiak, "One-Family Housing," *Polityka* (Nov. 27, 1971).

3. For an analysis of Poland's economic situation in 1971–73, see Michael Gamarnikow's essay in *Radio Free Europe Research, Poland* (April 19, 1972, Nov. 2, 1973), hereinafter cited as *RFER, Poland.*

4. In his programmatic speech of February 8, 1971, Gierek used the words "Communism" or "Communistic" only three times; the term "patriotism" was used twelve times, "fatherland" thirteen, and "nation" twenty times. Numerous observers of the Polish scene had noticed the deep emotional significance of the royal castle of Warsaw for the Polish masses; for a typical report on the subject, see Charlotte Sajkowski, "Polish Pride: Royal Castle," *The Christian Science Monitor,* Feb. 9, 1972. The American newspaperwoman remarked: "What Won't a Pole give for a Royal Palace! Women part with their rings, pensioners donate their blood, musicians turn over their concert fees, old folk assign their inheritance. . . ." The rebuilding of the castle is the final major step in the rebirth of the city Hitler had condemned to oblivion, "a miracle, a phoenix city risen from the ashes, alive and thriving" (Peter Daubeny, *My World of Theatre* [London: Cape, 1971], p. 265).

5. Renata Hammer, "Poland: Its writers and the censor," *Index on Censorship* (London) (Spring 1975). See also Richard Davy in *The Times* (London), May 25, 1971, p. 12, who writes that while Gierek's program includes the promise of a continuous "dialogue with society," which was widely interpreted as invitation to lim-

ited criticism, the scope of this criticism was circumscribed from the beginning. While the technical intelligentsia was wooed and encouraged to express its opinion more freely, ''the only people for whom the official nod of encouragement has been a little cool are the writers and intellectuals.''

6. On January 1, 1973, several large economic enterprises, most working for export, introduced new experimental principles of planning and management. Also starting January 1, 1973, a new organizational structure of crafts and artisanship came into effect. This was paralleled by the liberalization of tax policy affecting about 200,000 workshops employing some 450,000 people (*RFER, Poland*, Feb. 1, 1973). On January 1, 1975, the new labor code came into force. Together with the law on district labor and social security courts, it makes up the current system of labor legislation in Poland. While for the most part reaffirming existing regulations, the new code introduces a number of new points designed chiefly to ensure the equality of rights and duties between white-collar and blue-collar workers. The new code, however, in accordance with the principle of centralized management, does nothing to expand the powers of labor organizations representing worker interests, such as the trade unions or workers' councils. For an analysis of the new labor code see *RFER, Poland* (Feb. 19, 1975).

7. As an American observer of Eastern Europe pointed out: ''Last year, Poland kept price increases of food to 8 per cent on the official market, but in doing so, created shortages. People were faced with a choice between empty shelves and long lines at government markets, or going to the private market (not quite a black market). They could generally get what they needed at the private market, but there, price increases last year were about 35 percent'' (Malcolm W. Brown, ''East's Common Market Also Feels the Pinch,'' *New York Times*, Feb. 9, 1975).

8. Poland's overall energy policy is 80 percent coal-based. During the last thirty years the Polish coal-mining industry has increased its production to the point where it is the world's fourth largest producer and, after the United States, the second greatest exporter of coal. In that period, 3.1 billion tons of hard coal alone have been produced, of which 22 percent (678 million tons), with a total value of 35 billion exchange zloty, were exported. Brown coal has also made its contribution to the Polish economy. Even though there may be an upward trend in both home consumption and exports, known Polish reserves are sufficient to cover expected demand for approximately the next 300 years (*RFER, Polish Situation Report* [April 18, 1975]).

9. At the fifteenth plenary session of the party's central committee, which took place in Warsaw on October 22–23, 1974, Gierek, in reviewing the state of food production, declared: ''The future of our countryside is a highly efficient, modern, socialist agriculture, one that would ensure the country an abundance of food and provide agricultural producers with advantageous conditions of work and a rich cultural life'' (*RFER, Polish Situation Report* [May 16, 1975]; see also *RFER, Polish Situation Report* [Oct. 25, 1974]). Professor Ryszard Manteuffel, head of the depart-

ment of agricultural economics and farm management at Warsaw University, without saying outright that state farms in Poland have proved themselves over the years to be both inefficient and unprofitable, warned the authorities: "We cannot afford the kind of socialization that, as we all know from experience, leads to a grave loss of production for years on end" (quoted in *The Guardian,* Oct. 24, 1974). Professor Manteuffel's remarks are confirmed by many foreign observers; see, for instance, Eric Bourne, "Mixed farming pays off in Poland," *The Christian Science Monitor,* Dec. 12, 1974.

10. The importance of the USSR in Poland's economy may be seen from the following table in *RFER, Polish Situation Report,* May 2, 1975, based on *Rocznik Statystyczny (Statistical Yearbooks)* for the years in question.

	Foreign Trade Turnover of Poland, 1950–1974					
	Import			Export		
	(In million exchange zloty at [current prices])					
Year	Total	USSR	USSR as percent of total	Total	USSR	USSR as percent of total
1950	2,672.6	769.5	28.8	2,537.0	616.3	24.3
1955	3,727.2	1,254.3	33.7	3,678.7	1,122.0	30.5
1960	5,979.9	1,861.1	31.2	5,302.1	1,560.9	29.4
1965	9,361.2	2,913.7	31.1	8,911.4	3,125.5	35.1
1970	14,430.1	5,445.0	37.7	14,190.5	5,003.3	35.3
1974	34,822.9	7,816.5	22.4	27,624.8	7,875.3	28.5

For a short study of Poland's relations with the West and COMECON, see A. Gotowski's article in *Kultura* (Paris), no. 6/321 (1974).

11. "What Saudi Arabia and Iran are to the West, the Soviet Union has now become for Eastern Europe. In the immediately forseeable future, the East Europeans will have to transfer hitherto unanticipated and unplanned billions of dollars of their own resources to the Soviet Union. These forced transfer payments must tend to depress both investment and consumption levels in Eastern Europe" (*New York Times,* March 23, 1975).

12. According to Bogdan Melaniuk, "Polish Workers and Specialists Abroad," *RFER, Background Report/Poland* (April 28, 1975), there are some 30,000 to 40,000 Polish workers in East Germany, and 27,000 to 30,000 in Czechoslovakia. There have also been scattered groups of Poles working in the Soviet Union; the first such sizable contingent of laborers and specialists is now working in Kazakhstan to help construct the Polish section of the COMECON project known as the Orenburg gas pipeline. The pipeline will stretch some 1,800 miles from Orenburg to the west-

ern border of the Soviet Union. Five countries are involved in its construction: Bulgaria, Czechoslovakia, East Germany, Hungary, and Poland. Poland also temporarily exports teams of specialists not only to the countries of the Third World, but also to West Germany. This is especially true of construction workers, architects, and specialists in the reconstruction of art works.

13. *RFER, Poland* (April 11, 1975).

14. *RFER, Poland* (May 11, June 22, 1973). For an analysis of the program of educational reform (scheduled to go into effect in 1978) as a decisive factor in the party's youth policy, see *RFER, Poland* (Nov. 13, 1973).

15. *Dziennik Polski* (London), Feb. 11, 1975. For an analysis of the Vatican's policy toward the Soviet orbit, see Antoni Pospieszalski's article in *Trybuna* (Tribune) (London), no. 19 (1975), and Dominik Morawski's reports from Rome in *Kultura* (Paris) 7, 8 (1974), and 5 (1975). According to the Rome correspondent of a Polish émigré monthly, the cardinal insists that the church should be given a guarantee of complete freedom of pastoral activities, including the right of religious teaching; Polish Catholics should be granted equality in public life, including free access to mass media; they should be allowed to form religious associations, and not to be discriminated against in their social, cultural, and professional activities. Only after granting of these rights, believes the cardinal, would the signing of a formal agreement not amount to the Vatican's approval of the present discriminatory policy of the Polish government toward its Catholic subjects (Dominik Morawski, "A Correspondence from Rome," *Kultura* [Paris] Dec. 1974).

16. United Press International dispatch from Warsaw as summarized by *RFER, Polish Situation Report* (March 27, 1975).

17. *La Croix* (Paris), March 26, 1975.

18. The list of American companies doing business in Poland is long. For instance, Universal Oil Products' business division recently furnished the basic design for a new fluid catalytic cracking unit to Poland's Płock petrochemical complex. Universal's subsidiary, Procon Incorporated, is building two meat-processing plants in Poland. A. Epstein Companies were awarded contracts in excess of $60 million to design and build two slaughterhouses and meat-packing plants, and the same firm will design, build, and equip two food-processing and freezer storage plants in Legnica and Lagisza. International Harvester is expanding the steelworks at Stalowa Wola near Cracow to manufacture crawler tractors equipped with bulldozers, loaders, and pipelaying equipment. Universal Marketing System of Arlington Heights is actively participating in the import and export of electronic components to and from Poland. Koehring Company of Milwaukee granted the Poles manufacturing rights to produce excavators. The FMC Corporation of California and its Food Machinery International Division with offices in Chicago is updating or planning new systems in Poland's fruit and vegetable processing and freezing plants (*Zgoda* [Concord] [Chicago] Sept. 15, 1974). In 1973, U.S. exports to Poland showed a particularly rapid

285

increase, closing with a total of $350 million, an increase of 170 percent compared with the previous year. The principal Polish import from the United States was grain, particularly feed grain, followed by other agricultural and industrial semiprocessed goods and raw materials. These items made up about 80 percent of the total, whereas investment goods amounted only to some 20 percent (ibid., Jan. 1, 1975). See also M. W. Brown, "For Poland, the Zloties Outweigh the Ideology," *New York Times,* Oct. 6, 1974, and Don Cook, "Poland Taking an Uncommunistic Route to Economic Boom," *Boston Sunday Globe,* July 20, 1975.

19. "To further stress the new line, the thirtieth anniversary of the heroic fight of the Jews of the Warsaw ghetto who rose arms-in-hand against the German exterminators, was solemnly celebrated on April 18 and 19, 1973, by 'an evening of speeches, music and poetry.' Party, Government and Army delegates participated in the ceremonies" (*International Herald Tribune,* April 19, 20, 1973). Similar ceremonies took place in 1974 and in 1975.

20. Agence France Press, in a dispatch from Tel Aviv (Feb. 11, 1975), reported that the president of the Jewish World Congress, Dr. Nahum Goldmann, revealed that both Chancellor Willy Brandt and his successor Helmut Schmidt had agreed to pay about 250,000 marks to Soviet Jewish victims.

21. *New York Times,* Aug. 3, 1975. The paper commented that: "The agreement marks a turning point in West German-Polish relations almost as great as that of 1970, when they agreed to establish diplomatic relations. After that, 58,000 ethnic Germans emigrated to West Germany, but the flow became a trickle in the last two years." The people to be repatriated under the West German-Polish agreement reached at Helsinki are the last of the German families that found themselves under Polish control in 1945 at the end of World War II.

22. The sixth party congress laid down the guidelines along which relations between the Polish People's Republic and the diaspora of some 10 million people of Polish extraction should develop. For a background of the new course toward the "Polonia," see *RFER, Poland* (Oct. 16, 1972).

23. For interesting comments on the sixth congress, see Gotthold Rhode, "Der VI Congress der Polnischen Kommunisten," *Osteuropa* (Aug. 1972).

24. For details on the low-level administrative reform, see *RFER, Poland* (Oct. 5, 27, 1972); for the 1975 stage, ibid. (May 16, 1975).

25. While stressing the economic and social advantages of the reform, a French correspondent remarked that the increase in the number of voivodships is at the same time "a hard blow" to the local "chieftains," such as "certain first secretaries of big voivodships," as well as to the mid-level administrative party apparat, which is "used to a peaceful life among the district authorities." Gierek has decided "to start fighting bureaucracy, including the party one," Bernard Margueritte reported for *Le Figaro* on May 13, 1975. Another Western observer said about the reform: "It was the most beautiful example of gerrymandering Europe has seen in modern times" (*New York Times,* Oct. 19, 1975).

26. *Time,* Aug. 4, 1975; see also Joseph C. Harsch, "The Helsinki Texts," *Christian Science Monitor,* Aug. 5, 1975, and the editorial, "After Helsinki," *New York Times,* Aug. 3, 1975.

27. For a summary and analysis of the constitutional controversy, see *RFER, Poland* (Dec. 31, 1975; Jan. 16, Feb. 20, 27, 1976). For extensive documentation, see *Kultura* (Paris), nos. 1–8 (1976).

28. The original draft explicitly spelled out the "unshakable fraternal bond" with the USSR. Neither of these two adjectives appears in the final text, which simply states that Poland "strengthens its friendship and cooperation with the Soviet Union and other socialist states." A clause in the original draft amendments making citizens' rights contingent upon fulfillment of duties toward the state was toned down. In its new form the clause read: "The citizens of People's Poland ought to conscientiously fulfill their obligations toward the fatherland, and contribute to its progress." There is no mention of the possibility that they can be denied their civil rights if they do not comply with these measures.

29. For a summary and analysis of the food crisis, see *RFER, Poland* (Jan. 20, June 29, 1976), and Eric Bourne, "Poland's Food Price Controversy Simmers On," *The Christian Science Monitor,* Aug. 17, 1976. Malcolm W. Browne, writing in the *New York Times* (Aug. 15, 1976), quotes a Pole as saying: "If there is ever a revolution against Communism . . . it will be started by someone who had to stand in line too long."

9. THE POLISH PARADOX

1. Robert F. Byrnes, "Russia in Eastern Eruope: Hegemony Without Security," *Foreign Affairs* (July 1971). The problem of whether the present relationship between the Soviet Union and its vassal states is justified and lasting has also been raised in the USSR, especially among the dissidents. A Soviet scientist who now lives in the West had to admit that: "Already now the bulk of the Soviet divisions stationed to the west of our frontiers serve not so much as a shield against possible aggression by the Western powers as a guarantee of continued Soviet influence in the countries of Eastern Europe. An extension of socialist democracy in the USSR and in these countries would serve as a more reliable, cheaper and more effective guarantee of unity and economic and political co-operation and alliance between all the socialist countries" (Roy Medvedev, *New Left Review* [Sept.–Dec. 1974]. For discussion of the changing relationship between the USSR and its East European vassals, see Nish Jamgotch, Jr., *Soviet-East European Dialogue: International Relations of a New Type?* (Stanford: Hoover Institution Press, 1968), and Vernon V. Aspaturian, *The Soviet Union in the World Communist System* (Stanford: Hoover Institution Press, 1966). For a recent discussion of the present-day Communist regime in Poland, see Marek Taraniewski (pseudonym), *Rewolucia czy ewolucia* (Revolution and Evolution) (Paris, 1975).

2. "The expansion of Poland's contacts with different Western countries has

287

enhanced Poland's position *vis-à-vis* the Soviet Union. The greater Warsaw's influ-
ence is in Paris, Bonn, or Washington, the stronger is its voice in Moscow. The
Poles, then, can play a greater role in the formulation of the common policy of the
Communist bloc'' (Adam Bromke, ''Polish Foreign Policy in the 1970's,'' *Canadian
Slavic Papers,* nos. 1 and 2 [1973]).

3. For instance, in 1965 alone, about 5,000 Poles traveled abroad on the basis of
cultural exchange agreements with the West, while 4,000 foreigners visited Poland
(*East Europe* 3 [May 1966]: 53).

4. *Concise Statistical Yearbook of Poland* (Warsaw: Central Statistical Office,
1974), p. 189. According to official figures, the country was in 1974 second in the
world in the production of fishing vessels, third in the output of sulfur, fourth in
black coal, fifth in brown coal, and tenth in refined copper. In Europe, Poland's position is of course more prominent: it is Europe's biggest producer of fishing vessels
and sulfur, ranks second in coal-mining, third in oat production, fourth in milk, and
fifth in meat. Poland can boast 144 university students per 10,000 population—more
than England, East and West Germany, Switzerland, Hungary, Norway, Austria,
Finland, and Czechoslovakia. In 1974, 34 million Poles committed between them all
of 685 murders, or fewer than the residents of Detroit where the population is only
1.5 million. A one-year-old Polish female can expect to live another 75.2 years, or
about two and one-half months less than her American counterpart. By contrast a
Polish baby boy at that age has at least another 68.7 years of life ahead of him,
nearly a year more than the average one-year-old American. Poland has a divorce
rate of 1.19 per 1,000 population, which is considerably lower than in the United
States (4.3), the Soviet Union (2.8), and England (2.4), but higher than that of
Belgium, Mexico, or Japan. The Poles eat more meat than the Italians, Yugoslavs,
Norwegians, and Russians, but less than the Danes, British, Swiss, and French.

5. As a Polish sociologist put it: ''Manifestations of worker dissent in Poland became a recognized signal in the code of political communications, signifying the
presence in the body politic of serious tensions requiring drastic political change''
(Zygmunt Bauman, ''Twenty Years After: The Crisis of Soviet-Type Systems,''
Problems of Communism 20, no. 6 [Nov.-Dec. 1971]: 45–46).

6. For an analysis, see Ewa Wacowska's article on the Polish working class in
Kultura (Paris), no. 8/299 (1972). A look at the statistics illustrates the move to the
cities in Poland. During the twenty years of Poland's prewar existence, the migration
of the farmers to the urban centers proceeded at the annual pace of only 4 percent.
This meant that the increase of the urban population relative to the whole country
climbed from 24 percent in 1921 to only 28 percent in 1939. But during the postwar
years the percentage of urban population jumped to 31 percent in 1946 and up to
48.3 percent in 1969. Today well over half the Polish population of nearly 35 million
lives in cities. For an analysis of contemporary Poland from a sociological point of
view by a scholar who works in Poland, see Jan Szczepański, *Polish Society* (New

York: Random House, 1970); for a study from a Western viewpoint, see David Lane and George Kolankiewicz, eds., *Social Groups in Polish Society* (New York: Columbia University Press, 1973).

7. A student of the Polish educational system concluded that: "Rigid social stratification continues and is perpetuated because—despite the oratory on the importance of education as a big 'social leveler,' as the only rational vehicle for individual advancement—education remains a low priority item in the allocation of total resources, and educational opportunities are unequally distributed among the various sectors of society thus continuing old status distinctions. For, despite its low priority in terms of resource allocation, education is indeed a mark of status, along with family background and socio-economic position as it affects one's ability to pursue the 'good life.' The educational structure itself is highly differentiated, with lines of demarcation between status, and prestige. People's Poland is very much a class-conscious society despite declarations to the contrary and despite an official ideology which posits classlessness as an ideal. If the lines of social status and prestige do not correspond to income levels, such lack of relationship is not new to this culture whose elite was traditionally drawn from an impoverished gentry class which shared with the Marxist a common disdain for profit and money-making. Such traditional sociocultural pulls lead the Pole to prefer a classical and humanistic education over a technical and vocational one, thus further frustrating official goals and systematic plans relative to industrialization and technological advancement" (Joseph R. Fiszman, "Education and Social Mobility in People's Poland," *The Polish Review* [Summer 1971].

8. For the number of Catholic clergy in Poland, see *RFER, Poland* (Feb. 5, 1974). In an interview with the Vatican Radio, Cardinal Wyszyński declared: "In Poland the number of priests and nuns grows constantly. In 1972 some 500 priests were consecrated. In the higher secular seminaries we have 2,981 students, while the monastic seminaries number 1,073 candidates" (quoted by *Krajowa Agencja Informacyjna* [Polish Information Agency], Jan. 23–24, 1973). In Poland there are 44 monastic orders with some 500 houses, 7,700 monks and nuns, and 1,500 candidates (ibid.). Of the 59,000,000 Catholics who live in the Soviet orbit, 32,000,000 are to be found in Poland. One of the great events for Polish Catholics was the beatification of a Polish Franciscan brother, Maksymilian Kolbe, by Pope Paul VI in October 1971. During World War II, Father Kolbe was a prisoner in Auschwitz. When the Nazis condemned to death a fellow prisoner, Father Kolbe, although a stranger, voluntarily offered to die in the man's place. Pope Paul proclaimed Father Kolbe as a *Defensor Fidei,* defender of the Faith, in a ceremony attended by some 3,000 pilgrims from Poland. The delegation included the man whose life had been saved because of Father Kolbe's sacrifice.

9. Velizar Savić, *Politika* (April 14, 1968). According to the monthly *Znak* (The Sign), no. 214 (1972), among Poles eighteen years old or over, as many as "87 per

289

cent declared themselves as believers.'' Commenting on the figure, the Catholic periodical adds: ''Comparison of the results of various successive censuses covering the entire country during the years 1959–1968 indicates that among grown-up people the percentage of those who declare themselves as 'believing' and 'believing and practicing' has been on the increase.'' When an American journalist asked a pilgrim to the shrine of Jasna Góra why religion is so strong, the pilgrim answered: ''We have had the Church for over 1000 years, while the Communists were around for only 30 years'' (*Time,* Sept. 2, 1974).

10. As an American scholar wrote: ''The Catholic religion is experiencing a renaissance and is entering an age of inner maturity. . . . The Christian faith is becoming a faith of choice, a faith of constant and personal endeavor. Believers in Poland can no longer find support in what is institutional in morality, customs, civil law, tradition. . . . A new kind of religious life is being born in Poland. In the religious consciousness of the new generation in Poland a new ideal of Christian life is stirring. This ideal is oriented toward an active involvement of the Church into the contemporary world. . . . In the realm of moral life people are becoming more sensitive about their social responsibilities and the need for respect of personal worth of each human being. Greater demands are put on the Church and the clergy. The status and influence of a local pastor depends more and more on the integrity of his personal life, and no longer on his clerical prestige alone'' (Andrzej Woźnicki, ''Searching for a New Religious Image: The Spiritual Revival of Polish Catholicism,'' *Migrant Echo* [July-Sept. 1974]).

11. In May 1975, *Tygodnik Powszechny,* edited and published in Cracow, celebrated its thirtieth anniversary. This Catholic weekly, independent in the proper sense of the word (in contrast to the Pax press) has no parallel in the Communist world. The weekly was produced by the Metropolitan curia until 1953, and since 1956 has been put out by the Znak Social Publishing Institute. *Tygodnik Powszechny* has not been restricted to religious matters and receives regularly the contributions of many non-Catholics. Since its inception in the early spring of 1945, it has been deeply involved in socioeconomic and cultural problems in a progressive sense, and has sought to register the Christian presence in all matters of vital importance to the nation. A perceptive observer of the Polish scene remarked: ''The *Znak* group and the editorial board of *Tygodnik Powszechny* are a highly intelligent elite. Like the Warsaw philosophers they represent only a limited number of intellectuals. Nevertheless these two groups of Catholics and Marxists include some of the most interesting and constructive thinkers in contemporary Poland. Their activities are of great importance to their country, and the significance of their ideas extends beyond it'' (Richard Hiscocks, *Poland: Bridge for the Abyss?* [New York: Oxford University Press, 1963], p. 342).

12. Numerous observers of the Polish scene have noticed the deep emotional significance of the royal castle of Warsaw for the Polish people. For a typical report on

the subject, see Charlotte Sajkowski, "Polish Pride: Royal Castle," *The Christian Science Monitor,* Feb. 9, 1972. The American newspaperwoman remarked: "What Won't a Pole Give for a Royal Palace! Women part with their rings, pensioners donate their blood, musicians turn over their concert fees, old folk assign their inheritance."

The rebuilding of the castle is the final major step in the rebirth of the city which Hitler condemned to oblivion, like a modern Carthage, and which today is "a pheonix city risen from the ashes, alive and thriving" (Peter Daubeny, *My World of Theatre* [London: Cape, 1971], p. 265).

13. *Znak,* no. 214 (1972). For summaries of the polls, see A. Szczypiórkowski's article in *Polityka,* Oct. 13, 1974, and A. Micewski's essay in *Tygodnik Powszechny,* Nov. 10, 1974.

14. In this respect, see William Woods, *Poland: Eagle in the East* (New York: Hill and Wang, 1968), pp. 225–26.

15. Elizabeth Hardwick, "The Theater of Grotowski," *New York Times Book Review,* Feb. 12, 1971. An American historian writes: "Wrocław is the home of the contemporary theater's most significantly influential company directed by perhaps one of the world's most creative visionaries. I speak of the Laboratory Theater under the direction of Jerzy Grotowski. No other group and director in the world has had a more profound influence upon the techniques and artistic philosophies of the American avant-garde theater."

Further, the same author continues: "In my own mind and in the minds of many theater people in America, Wrocław has come to mean Grotowski and Grotowski has come to mean Polish theater generally. What I have discovered during my stay in Wrocław is the error of this assumption, for in this city alone, even aside from the work of the Laboratory Theater, exists one of the richest, most creative, and most active theatrical environments in the world. Indeed, I have discovered an extremely exciting theatrical milieu and at least one theater artist who may well deserve as much recognition and acclaim as Grotowski. I speak of Henryk Tomaszewski, director of Wrocław's Pantomime Theater" (Robert R. Findlay, "My Theatrical Pilgrimage to Wrocław," *Poland* [Feb. 1975]). See also Oscar G. Brockett and Robert R. Findlay, *Century of Innovation: A History of European and American Theatre and Drama Since 1870* (Englewood Cliffs, N.J.: Prentice-Hall, 1973), p. 747; and Oscar G. Brockett, *Perspectives on Contemporary Theatre* (Baton Rouge: Louisiana State University Press, 1971). Grotowski's work is described most fully in Jerzy Grotowski, *Towards a Poor Theatre* (New York: Simon & Schuster, 1970).

16. Britain's leading man of theater writes: "Mrozek is Poland's Ionesco, a brilliant and daring satirist. His plays find one of their most persistent sources of humour in exploring the immense gap between the world of reality and that recognized by Communist rhetoricians and bureaucrats" (Daubeny, *My World of Theatre,* p. 264). According to the German writer Karl Dedecius, Guenter Grass considers Mrożek as

291

the most prominent writer of our generation ("The German Chronicle," *Wiadomości* [News] [London], April 27, 1975).

17. As a noted Polish writer and musical critic observed: "The age-old church buildings have proved technically and materially ideal for the reception and recreation of avant-garde music. . . . These 'concert halls' are diversified, not banal but beautifully representing a wide gamut of forms and arrangements—splendid conditions for avant-garde music! But most interesting is the new audience, fresh, impressionable while at the same time capable of focusing attention and of displaying an understanding backed by a thousand years of tradition of deep and time-honored emotions. Where else could one risk undertaking the great work of renewal and synthesis; the synthesis of a new art with universal emotion and of the avant-garde with tradition?" (Stefan Kisielewski, "On Krzysztof Penderecki," *Poland* [Warsaw], July 1973).

18. *Kulturpolitische Korespondenz* (Bonn), no. 167/168 (1973). Since 1945, over 5,000 Polish books have been translated into 70 foreign languages; 145 were published in the United States, 128 in Great Britain, and 158 in France. Henryk Sienkiewicz has proved to be by far the most popular of Polish authors, with his books published in 465 editions. Among the most successful has been his Nobel Prize-winning novel, *Quo Vadis,* which has appeared in 203 editions (*News from Poland* [New York], Sept. 19, 1973). In the United States there is some interest in the Polish short story in English and a reawakening interest in Polish poetry and contemporary theatrical plays in English translation. In this respect, see Jerzy J. Maciuszko, *The Polish Short Story in English Translation: A Guide and Critical Bibliography* (Detroit: Wayne State University Press, 1968); Bolesław Taborski, *Polish Plays in English Translations* (New York: The Polish Institute of Arts and Sciences in America, 1968); Marion Moore Coleman, *Polish Literature in English Translation: a Bibliography* (Cheshire, Conn.: Cherry Hill Books, 1963). One should also point out the existence of some catalogues as compiled by Janina Hoskins, *Polish Books in English, 1945–1971,* which was published in 1974 by Library of Congress in Washington, D.C. The work provides a list of Polish books in English translation available in U.S. libraries. In the field of current registration of English translations of Polish literature, one should mention the *Bibliography of Polonica,* periodically published in the column of *The Polish Review.*

19. The invitations are issued chiefly for study and research purposes, he said, and their number has increased spectacularly since the conclusion of the 1970 agreement: from 196 in 1969 they rose to 575 in 1973, the total being equally divided between the two countries (*RFER, Special/Bonn,* Dec. 19, 1974).

20. *RFER, Polish Situation Report,* May 9, 1975. Jacobsen told the *Bonner Rundschau* (Oct. 24, 1974) that he spent one week in April and three weeks in September and October of 1974 lecturing in Warsaw, Cracow, Wrocław, and Opole. This spring he took a group of his students to Poland to acquaint them with Poland's

292

everyday life. According to Jacobsen, his students' interest in Polish matters is exceptionally vivid.

21. *Prawo i Życie,* Sept. 29, 1974.

22. Woods, *Poland,* pp. 225–26.

23. For an overall analysis of the transformation of Poland after World War II, see Szczepański, *Polish Society,* and Lane and Kolankiewicz, *Social Groups in Polish Society.* For a brief discussion of the issue, see Jan Szczepański, "The Polish Intelligentsia: Past and Present," *World Politics* 14 (April 1962); Alexander Gella, "The Life and Death of the Old Polish Intelligentsia," *Slavic Review* 30, no. 1 (March 1971): 17; and a study by a senior Polish sociologist, Józef Chałasinski, in his book *Przeszłość i przysłość inteligencji polskiej* (The Past and the Future of the Polish Intelligentsia) (Warsaw, 1958). For education in present-day Poland, see Joseph R. Fiszman, *Revolution and Tradition in People's Poland: Education and Socialization* (Princeton: Princeton University Press, 1972).

24. Fiszman, *Revolution and Tradition.*

25. J. B. Priestley, "A Sentimental Journey," *Travel and Leisure* (London) (June–July 1973). In what other country would a guidebook, after telling the tourist to obey all traffic signs, stay to the right of the road when driving, and to the left while walking, add: "Maintain and foster a sense of humor; it will keep you from many unpleasant confrontations." Priestley, while comparing pre-World War II Poland with the present, points out that: "Communism brought . . . a curious widespread anesthesia, a dusty gray tedium, certainly quite foreign to . . . the Polish character." But he also says, "I want to stand up and salute the astounding citizens of Warsaw . . . these incredible people [who] rebuilt the old city stone by stone." While there is no doubt that an overwhelming majority of Polish people supports the government in its effort to modernize the country and raise the standard of living, the support does not extend to the ideological premises of the Communist regime and many of its practices.

26. The official position is clear: a full and unquestionable identification with, and loyalty to, the USSR. In an article entitled "Our Place in the Alliance," a leading party spokesman, Ignacy Krasicki, declared: "In the present constellation of forces in Europe our country is the first ally of the strongest European power—one of the two world superpowers—the Soviet Union" (*Życie Warszawy,* Jan. 26, 1971). This view is not fully supported by the man-in-the-street.

27. The issue has been repeatedly raised both by Poles, for instance, by Stefan Kisielewski ("Poland: The Revolting Platform," *Tygodnik Powszechny,* March 15, 1959), and by foreigners. For a discussion of the problem by a British scholar, see Hiscocks, *Poland.* The book, besides drawing attention to Poland's mediatory role in West-East relations, has rightly stressed the increasing importance of the Polish contribution to the development of the Third World, where thousands of Polish technicians and educators have been working for well over a decade. This is especially

293

Notes

true of the Middle East, Asia, Africa, and Latin America. In 1973, there were about 5,000 Polish experts and technicians in Cuba alone. One of the signs of the growing Polish interest in the Third World has been the establishment in Warsaw of an Institute for the Study of Economic Problems of Underdeveloped Countries (*News from Poland*, Radio Free Europe, New York, May 16, 1973).

Bibliographical Note

⬧ ALTHOUGH THIS BOOK is based on sources in many languages, its nature, and the fact that it will be read mainly by English-speaking people, makes me confine these notes to a few basic books in English. Those able to use sources in Polish and other languages are referred to Paul Horecky's *East Central Europe: A Bibliographic Guide* (Chicago: University of Chicago Press, 1969), part five; to the bibliography of Oscar Halecki's *Poland* (New York: Praeger, 1957); and to the footnotes of this book. Such works as Richard F. Staar's *Poland, 1944–1962* (Baton Rouge: Louisiana State University Press, 1962), Richard Hiscocks's *Poland: Bridge for the Abyss?* (New York: Oxford University Press, 1963), and this author's *The Communist Party of Poland* 2d ed. (Cambridge: Harvard University Press, 1976) also contain fairly large bibliographies on contemporary Poland in several languages. The same is true of a symposium published in Poland by Aleksander Gieysztor and others, *History of Poland* (Warsaw: PWN—Polish Scientific Publishers, 1968).

The main periodicals worth consulting by the English-speaking students of Poland in the twentieth century are: *Canadian Slavic Papers—Revue Canadienne des Slavistes, East Europe, East European Quarterly, Journal of Central European Affairs, Problems of Communism, The Polish Review, Slavonic Review, Slavic and East European Review,* and *Survey.*

Among general histories of Poland that could serve as a background for contemporary developments, one should mention W. F. Reddaway's *Cambridge History of Poland,* 2 vols. (Cambridge: Cambridge University Press, 1941–50). The Jewish aspects of Polish history are extensively treated, up to the end of the eighteenth century, by Bernard D. Weinryb, *The Jews of Poland* (Philadelphia:

295

Jewish Publication Society of America, 1973). For the period after the Third Partition the best single book is by Piotr S. Wandycz, *The Lands of Partitioned Poland, 1795–1918* (Seattle: University of Washington Press, 1974).

An attempt at sketching Poland's reappearance as an independent state was undertaken by a diplomat-historian, Tytus Komarnicki, in his *The Rebirth of the Polish Republic* (London: Heinemann, 1957). There is no adequate, comprehensive single volume in English covering the contemporary history of Poland up to the present. One of the worthy attempts is that of a German scholar, Hans Roos, *A History of Modern Poland* (New York: Knopf, 1966); Antony Polonsky tried to cover internal affairs of the interwar period in his *Politics of Independent Poland, 1921–1939* (Oxford: Clarendon Press, 1972). Among the monographs dealing with important aspects of Polish domestic politics one should mention Edward D. Wynot, Jr., *Polish Politics in Transition* (Athens, Ga.: University of Georgia Press, 1974).

General short surveys of Polish economic history may be found in Ferdynand Zweig's *Poland Between Two Wars* (London: Secker and Warburg, 1944); while the Zweig work stops in 1939, Jack J. Taylor, in his *The Economic Development of Poland, 1919–1950* (Ithaca, N.Y.: Cornell University Press, 1952), covers also the early years of the post-World War II rehabilitation.

The only short one-volume treatment of Poland's foreign relations is Roman Dębicki's *Foreign Policy of Poland, 1919–39* (New York: Praeger, 1962).

Neither of the two great protagonists of the early twentieth-century Polish history, Joseph Piłsudski and Roman Dmowski, has an adequate biography in English. D. R. Gillie collected some of Piłsudski's writings in *Memoirs of a Polish Revolutionary and Soldier* (London: Faber and Faber, 1931). Two vital phases of Piłsudski's tubulent life have been covered in monographs, however; one by this author in his *Joseph Piłsudski* (Stanford: Hoover Institution Press, 1969), another by Joseph Rothschild in his *Piłsudski's Coup d'Etat* (New York: Columbia University Press, 1966). Charles H. Haskins and Robert H. Lord, in their symposium *Some Problems of the Paris Peace Conference* (Cambridge: Harvard University Press, 1920), have a brilliant chapter on the Polish settlement at Versailles. Norman Davies, in his monograph *White Eagle, Red Star* (New York: St. Martin's Press, 1972), revised some of the stereotypes concerning the role of General Maxime Weygand and his allegedly decisive role during the battle of Warsaw.

The vital initial phases of relations between Poland and post-revolutionary Russia are treated by Piotr S. Wandycz in his *Soviet-Polish Relations, 1917–1921* (Cambridge: Harvard University Press, 1969). Bohdan Budurowycz covers the period between the Polish-Soviet nonaggression pact and the outbreak of World War II in his *Polish-Soviet Relations, 1932–1939* (New York: Columbia University Press, 1963). Harold von Reikhoff has ably surveyed the relationship between Poland and Germany in his *German-Polish Relations, 1918–1933* (Baltimore: Johns Hopkins University Press, 1971), while Harry K. Rosenthal, in his *German and Pole—National Conflict and Modern Myth* (Gainesville: University Presses of Florida, 1976) tries to place the essence of this conflict in a broad historic perspective. Joseph Lipski's papers and memoirs, entitled *Diplomat in Berlin, 1933–1939*, edited by Wacław Jędrzejewicz (New York: Columbia University Press, 1968) give an insight into the German-Polish relations of those years. W. W. Kulski, in his book *Germany and Poland* (Syracuse, N.Y.: Syracuse University Press, 1976), brings German-Polish relations up to the present. Josef Korbel deals with the complex problems of the interwar period in *Poland Between East and West* (Princeton: Princeton University Press, 1963). Poland's dealings with the Western powers have no comprehensive treatment in English, but Wandycz's *France and Her Eastern Allies, 1919–1925* (Minneapolis: University of Minnesota Press, 1962) and Anna M. Cienciała's *Poland and the Western Powers, 1938–1939* (Toronto: University of Toronto Press, 1968) touch on the subject. Juliusz Łukasiewicz's *Diplomat in Paris, 1936–1939* (New York: Columbia University Press, 1970) gives an insight into Franco-Polish relations on the eve of World War II.

William J. Rose's article "Poles and Czechs as Neighbors" in

297

Journal of Central European Affairs, no. 2 (1951), is the best single and impartial treatment of this complex matter. Those more deeply interested in the subject may use C. M. Nowak's annotated bibliography, *Czechoslovak-Polish Relations, 1918–1938* (Stanford: Hoover Institution Press, 1976).

The dramatic story of Poland during World War II still awaits an adequate comprehensive treatment in English. Two works dealing with the campaign of 1939 are Nicholas Bethell's *The War that Hitler Won* (London: Allen Lane, The Penguin Press, 1972), and John Kimche, *The Unfought Battle* (London: Weidenfeld and Nicholson, 1968). The history of the Polish resistance against both Germany and Soviet Russia is told in such works as Jan Karski's *Story of a Secret State* (Boston: Houghton Mifflin, 1944); Tadeusz Bór-Komorowski's *The Secret Army* (London: Macmillan, 1951); Stefan Koroboński's *Fighting Warsaw* (New York: Minerva Press, 1956); and Jan M. Ciechanowski's *The Warsaw Rising* (Cambridge: Cambridge University Press, 1974). Janusz Zawodny, in his *Death in the Forest* (South Bend, Ind.: University of Notre Dame Press, 1972), has written the best book on the Katyń massacre. Zbigniew Stypułkowski, in *Invitation to Moscow* (New York: Walker, 1962), tells the story of the arrest and deportation of the sixteen Polish underground leaders by the MKVD.

The controversial Jewish-Polish relations during World War II may be studied in such works as: Philip Friedman, ed., *Martyrs and Fighters* (New York: Praeger, 1954); Joseph Tennenbaum, *Underground* (New York: Philosophical Library, 1952); Philip Friedman, *Their Brothers' Keepers* (New York: Crown, 1957); Kazimierz Iranek-Osmecki, *He Who Saves One Life* (New York: Crown, 1971); Władysław Bartoszewski and Zofia Lewin, *The Samaritans* (New York: Twayne, 1971); and Władysław Bartoszewski, *The Blood Shed Unites Us* (Warsaw: Interpress, 1970). Józef Garliński, in his *Fighting Auschwitz* (Greenwich, Conn.: Fawcett Press, 1975), tells the fascinating story of conspiratorial activities behind the barbed wire.

The only attempt at a comprehensive treatment of the Polish question as a major diplomatic issue during World War II is by Edward J. Rożek, *Allied Wartime Diplomacy* (New York: Wiley, 1958). Interested students may find a wealth of information in such collections of documents as: *Documents on Polish-Soviet Relations, 1939–1945*, published by The General W. Sikorski Institute in London, or Wacław Jędrzejewicz, ed., *Poland in the British Parliament, 1939–1945*, 3 vols. (The Joseph Piłsudski Institute, New York, 1946–59). The attempts to bring Poland and Czechoslovakia together are treated by Piotr S. Wandycz in his *Czechoslovak-Polish Confederation and the Great Powers, 1940–43* (Bloomington, Ind.: University of Indiana Press, 1956).

Some of the vital aspects of the war objectives of the Polish government in London are dealt with by Adam Pragier in his *Polish War Aims* (London: Max Lowe, 1944), and by Józef M. Winiewicz, *The Polish-German Frontier* (London: Polish Research Center, 1945). Jan M. Ciechanowski, in his *Defeat in Victory* (Garden City, N.Y.: Doubleday, 1947) takes a critical view of America and Britain toward Poland.

While Polish military contribution to the Allied victory in World War II has not been comprehensively treated in the West, Frederick W. Winterbotham's *The Ultra Secret* (New York: Harper & Row, 1975), has thrown some light on the Polish role in the field of military intelligence, especially the securing of the crucial "Enigma" code for the Allies. Jerzy B. Cynk's *History of the Polish Air Force, 1918–1968* (Reading: Osprer, 1972) treats the Polish participation in the Battle of Britain as well as other spectacular achievements of Polish aviation during 1939–45. There are many colorful memoirs written by Polish participants in World War II. As an example one may mention a volume written by General K. S. Rudnicki, *The Last of the War Horses* (London: Bachman and Turner, 1974), and Władysław Anders, *An Army in Exile* (London: Macmillan, 1949).

The postwar period of Polish history has a rich literature in English. One of the more significant books is Zbigniew Brzezinski's *The Soviet Bloc* (New York: Praeger, 1961), which has excellent passages on Poland. In addition to this panoramic treatment, the following monographs should be read: Ann L. Strong, *I Saw the New Poland* (Boston: Little, Brown, 1946); Stanisław Mikołajczyk, *The*

299

✑ Bibliographical Note

Rape of Poland: The Pattern of Soviet Aggression (New York: Whittlesey House, 1948); Arthur Bliss-Lane, *I Saw Poland Betrayed* (Indianapolis, Ind.: Bobbs-Merrill, 1948). The main economic aspects of postwar Poland are treated by T. P. Alton, *Polish Postwar Economy* (New York: Columbia University Press, 1955); see also Anthony Z. Kruszewski, *The Oder-Neisse Boundary and Poland's Modernization* (New York: Praeger, 1972); J. M. Montais, *Central Planning in Poland* (New Haven: Yale University Press, 1952); Stefan Jędrychowski, *The Fundamental Principles of Economic Policy in Industry* (Warsaw: Polonia Publishing House, 1957); Andrzej Korboński, *Politics of Socialist Agriculture in Poland, 1945–1960* (New York: Columbia University Press, 1964); and J. G. Zieliński, *Economic Reform in Polish Industry* (London: Oxford University Press, 1973).

The best biography of Władysław Gomułka in English is by Nicholas Bethell, *Gomułka: His Poland, His Communism* (New York: Holt, Rinehart & Winston, 1969). Flora Lewis, *A Case of Hope* (Garden City, N.Y.: Doubleday, 1958), and Konrad Syrop, *Spring in October* (New York: Praeger, 1957), both competently tell the story of the "Polish October" of 1956. Frank Gibney, in his *The Frozen Revolution* (New York: Farrar Straus, 1959), and S. L. Shneiderman, in *The Warsaw Heresy* (New York: Horizon Press, 1959) discuss various aspects of the Gomułka period. Both Hansjakob Stehle, *The Independent Satellite* (New York: Praeger, 1965), and Richard Hiscocks, *Poland: Bridge for the Abyss?* (New York: Oxford University Press, 1963), while focusing on the "Polish October" and its aftermath, interpret the phenomenon against a broad historic background.

Government on the local level has been analyzed by Jarosław Piekałkiewicz in *Communist Local Government* (Athens: Ohio University Press, 1975). David Lane and George Kolankiewicz, in their symposium *Social Groups in Polish Society* (New York: Columbia University Press, 1973), and Jan Szczepański, in his *Polish Society* (New York: Random House, 1964), deal with the social evolution of contemporary Poland. A book edited by W. J. Wagner, *Polish Law*

300

Throughout the Ages (Stanford: Hoover Institution Press, 1970), gives a historic perspective to the present legal system in Poland.

Those interested in cultural aspects should read Roman Dyboski, *Poland in World Civilization* (New York: Barrett, 1950), edited by Ludwik Krzyżanowski; Joseph Fischman, *Revolution and Tradition in People's Republic of Poland* (Princeton: Princeton University Press, 1972); Czesław Miłosz, *The Captive Mind* (London: Secker and Warburg, 1953), and Miłosz's *The History of Polish Literature* (New York: Macmillan, 1969), mainly chapters 9 through 11.

Index

303

⚮ Index

304

305

⚱ Index

309